GOD AND US

a life-changing adventure

*To my wife Judy,
and our children Luke and Anna-Marie,
who have been my cherished partners in
my exploration of God*

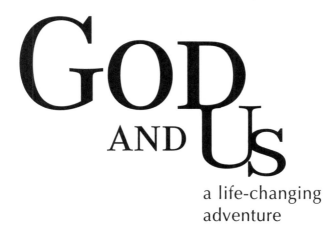

GOD AND US

a life-changing adventure

Keith Warrington

© Keith Warrington 2004
First published 2004
ISBN 1 85999 698 1

Scripture Union, 207-209 Queensway,
Bletchley, Milton Keynes, MK2 2EB, England
Email: info@scriptureunion.org.uk
Website: www.scriptureunion.org.uk

Scripture Union Australia
Locked Bag 2, Central Coast Business Centre, NSW 2252
Website: www.su.org.au

Scripture Union USA
P.O. Box 987, Valley Forge, PA 19482
Website: www.scriptureunion.org

All Scripture quotations, unless otherwise indicated, are taken from the Holy
Bible, New International Version, © 1973, 1978, 1984 by International Bible
Society. Anglicisation © 1979, 1984, 1989. Used by permission of Hodder and
Stoughton Limited.

British Library Cataloguing in Publication Data.
A catalogue record of this book is available from the British Library.

Cover design by David Lund
Printed and bound by Creative Print and Design (Wales), Ebbw Vale

✓ Scripture Union is an international Christian charity working with
churches in more than 130 countries, providing resources to bring the
good news about Jesus Christ to children, young people and families and to
encourage them to develop spiritually through the Bible and prayer.

As well as our network of volunteers, staff and associates who run holidays,
church-based events and school Christian groups, we produce a wide range of
publications and support those who use our resources through training programmes.

Contents

Introduction

A little boy once asked God how long a million years was to him. God replied, 'A million years to me is just like a single second to you.'

The little boy asked God what a million pounds was to him. God replied, 'A million pounds to me is just like a single penny to you.'

Then the little boy asked, 'God, can I have one of your pennies?'

God smiled and said, 'Certainly. Just wait a second.'

If there's one thing you can say about God, it's this: he's different. The amazing thing is that he invites us to explore him.

This book came about as a result of listening to my wife, Judy. She said, 'We don't hear enough sermons about God.' Her assessment was accurate. We hear sermons about how to be a better Christian; how to pray better; how to share the gospel more effectively; how to read the Bible enjoyably; how to be a better father, mother, son, daughter, husband, wife, pastor, elder. The list is endless. But sermons on God are comparatively rare. Is this because people have so many problems that need to be addressed in sermons? Or are we reflecting our age, which tends to be self-indulgent and focused on us, our concerns and our lives?

These issues have pushed aside the person of God so that he is largely undiscovered. The one who has established eternity for relationship with him is largely unknown and unexplored by many Christians. Yet he is the answer to many of our problems, and an investigation of his being may provide more answers for our contemporary dilemmas than we imagine.

But to attempt to explore the greatness of God is daunting. It would be impossible to scrutinise the wonders of the sea, to explore the unsearchable reaches of the universe, to probe every moment in the history of the world or analyse every intimate detail of creation. To attempt to explore God satisfactorily, let alone to complete the journey, is an impossibility that will defy even the endless aeons of eternity. But it is a voyage of delightful discovery and a privileged mission that has been granted to us, especially because the focus of our consideration takes us by the hand and opens himself to our gaze, allowing us an insight into the unimaginable.

Therefore, in the steps of others who have travelled as reverent adventurers into the greatness of God, I now tread. I hope to take you with me as we explore something of the mystery of the one who inhabits eternity because time is too small for him. This book will be an accessible, biblically based exploration of God with a personal and contemporary application. I hope to provide a stimulus to the intellect as well as to the emotions, with the aim of enabling you increasingly to realise the amazing nature of your God. Each chapter, which may be read in less than 15 minutes, includes some Bible references to ensure faithfulness to Scripture, and concludes with poetry that attempts to encapsulate the chapter's theme, followed by discussion questions to tease out some of the implications of the topic. The 12 main chapters are presented in couplets so that readers can explore, in parallel, issues that are associated with each other.

1 He's creative

Have you ever wondered:

- how God created something out of nothing?
- why God created humanity?
- how we can measure God's intelligence?
- how anyone can create a planet called Earth that weighs 66,000,000,000,000,000,000,000,000 tons?

God's creativity expresses his freedom

The Bible does not explore how God created, but it is emphatic in declaring that he did create and that he chose to do so freely. No one encouraged God to create. No one suggested the idea to him. It was not something that he had to do. Before God created anything and anyone, he existed in perfect, self-sufficient contentment. God needs nothing outside of himself. With this in mind, his creation of the world is a remarkable act of golden grace.

God's creativity reflects beauty

On a beautiful day when the world was waiting and the angels were watching, God created human life that reflected him. Adam and Eve were sparkling new. As with everything he had already created, his human creation was without comparison; it was good, exquisite and beautiful. Beauty exists because of God, whether it's the beauty of a butterfly, the awesome sight of a mountain range, a breathtaking sunset or a soft snowflake. Each is excellent in its own way, to be admired because it is exceptional.

God's creativity reflects meticulous precision

The chances of the Earth meeting the exact criteria needed for life to occur on it are astronomically small. God creates perfectly because he is wise (Ps 104:24; Prov 3:19). The Old Testament pictures of creation point to a Creator who may be depended on to create a perfectly designed and functionally reliable creation. The terms the Old Testament uses reflect a master craftsman or peerless designer who creates something carefully planned and perfectly executed (Job 38:4–6). Not only do his creative abilities not tire him; they are also way beyond our understanding (Isa 40:28; Rom 11:33–36).

There is precision about the creation of the Earth. The angle of its tilt (23.5° from the perpendicular) as it turns gives us the different seasons. If the tilt were less, much of the Earth would be uninhabitable. If the tilt were greater, extreme temperatures would make life intolerable. The speed of the Earth's rotation around the Sun (365 days, 5 hours, 48 minutes and 45.51 seconds, exactly) ensures that wind speeds on Earth are beneficial, unlike the climate of Jupiter, which rotates twice as quickly as the Earth, causing wind speeds of up to 1,000 miles an hour. A faster rotation would result in the Earth moving away from the Sun; a slower rotation would result in the opposite.

The balance between nitrogen, oxygen, argon and carbon dioxide in the air is just right for human life to be maintained. Although carbon dioxide comprises only 0.03 per cent of the atmosphere, it is crucial to life on Earth, for it is required by plants, trapping the Sun's radiation and enabling them to grow. If there were less carbon dioxide, plant life would decrease, resulting in less food for animals, and the food cycle would spiral downwards. An increase in carbon dioxide would cause a significant increase in temperature. The careful balance in the atmosphere acts as a giant protective umbrella. Without it, the Earth would be subject to a constant bombardment of meteors that would destroy life, but instead they burn up in the atmosphere.

The Earth's distance from the Sun is crucial to our existence. A few million miles closer and the glaciers would melt, causing the sea level to rise and cities and islands to be flooded. The increased sea cover would result in greater evaporation, and the increased release of water vapour and carbon dioxide would further raise the temperature of the world. If the Sun were further away, the opposite would occur, and the world would freeze to death. The ozone layer is the right thickness to keep out harmful ultraviolet rays from the Sun while letting in sufficient heat for us to live.

For many in the developed world, water is taken for granted. However, it is very rare in the Universe. In fact, it is known to exist only on Earth. The Earth has it in significant quantities, estimated at 340 million cubic miles, covering 71 per cent of the Earth's surface. Its physical and chemical properties provide an ideal environment as a primary component of life. One of its main functions is as a worldwide air conditioner, keeping the temperature of the land at a bearable level, the currents cooling the equatorial land and waters and warming the polar regions. It also acts as an effective recycling organism. Most of the Earth's carbon dioxide is dissolved in it, including the vast amounts created by the burning of fossil fuels, which would otherwise be released into the atmosphere, with cataclysmic consequences.

Another remarkable property of water is evident when it cools. As with most other materials, as it cools it contracts. But when the temperature sinks to 4°C it starts to expand – in contrast to most other materials – until it freezes. Ice then floats to the surface. If water continued to contract instead of expanding, it would become heavier, and ice would form on the *bottom* of the oceans, in the process killing many fish and lowering the temperature of the water until the sea froze from the bottom up.

The size and density of the Earth, the thickness of its crust, the fact that the Earth exists because of the Sun, its closeness to the Sun, the size and brightness of the Sun – these and many other features indicate that the creation is complex and precisely ordered. God is meticulous in all he does, exact in all he is.

He creates because he is God, because he is unselfish and wants to bless what he creates with his presence. He creates so that his creation can receive his smile. Those whom he forms feel his pleasure. Whatever he causes to come into being is crafted out of his desire to care for his craftsmanship. His creativity is channelled into being because of love alone.

The personal involvement of God in his creation is reflected in the way he creates. In picture language, the writers describe him using his fingers (Ps 8:3), shaping the mountains and creating the wind (Amos 4:13). His intimacy with his creation is demonstrated by the fact that it reflects him (Ps 8:1; 19:1) and praises him (Ps 104:31,32). God does not create in order to receive praise as if he needed it. Rather, what he creates is described as spontaneously and naturally expressing its pride at being created in such a perfect way by such a perfect Creator. The sixteenth-century Reformer John Calvin described creation as the theatre of God's glory. When we examine God's creation we recognise what a remarkable God he is. However, although his creation remains perfect when in relationship to the Creator, when the relationship is marred the creation is impaired. Sin has damaged God's creation, which longs to be renewed (Rom 8:21).

God does not absent himself from his creation

Psalm 104 tells us the trees are cared for by God (v 16) and young lions and fish depend on him (vs 21,25–27). When the writer to the Hebrews speaks of God's involvement with his creation, he states that through his Son he sustains it (1:3). He is not a giant Atlas who holds the world on his shoulders. Rather, his role as Sustainer describes not his strength but his authority. God controls the destiny of the world, determining its end from its beginning. He is not an absentee landlord but a governing God. Paul says God holds all things together continuously (Col 1:17). Jesus develops a similar theme, reminding his hearers that God cares for the inconsequential sparrow so they have no need to worry (Luke 12:6). Similarly, Peter reminds his readers, who are suffering persecution, that the Creator is faithful to those whom he has created (1 Pet 4:19).

God's creativity inspires worship

On 20 July 1969, Apollo 11 touched down on the Moon. For the first time, people could observe the Earth from another celestial body. The pictures beamed back were remarkable. Earth offers some remarkable sights, but the Universe is breathtaking. Although incompletely surveyed (there are probably over a hundred billion galaxies in the Universe), what has been discovered provides an overwhelming backdrop to the Earth, filling believers with humility and awe. The Sun is just one example of God's creation. Its energy is so enormous that the Earth harnesses only one billionth of its daily output. The Bible presents the unimaginable nature of God's creation in picture language. It describes him stretching out the heavens like a tent (Ps 104:2), scattering frost (Ps 147:16), holding the winds in his fist (Prov 30:4) and wrapping the oceans in his cloak (Prov 30:4).

God's creativity reflects him, and his creation carries an imprint of him. The more we consider creation, the more we are drawn to its Creator. Creation is one of his ways of getting our attention and transforming us into a congregation of watching worshippers. The more we examine the world and the Universe, the more we are moved to consider the magnitude and character of its Creator. God creates as a manifestation of his being. It is a defining element of his person. There is a mystery about the Universe. For instance, why do Venus and Uranus rotate in the opposite direction to the other planets in our solar system? Like his Universe, God's character has deep caverns of mystery.

Imagine the first day of creation. The angels are waiting and watching; they know something amazing is going to take place. Then God starts, and, in an explosion of colour and sounds, the Universe floods over the darkness. It's splendid. It's awesome.

It's God. Sparkling stars send pulses of light towards him; massive meteors move towards him and wait for his word of command; dazzling sunlight from a myriad stunning suns squeezes the darkness out of the scene. And the angels are astounded as he starts to create. In the words of the psalmist,

> *In his hand are the depths of the earth,*
> * and the mountain peaks belong to him.*
> *The sea is his, for he made it,*
> * and his hands formed the dry land.*
> *Come, let us bow down in worship;*
> * let us kneel before the* LORD *our maker.*
> (Ps 95:4–6)

God is still creating

The days of creation have not finished. The Creator is still creating. He's moving, stirring, tireless and enthusiastic in all he does. Lamentations 3:23 records that '[his compassions] are new every morning.' Isaiah states, 'See, I am doing a new thing!' (43:19), and 'From now on I will tell you of new things' (48:6). The psalmist (40:3) proclaims, 'He has put a new song in my mouth.' He is the God of the now as well as of the past; the God of the new as well as of the old. He is the active God, who intimately involves himself in our lives. He does not sit idly by and watch the world from a distance. Rather, he dynamically moves within our lives.

God's creativity is reflected in us

Although we are different from God, we share his characteristic of creativity. Just as God enjoys creating, so he has blessed us with the capacity to be creative. Genesis records that when God created the various elements of the world, he pronounced each of them good. A similar prospect, that of enjoying our creativity, awaits each believer created in his likeness.

Although God does not change, he creates change, developing new life, fresh experiences, unique lessons, innovative opportunities, progressive adventures, imaginative prospects and life destinies for us; creating what we shall be out of what we were. Our responsibility as believers is to gaze into the future with the recognition that a creative God is planning it. With the Spirit as our guide, and after identifying our gifts, strengths and passions, the next step should be to determine how to creatively develop frameworks for change within our lifestyles. Some of us may wish to write songs, learn to play an instrument, master an art form, engage in political life, develop social programmes, write a book or an article or research a subject. The list is potentially endless – projects to see through, trips to make, people to see, new habits to form. It can be broad-based and result in a two-year plan for change; it can be more narrowly focused on developing a greater vibrancy in our relationship with God; it can be relational or functional; it can be intimately personal or public.

The common denominator in each of these options is that they represent opportunities for change and a framework in which change can be achieved. Are we living in the present, realising that there is a future to be grasped, or living in the present as if the future didn't exist? AW Tozer wrote, 'Refuse to be average.' Only God knows the kind of person who is waiting to be developed within each believer, but, with his capacity to be creative, he encourages us to dream, and whispers, 'Be creative like your Creator.' Because of his creative artistry and wisdom, we should look for surprises with God.

Anyone can tell how many seeds are in an apple; only God can tell how many apples are in a seed. Take a leaf out of God's book and be creative, like your Creator.

He flung the stars out into space
and every one went to its place
and stayed.

He dropped the oceans in the sea.
The waters flowed obediently.
He tossed the sun and moon up high;
They shone for him in the darkened sky.

In his power and awesome might
he ordered the day to turn to night.
He commanded everything to be right,
for he, the Creator, ruled.

He reigned supreme, in splendour, awe.
His glory no one could endure.
And when the King whispered a word,
a myriad angels in glittering robes
pounced to obey his every word,
their King, their Lord.

But he cradles us in his arms.
He joins us in our storms and gently calms our fears.
He steps into our shoes, just where we are.
He shepherds us with tender care,
with fingers, hands,
love beyond compare.

He flung the stars out into space,
but he welcomes us with a warm embrace.
He shows us a glimpse of his eternal grace,
to us – members of a fallen race.
The King has a smile upon his face,
for the Creator has made us his own.

Questions for discussion

1. Why did God create the world? (Col 1:16; Rev 4:11)
2. What does creation reveal about God? (Ps 19:1; Isa 45:18)

3. What does creation reveal about the significance of humanity? (Gen 5:1,2; Heb 2:6,7)

4. How does creation encourage our readiness to trust in God? (Deut 32:6; Isa 40:26; 43:7)

5. What lessons for our lifestyle can we learn from the way that God created? (Gen 1:21)

Questions to think about

1. Can we be certain that God created the world?

2. What are the most significant aspects of God's creation?

3. What difference should the fact that God created the Earth make to our lifestyles?

4. What targets can we set ourselves as we reflect our Creator and honour the creative capacity he has given us?

2 He gives himself to us

Have you ever wondered:

- what life would be like if we were not Christians?
- what the word 'grace' means?
- whether God has planned abilities for us in this life?
- what abilities God has given us?

There's something satisfying about completing a project, whatever it might be. You invest time and effort, perhaps at some personal cost, and when the task is completed, like a cat who's found a lifetime's supply of cream, you purr with contentment. You've been released to enjoy life again and to relax for a while. It's time to reward yourself. If you had a day free after a busy week of creativity, what would you choose to do?

After God had packed into a week what we could not do in an eternity of weeks, he had a day free. What would you do with that day if you were God? Have a break, a rest or a holiday? Would you spoil yourself, go shopping, have a day in the country or socialise? Or would you take on an even bigger project? That's what God did. After God created the world, he created people.

But this was not as easy as it seems. Creating people meant more potential problems than creating the Universe ever did, because people were created with the ability to say 'No' to God. God wanted to create people who could enjoy a relationship with him. But he did not want to force that relationship on them; he did not want robots, people programmed to love him. He wanted them to love him freely. That meant that they had to be free to leave his love as an unwanted gift, to say 'No, thank you,' to God.

And God gave people that choice. Why? It's because he wanted our relationship with him to be based on love, freely offered and freely received. To do that best, he allowed us to say 'No'.

But in order to start that relationship with us, all he expects us to say is 'Yes'. When we recognise our need of God's forgiveness, which Jesus achieved when he died on the cross, God says, 'Welcome.' He accepts us unconditionally. We give him nothing but our sins and ourselves; he gives us his forgiveness and himself. It's an unequal, unfair transaction, but he enters into it willingly. That's why the word 'grace' crops up so often in the Christian life. Everything that happens to us is proof of his grace. As CS Lewis wrote, 'God, who needs nothing, loves into existence wholly superfluous creatures in order that He may love and perfect them.'

Before

His gracious activity towards us pre-dates us by centuries – before we were born, before our parents were born, before anyone was born. Before people ever think about God, God has already thought about them. Before they start to feel their way towards him, he has stretched his hands down to them. Before they bow the knee, he bends his ear; before they express hope, he has left heaven; before they dare to say sorry, he has died to save them. Before anyone proceeds towards a relationship with God, God starts the process (1 Tim 1:9). He leads us to himself – we who cannot search for him, we who cannot even accidentally bump into him. God is the God of the previous, who finishes before we start, who says 'Hello' to us when we're hiding from him.

Not only that, but he chooses to be our friend at the cost of his Son. If God were to accept me into his family by a statement of his will, that would be more than I deserve. But to enable it to happen through the humiliation of becoming a created being, the scandal of being treated as a nobody, the outrage of a painful cross, the shame of bearing the punishment for my sins, the degrading of God, is more than I can understand. At unimaginable cost to himself, he freely gives us what we need (Eph 1:6). At this point, we just begin to open the door of the vast treasure stores of grace, God's gifts to us.

Paul is clear that Jesus, the Spirit and the Father demonstrate grace to Christians. We cannot understand the concept of the Trinity. But we are told that all the members of the Godhead are united in everything they do, especially when it relates to the support of the Christian. Jesus redeems and forgives us (Eph 1:7), the Spirit enables us to be a home for God (2:22) and the Father gives us eternal life (2:4). In 2 Corinthians 13:14 Paul writes his only benediction, in which each of the members of the Godhead is mentioned: 'The grace of the Lord Jesus Christ and the love of God and the fellowship of the Holy Spirit be with you all.' Although God is a mystery, he wants us to recognise his commitment to us, and here Paul identifies aspects of this care. He is saying not that the individual attributes are restricted to particular members of the Godhead, but that all of them are intrinsically intertwined and all are dedicated to supporting us sensitively in every moment of our lives.

During

When a baby is born it enjoys the dedicated attention of a number of people, including hospital staff, parents, siblings, grandparents, friends – even the family dog, for a while. Through it all, the child is blissfully unaware that he or she has become the centre of a new world. This is natural when a baby is ushered into life with lavish love. Writing to the young Christians in Ephesus, Paul describes some of the gifts that God has lavished on them at the start of their Christian lives (1:8). He provides wisdom (1:17–19) and empowers them (3:16), while also giving gifts to them (4:7,8).

In a world of easy promises and empty pledges, it's natural to be sceptical regarding guarantees that seem too good to be true.

God's grace is one of those guarantees that seems too good to be true. Paul tells the Corinthians about one of these guarantees that God has given him: 'My grace is sufficient for you' (2 Cor 12:9).

When our children were much younger, we went for walks in the country. On one of these treks we crossed a stream that was too wide for their little legs. Although they had boundless energy, they lacked ability; they saw the other side, but focused on the gap. The crossing was easy for me, however, and because I carried them it was easy for them too. Similarly, God provides strength for our struggles, wisdom for our wilderness, love for our loneliness, friendship for our fear, forgiveness for our failure, hope for our heartache, joy for our journey and grace to reach the goal.

Paul makes a strange statement in Romans 8:26: 'the Spirit …intercedes for us'. That the Spirit prays for us is encouraging, because it's good to be aware that the Spirit is on our side. But the Spirit is God. So is God praying to himself? The Spirit can't be reminding God about my situation, because the Spirit is God. He can't be asking God for extra resources because, as God, he has them all already.

Paul is painting a picture with words to explore the fact that the Spirit in us works in partnership with the Father to support us in all our situations, not just when life is at its lowest but throughout all our days; when nightmares control our next steps; through the storms when all we can taste is our tears; in the hurricane when we hunt for a haven; and also when we can see a golden horizon, when dreams come true and life is too wonderful for words. God is there not just when we need him but also when we don't seem to. The Spirit is speaking out loud for our benefit so that we can hear his heartbeat for us.

The word used by Paul to describe the way the Spirit helps us is rare and includes the idea of support or partnership. He doesn't just help us from above, but comes alongside us and is with us; he steps into our shoes; not just once but continually and continuously. This is not support from a distance, not help from another world, but closer than a whisper. This word for 'help' is used once elsewhere in the New Testament, in Luke 10:40, where Martha asks for Mary to help her. She wants Mary to hold her hand in the helping process. God is so close that he can take our hand and charge us with his energy.

Within us

God doesn't just stand with us; he wants to work through us. Peter wrote to a group of Christians who knew what it was to feel unappreciated and impoverished. They had suffered for their faith and discovered that the world they lived in was an inhospitable place. They were alienated by its inhabitants; they belonged to another country, called heaven. Until they reached it, Peter told them, they must use the gifts they had received from God (1 Pet 4:10). The Greek word for 'gift' (*charisma*) comes from the same root as the word for 'grace' (*charis*). God's grace is reflected in us and activated in us in practical ways for the benefit of others.

When I was a young Christian and heard that God had given gifts to Christians, I pored over those listed by Paul (Rom 12:6–8; 1 Cor 12:8–10,28–30; Eph 4:11). But I couldn't identify any of them in me. I had never prophesied, spoken in tongues, given an interpretation or achieved any miracles or healings. I wasn't an apostle, pastor, teacher, evangelist or prophet. I had never ruled or shown much wisdom, never exhibited much knowledge. I faltered in my faith and didn't like giving too much. The conclusion was straightforward. When God looked in his barrel of gifts, he couldn't find one for me. Maybe he chose not to give me one. Who could blame him? If I were God I wouldn't have given one to me either! I didn't deserve one. I was just a young Christian, happy to be saved and knowing that I was going to heaven.

But then I discovered 1 Corinthians 12:4–7,11. I discovered that it wasn't because people were spiritual that God had given them his gifts, and that my task wasn't to ask for a gift from God but to discover what he had already given me and to use it. Paul's

lists are not meant to be exhaustive; he is simply giving exam-
ples of God's activity in his people. I learnt that these gifts are
varied. We are not to grab hold of them and tightly grasp them to
ourselves. They are gifts from God to enable us to reflect something of his grace to others. Becoming a child of God involves
becoming like a prism through which the greatness of God's
generosity and the intimacy of his compassionate care are radi-
ated to others who need to receive them. Exploring God's gifts
to us helps us appreciate the meaning of grace, because not only
do we not deserve them but we could not even receive them if
God had not made it possible.

After

Next time you look at a mountain, tell yourself that when the
mountain has been worn away by the winds of time you'll still
be alive; when the sun has cooled into a block of ice you'll still
be sparkling bright; when the rivers have all run dry you'll still
be bubbling with life because God has planned eternity with
you in mind. In giving himself to us he has changed us from
what we were and is committed to transforming us into what
he wants us to be – like him, so that we shall live our future in
the fullness of his life. Our future is based on the fact that God
is for us, unconditionally. That's grace. There's no satisfactory
reason, no understandable explanation; it's a marvellous
mystery and an inexhaustible journey of discovery.

Grace sums up God, who gives himself to us

The Father, Son and Spirit are committed to all aspects of
our salvation. A wealthy English family were horrified one
afternoon to hear that their young son Winston had nearly
drowned in the swimming-pool. He was saved by the gardener.
Years later, after Winston had become Prime Minister of
England, he was stricken with pneumonia. The King called for

the best doctor in England to ensure he recovered. The doctor was Alexander Fleming, the developer of penicillin and the son of the gardener who had saved him from drowning. Churchill had been saved by the father and the son.

God's commitment to us, however, is threefold, for not only has the Father saved us through the sacrifice of the Son but the Spirit guarantees to accompany us on our journey. One of the most famous paintings in the world is Leonardo da Vinci's *Mona Lisa*. One of its remarkable aspects is that her eyes seem to follow you wherever you stand in the room. God sees us not just from afar; he follows us with his eyes, hears our heartbeat, knows our name and stays with us when we stop.

One of the exercises I sometimes undertake with my students is to work through part of a Bible verse word by word. It's a form of meditation and allows them to savour the meaning of the words. God's promise to Paul, 'My grace is sufficient for you' (2 Cor 12:9) is a good example to practise on. Repeat the phrase aloud slowly, emphasising only one word every time you do, until you have spoken it six times (once for each word) and begun to explore some of its treasures. It will be our eternal destiny to explore his grace, so begin to enjoy it now.

When the world was dark and light was gone,
when creation groaned and the people mourned,
when evil creatures grinned and planned,
God stepped down and became a man.

When icy winds of fear and doubt
clutched at joy and threw it out
this world was lost and hope was gone.
But then, a child was born;
a child who sucked his thumb and smiled,
a boy who learned to sing and sigh,
a king who learned to fear and cry,
a baby who was born to die.

To show us God, to show us love,
his child stepped down from heaven above,
to say, 'I care, you're special to me.'
He left his throne where he reigned supreme
and came to earth so that we could see
his heart of grace for you, for me.

Questions for discussion

1. How has God shown his grace to you? (Rom 6:14; Eph 2:4–9; Titus 3:7; Heb 2:9)

2. How can you be certain that God has demonstrated his grace to you? (John 1:16; Rom 5:8; 2 Cor 8:9; Heb 4:16)

3. What are some New Testament evidences of God's grace in us? (Acts 14:3; 20:32; Rom 12:6; 2 Cor 9:8)

4. 1 Peter 5:10 describes God as 'the God of all grace'. What does this mean to you?

5. How can God's grace be reflected in us? (Col 4:6; 1 Pet 4:10)

Questions to think about

1. How can you ensure that you don't take the grace of God for granted?

2. Define the word 'grace'.

3. Identify an example of grace in the life of a Bible character.

4. How can you show grace to others today?

3 He lives in eternity

Have you ever wondered:

- what it means to say that God is eternal?
- whether eternity is more than endless time?
- how time and eternity relate to each other?
- whether eternal life gets better year after year?

Marshall Shelley is a husband and a father of five children, four girls and one boy, of whom three are living on this earth and two in heaven. Mandy was two weeks short of her second birthday when she entered eternity. Three months earlier, Toby had been born. He had departed from this life into eternity two minutes after he was born. Marshall Shelley and his wife struggled with the questions: Why would God create a child to live for two years, for two minutes? Why had God created a life that would last for only two minutes? They came to the conclusion that God had not created their daughter to live for two years. Neither had God created their son to live for two minutes. God had created them for eternity.

What a remarkable truth! God has created us not for two years, ten years or seventy years, but for eternity. We have been created, appointed and designed for eternity. Our life on this earth is only a parenthesis in the context of eternity, and God has programmed us for eternity. Thus Ecclesiastes 3:11 describes God placing eternity within our hearts.

But how can we understand the concept of eternity?

Eternity is not just endless time

In contemporary usage, the term 'eternity' tends to be used to indicate an interminable length of time. A journey to the beach with two 4-year-olds in the back of the car can seem like eternity. Waiting for your exam results, the outcome of an interview or a medical diagnosis can seem like eternity. However, eternity should not be viewed only in terms of length of time. Actually, it defines timelessness or boundless time rather than length of time. It provides a God-lifestyle of freedom from all that time precludes. God is eternal because he is free from any restraints of time. Eternity provides an extension of time in terms of its quality as well as its duration. It will be infinitely extended time. But also, it will be boundless time determined by the life of God as expressed in eternity in contrast to that expressed in the confines of life on earth.

Exploring the concept of eternity is easier said than done. There are difficulties in such a quest. The first is that it is beyond the finite mind to understand that which is outside time and to imagine beyond that which we know. Eternity, by definition, is beyond our current knowledge, as is the God who dwells within it. Secondly, the Bible does not reveal a great deal about eternity. Instead, it drops hints and encourages us to consider it, to allow our imagination to explore it, to savour the flavour of the life that belongs to God and to anticipate it.

Eternity is significant because of what it represents

The Bible often refers to the concept of eternity to stress the quality of salvation for the believer. Salvation will last for eternity (Heb 9:15), and believers are cared for by an eternally existing God (Rom 16:26), whose power is eternal (Rom 1:20). The Bible also uses the term to highlight the exalted nature of God by describing him as the One who 'inhabits eternity'

(Isa 57:15). Its most common occurrence is in the context of eternal life granted to the believer (John 3:15). Although this is often viewed as describing life after death, it is more accurately understood as a life in relationship with God that commences at salvation (John 3:36), but is fully realised after death; a life in which believers can benefit from all that God makes available to them as his children.

What is most important for us is not trying to understand how it can be that God never comes to the end of his existence (and never begins it, for that matter), but rather exploring the consequences of this fact. God's eternal nature does not have the negative associations of a static, unmoved, impersonal being who is unfeeling and remote. On the contrary, he willingly experiences some aspects of our lives (Eph 4:30). His nature does not change, although he adapts himself to identify with our changeableness. He is not frozen, but full of feelings for his creation; not wooden, but aware of how we are; warm, not cold; active, not passive; present, not absent.

God is self-existent: he does not depend on anything else for his existence (Exod 3:14). No one brought him into being, neither has anyone created any framework within which he must exist. Time is the context in which some of God's purposes are achieved. He is present throughout time, though eternity is the characteristic that best defines his being (Ps 29:10). God's eternal existence means that he is steady and steadfast, and provides safety and security (Ps 90:1). His promises (Ps 102:27), his certainty and trustworthiness (Rev 1:4), his experience and wisdom are unalterable. This means that God cannot be improved upon. Every decision he makes is perfect. He has no need to reconsider or change his mind (Mal 3:6). He never gets old and he was never young. He is as he always has been and as he always will be: perfect.

Eternity represents the antithesis of this life and its negative aspects. Eternity is an era of sinlessness, joy, fulfilment and unlimited access and proximity to God. In a world of changing values and uncertainties, the fact that God is eternal assures us of his open-ended commitment to us, unaffected by the variations caused by time.

The healthier and the more accurate our perception of eternity, the more positively it will impact our lives. Many of us make a considerable investment in this life. Our time, talents and gifts are poured into this life as if it was all we had. We need to be careful that the time-bound agenda of secular society does not determine our own destinies and programmes as Christians. Other issues may be more important than those that currently occupy our lives. We need to focus on these timeless principles that are vital to our existence, or we shall end our lives having failed to concentrate on what matters centrally to us, namely God and eternity.

Eternity is what Christians have been created for

I used to fear eternity because I thought that it involved only judgement. Picture the scene: God's eyes burning into my conscience; all my friends standing around me, staring. An orchestra of frowning angels plays a slow, throbbing dirge, conducted by an angel who keeps looking at me as if I shouldn't be there. A big bass drum is beaten heavily and monotonously. Christians are marched in, heads bowed. I'm third in the queue, following Billy Graham and the Pope. 'Silence!' The books are opened and it's my turn. Oh yes, I know I'm in the Book of Life. It's the other book that troubles me – the one that measures my words, deeds and thoughts. I don't want my worst moments shouted from the housetops. I don't mind eternity; it's the first few minutes that trouble me!

Some people think of eternity as the time when normal activity ceases, to be replaced by month-long choir practices and year-long prayer meetings. Little wonder that few sermons get preached about heaven nowadays! Do many people relish that kind of heaven? Even though most Christians recognise that these pictures are caricatures of the life hereafter, the realities of eternity and the life to be enjoyed within it are still, to a large degree, unexplored mysteries.

Rather than seeking to identify details of the life to be experienced after death, it is more productive to recognise that, whatever it will be like, it is that for which believers have been created. Eternity is not the full-time whistle; it's when the fulfilment actually begins. Eternity is not the end of time; it's the start of endless time. It's not the final scene; it's not the moment of applause. Eternity is the start of the performance of our lives. Believers are ushered through this life for the purpose of eternity, destined for eternity. Eternity is not the reward for life on earth; it's not the bonus; it's the reason for our creation. Life on this earth is not the reason for our salvation; it's just the entrance porch, the waiting-room, the gateway to our destiny, which is eternity.

Life doesn't end when eternity begins; to a very significant degree, it begins. Death is the magic carpet that releases us into the glory of eternity. Eternity is the time when we shall do best the task for which we were created – endlessly exploring God. Now, we are like yachts in the harbour, ready to sail on the ocean of God's greatness, but becalmed because of our intellectual weakness and sinful tendencies. In eternity, we shall be transformed and shall endlessly discover the infinite clarity and sparkling treasures of the depths of God's glory. Eternity is not an uneventful, static and quasi-frozen state. John Baillie wrote: 'I thank Thee, O Lord, that Thou hast so set eternity within my heart that no earthly thing can ever satisfy me wholly.' Only then will all out longings be satisfied.

Eternity is a quest to be commenced in this life

We have all eternity to be intrigued by God. It will be a time to explore the innumerable mysteries of God: how he hears a leaf floating to the ground in the depths of the deepest forest and also our heartbeat; how he sees the future and the heartbreak of an orphan; how he feels the weight of the pain of his world and our tears; how he can be touched by our sorrows but not contaminated by our sin; how he could save the world and us.

God is endlessly intriguing. He cannot be completely known or understood, and he creates us for eternity to enjoy an endless exploration into him. Eternity awaits us with endless life of a quality that we can only dream of. This brief period of time on earth is a moment when he holds his breath, when he blinks his eye, but he inhabits eternity. That quest is to be commenced in this life and continued into the next.

I stand,
a lake of tranquillity stretched out before me,
serenely vast – it stills my soul.
Chameleon horizon envelopes my vision,
unique clouds blurring into forms I cannot define,
revealing glimpses of glorious colours.

Unweary rays of light melt upon my face;
magical gifts from a supernatural sun,
so pure its light, so true its intensity,
so passionate its warmth.
Such beauty inevitably reminds me of you,
the eternal Creator.

You who give orders to the morning and show dawn its
place;
you who bring forth the constellations in their seasons;
you who send lightning bolts on their way;
you who shut the sea behind doors when it bursts forth
from the womb.

You who know when the mountain goat gives birth
and watch when the foal bears her fawn.
You who give the horse its strength
and clothe his neck with a flowing mane.
You who endow the heart with wisdom

and give understanding to the mind.

You who hunt the prey for the lions
and satisfy the hunger of the lions when they crouch in
their dens.
The hawk takes flight by your wisdom
and spreads his wings towards the south.
The eagle soars at your command
and builds his nest on high.

I stand,
delighting in the majesty of my God.
So little do I comprehend of your creation.
I'm like a child with a picture book.
Angels, as bumble bees in a field of daffodils,
whisper in my ear,
and I turn to the one who's been holding my hand.
A contagious smile creeps on to your face
as we walk down the yellow-bricked path of eternity
towards my Father's Paradise.

Luke Warrington, based on Job 39

Questions for discussion

1. How can we know that we have eternal life? (John 6:47;
    Titus 1:2; 1 Pet 5:10; 1 John 2:25; 5:11)
2. How can we understand eternal life better if we think of it
    as knowing God? (John 17:3)
3. How can the fact that God is eternal make a difference to
    our sense of security? (Deut 33:27)
4. How can the idea of eternity change our lives? (Eccl 3:11)
5. What impact does the fact that God is eternal have on our
    relationship with him? (Heb 13:8)

Questions to think about

1. What impact can the fact that God is eternal have on our lives and futures?
2. In what ways is eternity more than endless time?
3. Shall we grow in knowledge in eternity?
4. What is the relationship between time and eternity?

4 He's beyond us but he beckons us

Have you ever wondered:

- whether we shall ever fully comprehend God?
- why God created humanity?
- why God gives people the opportunity to have a relationship with him?
- why God wants Christians in heaven, with him, for ever?

The answer to each of the last three questions is the same. It has to do with the fact that God wants Christians to enjoy him; to enjoy not simply a relationship with him but also to enjoy *him*. The answer to the first question is that not even eternity will be long enough to appreciate God fully, but it will provide us with the opportunity to explore God, in his presence, for ever. The seventeenth-century writer Jeremy Taylor wrote, 'A religion without mystery is a religion without God.' God is full of mystery, but he helps us feel our way to him.

Some while ago, I was wondering what I should speak about to a large group of theological students. My thoughts went like this:

'Lord, what shall I talk about?'

'Tell them about me.'

'But I don't know enough about you.'

'I know. You never will; neither will they; so journey together into me and, as you do, you will arrive at worship.'

One of the miracles of Christianity is that God, who is far beyond us, has enabled us to focus on him intimately. This opportunity to gaze upon God is to be our eternal destiny. This destiny shows why God created humanity in the first place and why he welcomes us into an active relationship with him that commences in this life. To be certain of the welcome and to discover how to develop it in this life should be our constant preoccupation as believers. The invitation that God whispers to us every day is to take pleasure in him passionately.

God is glorious

But first, it's important to remember how different God is from us. The Bible describes him as glorious. The concept of 'glory' is not easy to define. Often the Bible speaks of people seeing God's glory (Isa 6:1–3; John 1:14). It is best to understand this as becoming aware of God as he manifests himself in a particular way. The concept of glory is also associated with the kingdom of God (1 Thess 2:12).

The word 'glory' may mean splendour, majesty or magnificence. It is best used as a superlative when attempting to describe something or someone superior to all others. The Greek word used in the New Testament is *doxa*, from which the English word 'doxology' is derived. In the Greek version of the Old Testament, often used by the writers of the New Testament, this word often translates the Hebrew word *kabod*, which describes someone who has influence (Gen 45:31), riches (Gen 31:1) or power (Isa 8:7). It is used to refer to someone or something that makes an impression. God is impressive, and the term 'glory' indicates this. As the cloud that signified God's presence weighed down upon the tabernacle (Exod 40:34), the picture of God is well expressed as one who is substantially important. He has presence. He has weight, influence and authority. In this regard, the word 'glory' is best used of God. He is superior to all and the word that is used to represent his deity

('Godness') is 'glory'. What defines God most completely is that he is glorious, and in that he is unique.

To attempt to describe the supreme magnificence of God is difficult because of the limitation of language and our inability fully to comprehend his splendid majesty. This is where the word 'glory' is particularly useful, as it is our best attempt to represent something of the radiant grandeur of God. He is glorious; as such, he has no equal. Where he is, it is glorious, and he manifests himself gloriously (Exod 24:17). Charles Spurgeon, the nineteenth-century preacher, writes, 'There is nothing little in God.' Everything about him is best expressed in superlatives, for he is awesome. God is different, set apart, incomparable, unique. We may use pictures to seek to define just how uniquely excellent he is, but they all fail to do justice to his unrivalled distinctiveness.

Windows into God's glory

The biblical writers express the glory of God in superlative language and record a few incidents that paint pictures of his radiance. The best picture of God's glory is the person of Jesus, who reflects God and radiates his character. Thus, the perfect nature of Jesus reflects the peerless character of God, which cannot be improved upon.

Throughout the New Testament we catch glimpses of this glory when a bright light expresses the intensity of his magnificence. In the birth of Jesus, a star illuminated the way to him and God's glory shone around the shepherds. In his transfiguration, a bright light enveloped the disciples. In his exalted state, he dazzled the inhabitants of heaven (Rev 21:23) as he did Saul (Acts 22:11). John's vision presents him as a superior being whose presence radiates the most intense brightness imaginable (Rev 1:16). This concentration of light creates the sense of purity and distinctiveness. The miracles of Jesus also manifested his glory, revealing something of his being (John 2:11); and his ascension is encapsulated by the word 'glory' (1 Tim 3:16).

However, this glory is also seen in his death, for in that event the love of God is most clearly expressed (John 12:23). Glory is demonstrated not only in the magnificent light of God's transcendent authority, but also in the pain of darkness, when he humbles himself to take on fragile weakness. Wherever God is, there is his glory. His very existence causes him to radiate some of that which makes him impressively unique.

Believers will participate in his glory

Although, as believers, we would naturally withdraw from God because of our imperfections, he beckons us to him and invites us to explore his person. Why? The *Westminster Shorter Catechism* states that our chief purpose is to glorify God and to enjoy him for ever. This is our eternal privilege: to enjoy admiring the glorious aspects of God.

Although God's glory is what makes God unique, Paul (Rom 8:17,18) and Peter (1 Pet 5:1,4) state that believers will participate in that glory, enjoying God's presence so intimately that we shall be infused with some of his glorious characteristics. This will be partially because the new bodies that we shall receive will share some of the properties of the resurrection body of Jesus (Phil 3:21). Consequently, Paul says we shall experience 'glorious liberty' (Rom 8:21), and that God is preparing a 'weight of glory beyond all comparison' for all believers (2 Cor 4:17). The picture he paints is of a vast collection of presents, flowing from his lavish generosity, that God will bestow on believers. And if we feel unworthy of such liberty and generosity, the Spirit who lives in each of us guarantees that this will happen (Col 1:27).

An awareness of his glory leads to worship

We do not give glory to God. It already belongs to him (1 Pet 4:11). Our role is to acknowledge that he is glorious and to appreciate its significance for our own lives. When we become aware of the awesome majesty of God we shall naturally feel fear and uncertainty in the presence of such a powerful, unknowable being. But everything we know about his attitude to believers leads us to experience very different emotions, best expressed in worship.

The angels can teach us how to worship God as we increasingly appreciate his glory. Who knows God better than the angels, who live in his presence? Their worship of God is based on 'quality assessments' of him. In other words, their awareness of his character is what stimulates their worship. Seven words form the basis of their worship: 'Blessing, and glory, and wisdom, and thanksgiving, and honour, and power, and might, be unto our God for ever and ever' (Rev 7:12, Authorised Version).

The first word, 'blessing', fundamentally means 'happy'. To bless someone carries with it the idea of making that person happy. The angels are engaged in an activity that is intended to give God pleasure. In seeking to bring pleasure to God, they rehearse his attributes and his intrinsic worth, which inevitably leads them to worship him.

The result of this exploration of God should be threefold. It should result first in an increased sense of awe; secondly in changes in our emotions, our lifestyles and our readiness to follow him closer; and thirdly a recognition that this is a precursor of worship to be developed, for it will be the basis of our eternal worship. God is infinitely to be explored and therefore infinitely to be worshipped.

Though he's beyond us, he beckons to us

This is an anonymous imaginary conversation between God and a Christian that I came across some time ago:

When I said to the Lord, 'I am so short of where you want me to be,' he gently answered, 'That's OK. That's all the farther you and I can walk together.'

When I said to the Lord, 'I don't know who I am,'
he gently answered, 'That's OK. I know who you are.'

When I said to the Lord, 'I am so tired of fighting,'
he gently answered, 'That's OK. Satan is down for the count.'

When I said to the Lord, 'My mind is corrupted,'
he gently answered, 'That's OK. Use mine for a while.'

When I said to the Lord, 'I don't know how to love,'
he gently answered, 'That's OK. I will give you free lessons.'

I want to worship, Lord, but I'm not sure what to do.
Do you want me to sing a song to you? Should I sing it soft
or loud?
What would you prefer me to do?
Should I stand or sit or clap my hands? Should I raise them
high or laugh or cry?
Should I join with others or get alone,
where I can be at peace with you?

Should I sit in a church and join with the crowds
or go to the country and gaze at the clouds?
Should I praise you now for all you are, or thank you for all
that you've done?
I really want to worship you, Lord, and hear you say,
'Thank you, my son.'
But how can I worship you? Please tell me how.
What pleases you most when before you I bow?
What can I give you, since you are complete?
How can I worship while I kneel at your feet?

'Son, I don't depend on your worship;
I don't need it in the way you assume.
There are no rules for worship before I give you more room
in my heart. I don't count up the minutes you praise me.
I'm not disappointed with you.

When I call you to worship, I call you to me,
to the me that's important to you.
And when we're together in worship, you see,
it's not your praise or thanksgiving I need.
It's giving you the chance to gaze upon me.

'Take time to explore me with all of your mind;
discover how I'm mighty and awesome and kind;
hear the whisper, the King of Glory has stopped for a show.
I'm the show; you're the guest, the audience is you.
Sit down and see, come and receive.
I know you wish you could give more to me
but I'm asking you now to just come and watch me.
I expect a lot less than you think.
I give a lot more than you know.

'For I'm the one who has so much to give. There's nothing I
need now from you.
I'm the treasure, not your worship. I'm the gold, not your
praise.
I'm the pearl of greatest price, your wonder of endless days.
You're the watcher, the explorer, the child with a toy of its
dreams.
I'm the giver of glory for you.
Come, enjoy me for all I'm worth.
I'm worth it for you.'

Questions for discussion

1. Define the word 'glory'.

2. How can we see the glory of God? (John 14:8,9; Rom 1:20,21)

3. In what ways will our bodies be glorious in heaven? (1 Cor 15:42–44; Phil 3:21)

4. Which attributes of God help to stimulate worship? (Ps 29:10; 102:25–27; James 1:17; 1 John 3:20; Rev 19:11)

5. How can God's glory be manifested in times of weakness, such as the death of Jesus? (John 12:23; 2 Cor 4:9,10)

Questions to think about

1. Which characteristics of God are most important to you?

2. Which aspects of God lead you to worship him the most?

3. How can you develop your worship so as to incorporate a greater assessment of his attributes?

4. In what ways are you aware of God's glory being manifested in your life?

5 He forgives us

Have you ever wondered:

- how a holy God feels about me because I'm not holy?
- whether God will forgive me for committing the same sin again and again even though I wish I could stop?
- whether he forgives me for the sins I've forgotten about?
- whether he forgives me for the sins I didn't realise I'd committed?
- whether I need to apologise to him before he'll forgive me?

Holy Joe lives in my town. He used to carry a big Bible and dress in black with a grey tie and scruffy laced-up shoes. Sunday was his favourite day. He's different nowadays, but holy Joe still thinks he's 'holier than thou'. It all started with my new car. It rested in the church car park looking sleek and menacingly fast. Holy Joe parked his Robin Reliant next to mine and lifted his eyebrows as he watched me get out. I could read it in his eyes. My car represented extravagance: his represented holiness. Mine stood for luxury: his for necessity. He was a saint: I was a sinner. His sins were forgiven: mine were too big.

We walked together to church, sat together, sang together. He prayed – loud enough for me to hear. He prayed *at* me by asking God to help him to be holy and not squander his money. The pit he was digging for me was called guilt. I accidentally dropped my car keys down the drain on the way home and had to have a lift with holy Joe. It was clear what he was thinking: judgement for my sinful ways. We chugged to my house for the spare set of keys and chugged back. All the while, he talked of the missionaries in the steaming jungles, eating mangoes and bananas and riding bicycles.

That night holy Joe came to visit me and brought with him some of his friends. They sneaked into my house, into my bedroom and into my dreams. Joe introduced them to my sleeping mind. First, there was Anthony. He'd lived 1,900 years ago. He'd sold everything he had, ate just once a day and then only bread, salt and water. Joe reminded me of the meal I had eaten the night before. Not only had I eaten it, but also I'd enjoyed it, and the bottle of wine that went with it so well. In addition, even though my friend Neil had eaten much more than I had, Anthony still looked at me in a patronising sort of way.

Jerome then joined the happy crowd. He had spent his life in Palestine, escaping the temptations of Italy. He lived in a tiny room, but felt guilty for keeping a library of non-Christian books. Holy Joe sneaked up on me again and reminded me of the novel I was reading. 'Wouldn't God prefer you to read the Bible?' he softly whispered. I felt certain that he would, and slunk further back into the corner.

The great Augustine, champion against pagans and heresies, strolled in. I knew he was holy; he made even Joe look like a pagan. Augustine said holiness was a never-ending battle and went on to deplore the pleasures of the senses. Joe just looked at me. It was enough. The corner wasn't big enough for me as I tried to recede into its darkness. I knew that if that was a catalogue of holiness, I was certainly a sinner. Joe was right. The car would have to go, and my credit cards, and the freezer, and the tumble dryer, and the washingmachine (we could make do with a clothes line, couldn't we?), and the TV – *the TV*!

It was then that I woke up, my heart thumping, my eyes staring. I looked under the bed, but Joe wasn't there. I opened the curtains thinking I might see Augustine trotting down the road, but I didn't. I looked at the side of me, and it wasn't Mother Teresa lying there, but Judy, my wife. The birds were singing, the sun was shining, the kids were sleeping; it was Saturday. It had all been a diabolical nightmare.

And Joe? He crashed his Robin Reliant and the insurance

gave him a BMW. He avoided my eyes when I saw him in it. I gave him my best condescending grin, waved from across the car park and rushed into church ahead of him because I knew he wanted to explain. Actually, I think he likes it and that's why he thinks it's evil. Poor old holy Joe!

I'm forgiven, really

OK, so I'm a sinner – not because I may have a new car but because I don't meet up with God's standards. He is holy, and that means everything he does is perfect. He cannot make any mistakes, because he is perfect. The problem is that I am not, and when I think about God I feel my imperfection acutely. What should I do about it? Well, according to 1 John 1:8, I should acknowledge it, not deny it. John encourages his readers to accept that they are sinners but not that they're unforgivable. In 1 John 2:1,2 he reminds them and us that if we sin, Jesus takes it upon himself to speak on our behalf; he came to forgive our sins. Thus the holiness of God does not become a barrier between us and God; instead, he chooses to embrace us and welcome us as forgiven sinners who then commence the journey to holiness.

It was 9.45 on Saturday morning, 22 January. I had just returned from an elders' prayer breakfast and the house was quiet. Anna-Marie, our daughter, was in her bedroom; Luke, our son, had just returned to university and Judy was in the conservatory. I walked through the house and saw her crying on the settee. My first reaction was that she had received some sad news, but her Bible was on her lap. When I asked why she was crying she replied, 'I've just been thinking how much I've been forgiven by God.' Her reflection on this truth had moved her to tears of joy. As Christians we have been invited to explore God's forgiveness and to relax in the recognition that God has forgiven us.

The fear of taking God's forgiveness for granted is sometimes so great that we fail to take time to enjoy the fact that we have been forgiven. I get concerned that I might get blasé about sin and fall into it too easily if I concentrate on God's readiness to forgive me, so I choose not to think about it much. I am learning to recognise the fact that, though I never want to be insensitive to my sin, God encourages me to be fascinated by his forgiveness.

As believers, we regularly find ourselves making our way back to God in shame, and sometimes despair, with the same words on our lips, 'I'm sorry.' Sometimes we scarcely want to raise our heads, for we are embarrassed by what we have done. We're in good company. David, the man described as being 'after God's own heart' (see Acts 13:22), knew what it was to say sorry to God (Ps 38:18). However, God restores us because that's the amazing kind of God that he is. In addition, although we must never take him or his forgiveness for granted, it's appropriate to acknowledge it and enjoy the incredible nature of such mercy. I'm learning to recognise that it's not the act of falling in sin that's the problem – but staying down in the dust, afraid to look up. Abraham Lincoln said, 'I am not concerned that you have fallen – I am concerned that you arise.' It's important to recognise the significance of our sin and not to assume quickly that it doesn't matter. But, at the same time, wallowing in guilt and self-condemnation is not God's plan for us. He would prefer us to recognise our mistake, ask for his forgiveness and move on, determined not to fall so easily next time.

Knowing I'm forgiven helps me relax

In an article entitled 'Finding the Eye of the Storm', Craig Barnes discusses how to enjoy God's grace during the storms of life. He writes, 'When you're convinced of God's love, you're not so frightened. I don't have to succeed as a pastor: I just have to be convinced I'm forgiven by my Father ... If I know that, I'm free to enjoy being a husband and a dad and a pastor.'

Billy Graham states, 'In these days of guilt complexes, perhaps the most glorious word in the English language is "forgiveness".' Knowing I'm forgiven by God helps me relax. I'll make lots of mistakes in my life and, while I'm not indifferent to that, I know that my sins have all been forgiven and now I'm his child. The world looks different from the resurrection side of the cross. Knowing we're forgiven by God puts life in perspective. We don't realise just how forgiven we are because we don't know how much we are loved. In addition, we start this adventure of exploring God's forgiveness knowing we're never going to reach the end.

My children don't realise how much they are loved. The more they do, the more they'll be able to relax. Will they be tempted to take advantage of my readiness to forgive them? It's a risk – but you see, they're my children and I'll love them anyway. I want them to relax with me, enjoy my presence, and know they're accepted. And God's the same – only better.

Do you remember that, when Peter lacked trust in Jesus when walking on the water and thought he was going under, Jesus took him over to the other side? My sins will often cause me to go under the waters of guilt, but God is prepared to take me over to the other side of forgiveness and restoration. Peter learned the reality of this process; painful but not pointless, and ultimately productive.

Knowing I'm forgiven keeps me going

Do you remember the occasion when Elijah had let God down big time? He'd run away from Jezebel. God had used him in a remarkable way to humiliate the prophets of Baal by the miracle of fire on a drenched sacrifice. He'd fearlessly preached to the Jewish people and, with incredible courage, had told King Ahab what God thought of him. He'd ordered those prophets be put to death. He'd seen rain for the first time for three years as a result of what God did through him. Finally, God miraculously turned him into an Olympic sprinter and he ran home, overtaking Ahab's chariot on the way. He'd seen more miracles in one day

than most of us see in a whole life (1 Kings 18). However, three
verses later he was running scared (19:3). He failed to trust that
same God and, in fear, he ran from a mere mortal.

What did God do?

God sent an angel with a miraculous breakfast in bed: freshly
baked bread, still warm, a jar full of water – all within arm's
reach. It sustained him for forty days. God reminded Elijah of
his closeness to him, despite what he'd done. When he did speak
to Elijah, he spoke in a gentle whisper and said, 'It's OK. I've got
another job for you to do' (see 1 Kings 19:15).

Recognising that God forgives us provides a platform for us
to proceed. God knows you'll fail before you do. It's no surprise
to him when you blow it. He knows us better than we know ourselves and he's still committed to us. He's not surprised when he
has to forgive us again, and again, and again.

A friend of mine felt he had let the Lord down badly, and for
a long time he found it difficult to accept that God could forgive
him. Eventually, he confronted his fears and explored God's forgiveness and said sorry. He summed up his experience in these
words: 'I wish I'd realised how ready God was to pick me up,
dust me down and start me off again.' Knowing we're forgiven
because we're loved keeps us going.

Knowing I'm forgiven keeps me in awe of God

Centuries ago, a man called Anselm wrote a book called *Cur
Deus Homo*. Thankfully it's been translated from the Latin!
The title means *Why God became Man*, and Anselm sought
to respond to this question. I have often wondered about it too.
Why did God bother? What did he hope to get out of it that he
didn't already have? He doesn't need our service or worship.
He is completely self-sufficient, in need of nothing. Why get
involved, especially when he must have known that we'd spoil
his dream? What was the point, especially when achieving
our salvation would cost him the life of his Son? Why did God

become our Saviour?

God didn't save us because *we* were special. He saved us because *he's* special, and he wanted us to have the chance to explore just how special he is. The gift of forgiveness is his eternal prism that radiates his grace to us, and the sight and the beauty of that forgiveness are awesome. Through the lens of forgiveness, the portrait of God is unbelievable. It's what gives him the eternal 'wow' factor.

For me, confession is very important – not because it gives me an opportunity to whip myself metaphorically over all my sins, but because it gives me a chance to know his forgiveness. Confession, for me, isn't proof that I'm good at saying sorry. It's an opportunity for me to be in awe of his graciousness in forgiving me. God's forgiveness is thorough; it's final; it's a present possession; it's an experience to enjoy.

Recognising we're forgiven is the strongest impetus for us to love God. I don't love God because he's mighty or because he knows everything or because he can answer all my prayers, but because he's so lovable, so full of grace and forgiveness. His willingness to forgive demonstrates his love at its most intense. God is never concerned that he might be forgiving us too much. Worship is the inevitable result of considering such forgiveness.

Knowing I'm forgiven leads to an inevitable response

Remember, we're all different and we respond to God differently. My wife Judy responded to God's forgiveness in tears. One man, who had just completed a long term in prison, responded to God's forgiveness by shouting at the top of his voice, 'I'm saved! I'm saved! I'm saved!' My own response is to think about it, discuss it, explore it, probe it, like a little boy who has been given a tantalising present, because it seems too good to be true. I want to taste my forgiveness, like some new fruit that's juicier than all others.

The form of our response is not particularly important. What really matters is whether our response draws us deeper into God's love and to a more godly lifestyle (Rom 6:17,18). Forgiveness is for real. What's important is that we explore the reality of this gift. We don't have to look at the awfulness of our sin to recognise how much God forgives us. The devil would prefer us to remember our sin. Our Father wants us never to forget his love. Isn't that how good parents treat their children? Would you want to keep reminding your children of their mistakes, rubbing their noses in the way they've spoilt themselves? No, you want to rescue them, lift them out of their problem, sort them out, love them, forgive them, let them feel they're forgiven, let them be part of you again. Jesus came to earth not simply to tell us that he was ready to forgive, but actually to forgive.

Do you remember the paralysed person whose friends brought him to Jesus for healing? The first thing Jesus did was to forgive him for all his sins (Matt 9:2). It wasn't that his sin had caused his paralysis; it was that sin was his biggest problem, the one that Jesus wanted to sort out first. He could still get to heaven as a paralytic, but not if his sins remained unforgiven. But do you notice there is no record that he repented or even acknowledged his sins? Jesus had come to forgive. Imagine if he had said, 'Wait, Jesus, I haven't said sorry yet. Don't forgive me until I've repented.' Too late! Jesus had already forgiven him. That's the quality of Jesus' forgiveness. Jesus wasn't going to wait. He forgave the man before he had had a chance to ask for forgiveness. When John tells us, 'If we confess our sins, he is faithful and just and will forgive us' (1 John 1:9), he is describing not so much a process as the inevitability of forgiveness for those who confess their sins to God.

Forgiveness is an adventure in understanding how to say 'Thank you' to God; an opportunity to pursue a kind of shyness that says, 'Can it really be true? Can I really be that forgiven? Do you mind if I ask you again about my forgiveness? Can I say I'm forgiven, really, for good; for ever?'

Forgiveness: an opportunity to hear God whisper into my mind the words of Hosea 11:7,8, 'How can I give you up' even if you 'are determined to turn from me'? These words scare me because they express a love I don't understand. I am left in awe of a Father who can forgive so much for so little in return and for ever. I may cry, laugh, shout, sing – but I shall always want to bow before such a God.

Learn to explore your forgiveness; celebrate it; feel it; and never forget that it's God's greatest gift to you.

Can it be that
my sins of yesterday are forgiven,
my sins of today have been forgiven,
my sins of tomorrow will be forgiven?

Can it be that
God has welcomed me as his child?

Can it be that
I am forgivable,
I am acceptable,
I am accepted,
I am forgiven?
Yes,
even me?

But my sin looms like a wall before my eyes.
It blocks my sight of God;
it blots my life;
it bruises my best intentions;
it breezes its way into my life
again
 and again
  and again;
it breaks my heart.

Before my burning bush,
I bow my head.

Words drift into my mind.

'Your sins of yesterday are forgiven;
your sins of today have been forgiven;
your sins of tomorrow will be forgiven.
It is certain;
it has been decided by me, your God.
I have welcomed you as my child.

'Therefore,
you are forgivable,
you are acceptable,
you are accepted,
you are forgiven.

'Yes,
especially you.'

Questions for discussion

1. Does God forgive our sins if we've forgotten to apologise to him? (Ps 130:3,4)
2. Does God forgive sins that we commit again and again when we're sorry that we have done so? (Ps 103:10–12; Neh 9:17)
3. Is there any sin too serious for God to forgive? (1 Kings 8:50; Jer 33:8; Luke 23:34)
4. Does God forgive deliberate sins as readily as accidental sins if we are sorry? (Ps 32:5; 1 John 1:9)
5. Will God still punish us even though he has forgiven us? (Isa 6:7)

Questions to think about

1. If we died before we had confessed some sins to God, would he still forgive us?
2. Does God forgive the sins that we're not aware of having committed?
3. Why is 'blasphemy against the Spirit' (Matt 12:31) viewed as unforgivable?
4. Does God forgive us because we're his children or because we ask him to?

6 He's adopted us

Have you ever wondered:

- what it means to be a child of God?
- why Paul uses the image of adoption?
- how God can adopt anyone?
- why God adopts anyone?

Socrates said, 'Wisdom begins in wonder.' When I think about God and reflect that I can call him Father, I often wonder, 'Why?' Why did he choose to be my Father? Calling him God or King would have made more sense, but to call him by such a personal term as Father seems a luxury I don't deserve.

Of course, too many people have a poor experience of their fathers in childhood. However, our failure to appreciate God's fatherhood adequately is due not so much to that experience as to a limited awareness of the perfection of his fatherhood. The Bible offers analogies from human fatherhood, but only as a springboard to explore the much more remarkable aspects of God's fatherhood. God does not have natural children, since everyone has been created by him; but the concept of *adoption* helps us to discover the incredible fatherliness of God.

Adoption of a child is one of the oldest expressions of social harmony and love, dating back to the ancient Babylonian and Egyptian empires. Every reference to adoption in the New Testament is by Paul, and most of them refer to Christians. The question to be explored is; why did Paul choose to use this term to describe the relationship between God and his people? One answer is that 'adoption' describes the greatest privilege available to humanity, more significant even than salvation itself.

Adoption before the time of Jesus

Central to the act of adoption was the privileged position of the one adopted and also the significance of the one choosing to adopt. Two of the most celebrated people in the Old Testament had one thing in common. Moses, who rescued the Jewish people from slavery in Egypt, and Esther, who rescued them from being massacred by their enemies, were both adopted. The activities of both are celebrated annually in the feasts of Passover and Purim respectively. Two people with initially limited prospects fulfilled great objectives because they were adopted. Being adopted offers people the chance to achieve their full potential.

Taken from obscurity as just one group of people out of many, the Jews were adopted by God (Rom 9:4). God now became their Father and provider. They would be granted the privilege of knowing him as well as being known by him. No group other than the Jews was ever granted this privilege. When Paul wanted to describe God's relationship with Christians, he chose to use the same word used for the adoption of the Jews. But he extended its meaning to reflect the relationship that Christians have with God, which exceeds even that enjoyed by the Jews in the Old Testament.

Adoption in the time of Jesus

There is no evidence that the Israelites practised adoption in the Old Testament. All its references to adoption are to non-Hebrew people. Not surprisingly, therefore, John and Peter, writing to Jews, use the image of sonship, not adoption, to describe the Christian's relationship with God. Only Paul, writing to Gentiles, uses the term 'adoption'. Not only do the Old Testament pictures of God adopting the people of Israel parallel the way God has rescued unbelievers and transferred them into his family, but adoption in the non-Jewish world of the time sheds further light on what God has done for us. Paul's readers, aware of the custom, would understand what Paul was getting at. What then did adoption involve?

Adopted people enjoy an exalted relationship with a father, experienced by no one else but natural-born sons, and shared equally with them. Adoption becomes the basis for knowing God (Gal 4:4–9). The adopted child can call God '*Abba*, Father' (Rom 8:15). The word *abba* means 'father', and was the word Jewish children used to address their fathers. Only two children in the world can refer to me as their father: Luke and Anna-Marie. It is a relationship that only they can enjoy with me; they are my children and I am their father. There is a special exclusiveness about this bond. This is what makes adoption even more remarkable than salvation. It is one thing for God to forgive us our sins; it is another for him to welcome us as members of his family. It is true that before we can become members of his family we have to be forgiven, but being forgiven does not inevitably entail being allowed to be his children.

When we became Christians, it was because our sins were forgiven. That is a gracious gift, far greater than we deserved. But God went beyond that and welcomed us into his family; not just for the afternoon, dressed in our best clothes, but for eternity; not just to be shown around as if exploring a historical mansion, but to be ushered into the guest bedroom and given the key to the front door; not to function as servants and domestics, but to be sons and daughters (Gal 4:7); not as fee-paying visitors, but as valued friends (John 15:15). If we are to call God Father we need to feel confident with him, and God adopts us to make sure we do.

Adopted people are released from previous relationships and welcomed into a new family. Children are not just adopted for Christmas and then sent back to the desert of loneliness; it's a lifetime choice, and the process leading to it is carefully controlled. Christians have not been conscripted into an army or marched into a monastery; we have not been forced into a fraternity but welcomed into a family. Heaven is where friends are reunited for ever.

An adopted person becomes an heir of the father who adopts him or her and generally receives a new name. As heirs, adopted children have every right to be confident in the presence of their father. They don't have to beg permission to see him or book an appointment.

Adoption is motivated by love (Eph 1:5), not by the hope of reward or service. Adopted children are chosen. They cannot choose who adopts them. A Roman would sometimes adopt an heir if he needed a servant or slave, so it was not common for young children to be adopted. Alternatively, a man who needed an heir to carry on the family name might adopt a son. In either case the adoption was primarily for the benefit of the adoptive father. God is different. He adopts us not because he needs us. Rather, he volunteers to love us and chooses to adopt us because of it.

Adopted people are legally protected in their new relationship. God sees us when we're at our worst, when we don't know he's even looking at us; then he adopts us even before we've smartened up, and binds himself to that adoption by coming to live in us and improving us from the inside out (Rom 8:16,17). The Spirit who was given to us when we became Christians is the eternal evidence that our adoption is certain; he is a watertight guarantee that our adoption is irrevocable, immediate and eternal (Eph 1:13,14). Adoption unlocks God's resources for the person adopted but cannot itself be unlocked; there is no key.

Adoption results in God making himself vulnerable; he can be hurt and even rejected by his children. Fatherhood brings pleasure but also potential pain. The pleasure parents take in the first steps of their baby contrasts with the pain of those who see their child taking the first steps towards rebellion. Children sharing smiles with their parents bring pleasure; children who slam the door, refuse to do as they are asked or shout expletives cause their parents pain. Parents allow themselves to be vulnerable because they love their children more than their children know. God does the same. The question remains: 'Why?' Heaven doesn't need to be repopulated. But the God who is joy willingly adds potential pain to his untroubled existence as part of the package of adoption.

Adoption means that the resources of God the Father are made available to his adopted children. Picture the scene. The earth is scorched, the land is flat and barren as far as the eye can see. The wind whistles around you. You step on a twig, and the sound of its crack lingers in the air. The blown sand drifts against ruined walls and settles there. Your home and future are buried beneath it. Life has retreated from this desolation.

Where are the laughing children, the farmyard animals, the flocks of sheep on the hills, the footprints in the sand? There's nothing but a few lonely trees, crumbling walls, dashed dreams and hollow hopes. The flocks have gone; the people are dead or exiled; the city that once was Jerusalem has been destroyed and the land lies close to death; the crown of Israel has been robbed of its precious stones. Numbness fills the few who escaped the carnage and, as they brood over their troubles, they begin to sense despair.

This is a time when the people need someone to cling to, a big brother, a father who can soothe their fears and tell them everything will be all right. God sends a young man with limited powers but a life changing promise. The prophet Jeremiah introduced a new name for God that the people needed to hear: 'the LORD our Righteousness' (Jer 33:16). God's promise to the people through Jeremiah was that he was on their side. Although the situation was desperate and the forces against them were frightening and deadly, someone whose power was unimaginable was closer to them than the sand that clung to their clothes. His role was to make right what had been wrecked, to restore what had been ruined, to vindicate the victims and to be a father to the frightened. The king who reigned in Jeremiah's time was Zedekiah (whose name means 'The LORD is my righteousness/vindication'). Jeremiah's message was that, when the people trusted this king whose name signified certainty and assurance, he failed them. That would not happen with God. His dedication to his children is unshakeable.

There are times in the lives of all of us when dreams become disasters and hopes are torn and shredded, left to blow in the wind that always seems to be against us, bringing with it cold fears and stinging pain. But the promise remains the same, for although we may be children newly added to the family, the Father does not change (Mal 3:6). Even though others hurt us, he remains the Father who views each of his children as priceless and who cares for them sensitively; and all the bills for these services are sent to his account.

Conclusion

When God adopts us as his children we become co-heirs with Christ and share in his glory (Rom 8:17). Of course, adopted children have responsibilities as well as privileges in their new families. Matthew says that God's children are to love those who are unfriendly or hurtful (5:44). Similarly, because we are children of God, he chooses to improve us, and sometimes that can be painful (Heb 12:5–11). Chasing after sin will result in chastening by God. He does this because we matter to him, not because he's enraged by our behaviour and determined to punish us so that we cower in fear. He punishes us as a good father punishes his child, for whom he would willingly sacrifice his life. He wants his children to be the best they can be, and he helps them in that direction because he loves them (Rev 3:19).

Becoming a child of God stills sounds too good to be true, but it *is* true. Adopted children don't change to look like their father, but Christians do. That's because of the Spirit, one of whose roles is to work on our characters, improving us and helping us to change. This proactive commitment is based on his dedication to our development as children of God. Explore what it means to be a son or daughter of God now, and then imagine what it will be like in heaven. Just as a baby doesn't appreciate what it will achieve as a child, so our future too is unimaginable.

Before time's fabric was begun,
before anything was said or done,
you know you've always been the only one.

In Paradise full, fresh, man dwelt with you,
among bluebird songs, nature's palette true
till an inverse 'son'rise. With pride he withdrew.

At so many 'cross'roads have you yearned for him,
tear-stricken eyes felt adoration grow dim,
each generation, consecration more thin.

Here I exist, sliding into the mould,
another deserter, heart hanging old,
the worst of all brothers, my rationale cold.

I didn't know you when you offered to me
the sole way to freedom, a misshapen tree;
by your spear-torn side, life for eternity.

Can such blood-blind eyes receive grace and see?
Your precious Son, he more than died for me,
his executioner, at Calvary.

The wilful slayer of the Servant King
has been shown forgiveness and welcomed within,
a choir robe given as heaven's angels sing.

Like the dazzling sun, so bright, shining high,
eternal gold in a sapphire sky,
your holy light shames me as I stand by.

But then I'm brought to life by sun-beam love.
Rainbow hope rises like a star-bound dove.
How can I say just what you mean to me?

And when I offer up the best of me,
it's a poor exchange for the perfect Three.
My heart is warmed with joy – thermals from thee.

So will you please accept my tears
and love away my shame and fears?
Lord, come and take me by the hand;
please lead me to the Promised Land.
For I just want to smile at you,
for all the good things that you do.

And finally now the time has come,
when everything's been said and done.
You know you're still the only one
for me.

Luke Warrington

Questions for discussion

1. How do we know that we have been adopted by God as his children? (John 1:12; 1 John 3:1,2)

2. How does being adopted as God's children help us in our relationship with God? (Matt 6:9; Heb 12:5–10)

3. How does the fact that we are adopted by God make a difference to our sense of security? (Rom 8:14–17,23)

4. How can the fact that we are God's adopted children affect our relationship with other believers? (Eph 5:1,2; 1 Tim 5:1,2)

5. How does the term 'Abba, Father' help us in prayer? (Rom 8:15; Gal 4:5)

Questions to think about

1. What impact does the fact that we are adopted as sons and daughters of God have on our lives and futures?
2. What differences can we make in our lives in order to be more like God, our Father?
3. Why did God choose to adopt us as his children?
4. Identify three practical ways in which knowing we are God's adopted children can affect our relationships with other Christians.

7 He's all-powerful and we're not

Have you ever wondered:

- whether God could ever lose a battle?
- if God is all-powerful, why life is so unfair?
- if God is all-powerful, why I am so weak?
- how much less powerful than God the devil is?

How big is your God?

Many years ago, JB Phillips wrote a book entitled *Your God is Too Small*. In a world that believes its own press about its own accomplishments, we are in danger of losing sight of the greatness of God, whose unique might, ingenuity and authority are awesome. The Bible is clear that God is all-powerful. It describes him as sitting above the earth, the people like grasshoppers, people-powers being as nothing in comparison to his power (Isa 40:22). The nations are described as drops in a bucket, dust on a set of scales (Isa 40:15). But these expressions of God's power sometimes fall flat because they do not seem to be borne out in reality in this world and in our lives. We can even be tempted to think that if we had God's power we would make some changes, which raises the question, 'Why doesn't he?'

Why doesn't God do what we expect?

The village of Corozalito is filled every day with the screeching of colourful parrots, the call of howler monkeys and the bustle of the 94 people who live there, deep in the heart of the Columbian jungle. Most of them are Christians, due to the witness of an uneducated farmer named Victor. Victor came from a profligate background, operating a brothel, living with three women simultaneously while being addicted to alcohol. But he became a Christian and led his whole family to the Lord, followed by most of his village. From Corozalito he began to reach out to the surrounding villages, establishing groups of believers wherever he went, travelling by horseback, dugout canoe and on foot. Over about 15 years Victor led hundreds of people to Christ, as a result of which dozens of churches sprang up in Northern Columbia. The power of God was clearly seen.

Then he heard of an Indian tribe deep in the jungles of the Choco region, near the border with Panama, who had never heard of the name of Jesus. He decided to move there. In order to learn their language he lived with them, hacking a small farm out of the jungle in order to survive. Fifteen years later, at a conference for Christians in one of the bigger cities, he was with friends who wanted to know what progress had been made. His reply was startling. Although he had been there for 15 years, the Indians were so nomadic and volatile that no church had yet been established. After seeing dozens of churches established during the first 15 years of his ministry, it was almost inconceivable to see the opposite result in the second 15 years. Success and failure? Victory and defeat? The sight of God's blessing and God's turning away? The presence and absence of God's power? We shall see Victor's response later.

In my first week as a minister pioneering a church in Bootle, Merseyside, a young Christian asked me to pray for his young wife, who was dying of cancer. I visited her with my wife Judy and we prayed that her ravaged body would be restored to health by God's power. But a few days later she died. Her desperate husband rang me to tell me the sad news and asked me to come and pray for her again. He had read that Jesus had raised people from the dead and wanted me to ask him to do it again. Of course, God _could_ do it again; the question was whether he _would_. An aspect of God's character that needed to be considered alongside his power was his _will_. The distraught husband's question was, 'Why _wouldn't_ he restore her?'

In order to answer that question and understand Victor's experience, one needs to revisit the scene where God's power is most clearly married with his wisdom. At the end of his life, Jesus cried out, 'It is finished' (John 19:30). So his mission must have succeeded. To nearly everyone watching, however, it looked as if he had failed, because he had died. God did not seem to be manifesting his power, intruding in a cataclysmic manner or mightily breaking into the desperate weakness and ignominy of death. Yet in the weakness of death new life was born. Jesus' death looked like a pathetic failure, but it was the climax of his perfect obedience to God's wisdom. Success was achieved in the midst of apparent failure .

The fact is that God operates by a strategy different from that which we might prefer. It is not power that determines his activity, but wisdom. When we see a problem and have the resources to deal with it, we often do so decisively, quickly, energetically and powerfully. But God's priority is seldom to effect change by the use of power. He has another agenda and operates his divine strategy to achieve it. His power is always linked to his priorities. He functions not with red-hot, raw energy, but with careful, unruffled authority.

What should we do when God doesn't do what we think he should?

When we don't see God working as we think he should, we often get confused and worried. Our logic tells us God can do anything, so when there's a problem he doesn't solve, or a prayer he doesn't answer in the way we asked, or guidance he doesn't clarify, we assume we're to blame or the devil's too strong. Perhaps we think:

- We need to do more to get God to release his power
- We should pray or fast more to see the answer to prayer
- It must be something in our character that's holding him back
- Personal sin must be clogging the channel of power from God to us
- The devil is stopping God doing what he wants to do
- God loves us less than he loves others

Most of the time, none of these is relevant. It's just that our conclusions as to how to resolve the situation are often not the same as his. When Paul wrote to the church in Ephesus, where he had spent three years as their first pastor, he introduced his letter by reminding them that God achieves everything 'in conformity with the purpose of his will' (Eph 1:11). This was important for the Ephesians because they were aware of other forces that would attempt to destabilise them. At the time, Ephesus was one of the most important occult centres of the Roman Empire. Magical charms known as 'Ephesian letters' were bought by many visitors who sought protection on long journeys or to have their wishes granted. It was in Ephesus that sorcerers' possessions were burnt on a bonfire after their owners became Christians. They knew the power of the supernatural and could harness it. Paul's message to them was not just that God had greater power but that his power was demonstrated in harmony with his will. And since God always acts perfectly his power is never arbitrary. It does not control his actions. It is not the central part of his character. His perfection is. His power is always perfectly manifested.

Similarly, there is no danger that the devil might stop God doing what he wants to do. The devil is not a competitor to God, nor is he a dark force that comes close to winning the war. He was always only a creation of God, an angel who thought he could replace God. At the moment of his rebellion he was defeated. His demise was affirmed by Jesus in his death and resurrection, and his destiny had been determined by God before he was created.

Likewise, there is no danger of God loving us less than he loves other Christians and thus responding to our situations with less care than he does to others. At this moment, God loves us as much as he will do in a million years' time. His love for us is based not on our performance as Christians but on our position as children of God.

God has power, but priorities too

When Peter searched for Jesus early one morning and told him that a crowd of people were looking for him, Jesus went away to a different location. His priority was not to heal people just then. At that moment, his priority was prayer (Mark 1:35–38). When Jesus went to the pool of Bethesda in Jerusalem, he healed only one man, who didn't even ask to be healed. Of course, he had sufficient power to heal them all; but only one man was chosen, a man who didn't even know who Jesus was. His priority was not to release his healing power but to present himself as a Saviour worthy of their trust (John 5).

When Jesus heard that his friend Lazarus was sick, John records that Jesus stayed in Jerusalem for two more days. By this time Lazarus had died (John 11:1–6,14,15. Jesus' itinerary was determined not by his power to perform but by the priority of following his Father's agenda. That's why he didn't obliterate the devil and all his demons in one demonstration of power at the commencement of his ministry. That's why he didn't make it easier for the people to accept him by devastating the Roman occupying forces from the land. That's why he didn't step down from the cross and unleash his power against those who had put him there. His power is best demonstrated in weakness because that's the way God chooses it to be.

We have questions: God has reasons

God's logic is often very different from our own, and we can too easily assume that our conclusions, based on our logic, are right. Often they are not. Our role is to trust God. Elisabeth Elliot was the wife of one of five young American missionaries who went to the Amazon jungle to share the gospel for the first time with the Auca Indians. On 11 January 1956, after the missionaries had failed to radio their families for five days and two bodies had been seen floating in the water, she wrote these words, knowing that her three young children would probably not see their father again this side of heaven: 'I have no idea what I will do if Jim is dead, but the Lord knows and I am at rest. We hope for final word tomorrow and trust our loving Father who never wastes anything.' After it was confirmed that her husband Jim and his colleagues had been killed by the people they had gone to save, she wrote, 'God knows what he is doing and he is not under any obligation to make us any explanations.'

Sometimes, there are no answers to our problems. Take Job. He lost everything. Carnage visited the greatest man in the East, devastating him and nearly destroying him. His seven sons and three daughters were cruelly snatched from him and Job began to endure his darkest hour. But the end of the story records that Job had seven more sons and three more daughters, who were the most beautiful girls in the land. So it all worked out for the good in the end. There's your answer!

But *was* that an answer? Was that enough to silence the questions in Job's mind? Was that sufficient to compensate for the pain of the loss of his children? God appears to allow a man to be robbed of his precious children and then simply replace them with others by way of compensation. Is that picture accurate and helpful? Job was fully aware that God had unimaginable resources of power at his disposal. But even after the story had ended Job didn't seem to know why God hadn't responded in power to stop the path of pain before it had begun (42:11). What we do know is that, in the context of his own powerlessness and God's non-use of his power, Job trusted God. Not easy, but he did.

The eternal future may unlock the reasons for our present sufferings. The answer is not that God cannot help, or that he is unaware of our situation, or that he doesn't love us. The answer lies in his priorities, which are often beyond our understanding. Of course, accepting this demands faith on our part. It's helpful to remember what God said through Isaiah to the Jews who were struggling to work out what was happening to them in exile: 'my thoughts are not your thoughts, neither are your ways my ways' (Isa 55:8). What we do know is that his ways are fair (Deut 32:4), right (Hos 14:9) and holy (Ps 77:13), even though we may not understand the reasoning behind them. We can commit our ways to God (Ps 37:5) because nothing happens to us that his power could not change if it was not in his perfect plan.

God's power is for overcoming life's problems, not for escaping them

Pedrilo was a feared member of one of the most violent gangs in Manila, the capital of the Philippines – the Sigue Sigue gang. Now, he is a Christian and a leader in the largest church in Smokey Mountain, the name of Manila's biggest rubbish dump. Twenty thousand people live there, their only income earned from selling whatever they can scavenge from the trash discarded by others. God has changed Pedrilo's life except in one respect, found in the name of his former gang. 'Sigue, sigue' means 'Keep going, keep going.' Life is a struggle at times; occasionally, it's an endurance test. But our role is to keep going because we have a destination, a hope and a future. We keep going in order to arrive, to reach the finishing-mark, to complete God's agenda for us, to achieve our eternal destination: the powerful presence of God.

God's power is awesome. But his role isn't always to make the mountains melt, but to make them manageable; not always to make the desert disappear, the darkness depart or the fog fade away, but to keep us, care for us and carry us through, enabling us to grow in the process. Against the forces of the evil foe, the finger of God is enough to keep us safe. When I think he's removed his finger from my life, I'm wrong. I may not know all the answers, but I am learning to trust the one who has set the agenda.

He holds the foe as he tries to push in
with an empty heart and malicious grin.
He cups his hand and shelters me there
in a cradle for him and me to share.

> *And the enemy writhes in anger and pain;*
> *desperate to unleash his evil and stain*
> *my peace with a blot of fear,*
> *to take my smile and smudge it with tears,*
> *to take my calm, my innocent joy*
> *and shake me and hurt me*
> *like an old, worthless toy.*

But there's someone between us and he can't get in.
Although he'll pretend he's a powerful king,
he's simply a bully, a thief and a fraud;
we look at him calmly
through the fingers of God
for ever
folded
around
me.

Questions for discussion

1. What powerful acts has God done in your life? (Rom 1:16; 5:1; Col 1:10,11; 2 Pet 1:3)

2. How can we access some of God's power? (Rom 1:16; Eph 1:18,19; 3:16; 6:10,11)

3. How can the fact that God is all-powerful make a difference to our sense of security? (Rom 15:13; Phil 3:10,21)

4. How is God's power manifested in the world? (Jer 10:12; Col 2:10)

5. Why does God choose to manifest his power in our weakness? (2 Cor 4:7; 12:9; 13:4)

Questions to think about

1. What is the difference between God's power and his authority, and which is more important?

2. How can you see God's power manifesting itself in your own weakness?

3. How can you help others recognise God's power when they feel powerless?

4. What would have been the result if Jesus had exercised his power and stepped down from the cross?

8 He's holy and we're accountable

Have you ever wondered:

- whether God could ever sin?
- whether God could make a mistake?
- whether God can make us holy?
- what it means to say that God is holy?

When we refer to God as being holy, it doesn't simply mean that he has never sinned or made a mistake. It does not simply refer to the fact that he is perfect and that everything he does is flawless. It's much more significant than that. God is not just the one who has never sinned, broken the law or had to say sorry. He's more remarkable than that, much more.

He's different

The fundamental meaning of the Greek word regularly translated 'holy' describes God more completely. It means 'set apart', 'different'. It's not that God is unusual, but that he is unique; he's not just out of the ordinary but one of a kind. That's what it means when he is defined as being holy. Isaiah 40:25 says, 'To whom will you compare me? Or who is my equal? says the Holy One.' Sinlessness is just part of what makes him different, but he is much more than sinless. He is set apart from anything anyone can imagine, unequalled, incomparable, irreplaceable. He's holy.

One of the reasons God is so different is that he cannot improve himself or be improved; he can't get better or worse; he can't be developed or refined; he's already ideal, and always has been and always will be. It's a rare person who is satisfied with his or her workmanship whether as a composer, author, painter, craftsman or musician. But people are even less prepared to acknowledge that they have achieved perfection in their art when a superior authority examines their work. They may have done the best they could, but they will acknowledge that it is not the best that could be achieved. But when God designs, creates or achieves anything, it is simply the best that it could be. It is not just that he has nothing equally good to compare it with; he compares it with his character, which is perfect. Everything that flows from him is flawless. He's holy. He's different.

He's definitely different

Joshua describes God as being holy because he protects his people (Josh 24:19). Joshua lived in a world where the gods were worshipped not because of their faithfulness to their subjects but because they were feared. God is different.

Samuel describes God as being holy because he is a rock (1 Sam 2:2). Unlike other so-called gods, God is dependable, safe, unshakeable and trustworthy. He's different.

Isaiah describes God as being holy because he is righteous (Isa 5:16). He doesn't make mistakes; he never worries whether he's made the right choice; he never needs to change his plans; he doesn't need an eraser. God is always right. He's different.

The same prophet also describes God as being holy because he's almighty (Isa 6:3). It's not just that he's powerful; he's all-powerful; not just that he's strong, or even very strong, but that strength resides in him. The authority of the most authoritative empire, the power of the most powerful bomb, the influence of the most influential person, the dominance of time over our lives are all but whispers in the wind of God's strength. The most powerful force is a fragile leaf blown by the breeze when compared to God. He is supreme. He's different.

For Isaiah, one dimension of God's holiness is that he redeems his people (Isa 43:14). This is something else that emphasises how different God is. When people angered the gods they expected nothing but punishment. Sickness, suffering, storms and even death were the shadows that stalked the ancient world, sent by the gods when the people upset them. But God is different because he made the first move to restore the relationship with himself that people had broken. He did not inflict malicious punishment but showed merciful patience at cost to himself. He buys us back. He's different.

He calls us to be holy

One of the most frequent commands of God to his people is to be holy because he is holy (Lev 11:45; 20:26; 1 Pet 1:16). If we think this simply means that we should be sinless, we are in for some worrying times. We may feel that God is asking us to do the impossible, since we cannot be sinless until we are in heaven (1 John 1:8). We may feel further aggrieved because we know that God knows we cannot be sinless until we get to heaven; so why does he tell us that we should be? Perhaps God is encouraging us to raise the standards of our lifestyles so that they reflect the character of Jesus. More fundamentally, however, he is asking us to recognise that he has set us apart for himself and to consecrate ourselves in practical ways to that mission. Moses explains that to be holy means to be consecrated to God (Lev 20:7), to acknowledge daily that he controls our actions, thoughts and words.

To be holy means to be set apart for God

When the word 'holy' is used in the Bible, it regularly means 'set apart for God'. Holy fruit (Lev 19:24) isn't fruit that has no bugs but fruit that has been set apart as an offering to God. The priests are called holy (Lev 21:7) not because they do not sin but because they are consecrated to God. A holy field (Lev 27:21), holy ground (Josh 5:15), a holy temple (Ps 64:5) and a holy mountain (Ps 99:9) are not uncontaminated by sin but consecrated to the service of God.

Similarly, when Paul speaks to the Christians in Corinth, he describes them as being a holy temple (1 Cor 3:17). He doesn't mean they're sinless or even good Christians. In fact, many of them were battling with a variety of sinful tendencies and habits. He is reminding them of their position as people set apart by God for a personal relationship with him and to be his messengers. That's the meaning of the word 'saint'; in the Greek it is related to the word for 'holy', and describes a person who has been set apart, by God, for God. It is a mark not of sinlessness or superiority but of sole ownership and consecration. It's not a cause for pride in what we have done but a challenge to pursue whatever God wants us to do. It's not a sign that we have arrived but a reminder that God has arrived in us.

To be holy means that we belong to God

When God described the Jewish nation as 'holy' (Exod 19:6), he was saying that he owned them. No longer were they owned by the Egyptians; now they were owned by God. Because of this, God told them, he had carried them 'on eagles' wings' (19:4). This is the kind of care that goes with the package of being under heavenly management.

Of course, there are personal implications of this new ownership: responsibilities as well as rights, prohibitions as well as privileges. In a list of guidelines for behaviour written for the Christians in Ephesus (4:17 – 6:9), Paul gives them the fundamental reason why God adopted them. In 4:30, he reminds them that sin grieves the Spirit of God, who is described as holy and the one who is committed to their salvation. This is the only time Paul describes the Spirit as 'the Holy Spirit of God' – a graphic reminder of the Spirit's status. Paul recommends his readers to consider how humiliating it would be to embarrass this Spirit by letting him down and thereby bringing his reputation as a guarantor (someone who presents them positively before God) into disrepute. It would be the height of ingratitude for people to hurt a Person who was doing this for them. Belonging to a holy God has strings attached. If we're not serious about being holy, God feels sad. It's a sobering thought that mortals can cause the immortal God to feel sorrow.

To be holy means to be different

The final reference to being holy in the Bible is in Revelation 22:11. People who are holy are contrasted with people who do wrong and compared with people who do right. Holy people are those who are trying to be better, to stamp out sin, to be thoughtful, not thoughtless, to be sensitive, not indifferent, to be as they ought to be, not as they are or were. Such people are different and holy. To be holy is thus not simply a destination but a daily process of deciding to be different.

A friend of mine has a Highland terrier, a pure white pedigree champion. She keeps it in pristine condition, bathing it regularly so that its white fur is spotless. On a winter's day after it had snowed all night, she looked out of her bedroom window on to the garden below and saw a dog run across the lawn leaving pawprints in the fresh snow. She could not understand how the dirty dog had strayed into her garden, and asked her husband to chase it away. 'But it's *your* dog!' he said. The animal that normally looked so clean and white seemed dirty compared with the sparkling snow. Our task is not to compare our lives with those of others or with our own best intentions, but with God. Aiming for his holiness is not a burden but a benchmark; meant not to inspire guilt but to encourage us to receive his grace to go forward. He has already set us apart; now he motivates us on.

How to be different

We cannot become like God quickly; it is a lifetime process, and even at the end of our lives, we shall still not have achieved our target completely. I am discovering a number of principles in this lifestyle of development.

The first priority is to *set small targets*. Rather than deciding to read the whole Bible in a month, read a chapter a day. Instead of planning an hour a day in prayer, commit to ten minutes. Don't plan to memorise a verse of Scripture every day, try one a week. Just as a golfer doesn't expect to hit a ball from the tee into the hole, so we need to be realistic in setting achievable goals.

A second principle is: *don't try to achieve too many targets at one time*. Imagine trying to keep table-tennis balls under water using only one hand. Keeping two under is not too difficult, but it gets progressively more difficult the more balls you add. Sometimes, we get into difficulties because, in our enthusiasm to be better, we try to do too much too quickly and end up failing in most attempts. It's better to be thoughtful in the choice of targets and realistic in deciding what can be achieved.

The final principle is to *set a time in which to achieve the goals*. This allows you to choose various tasks, giving you the opportunity to progress in different aspects of your life. It also helps you keep a check on how you have progressed in the time allocated. It is more important to see that you have moved forward than to worry about having missed the target if you don't achieve it in the time set. One of the practices that I regularly undertake with some friends is for each of us to set a target relating to an aspect of our growth as Christians, write it down, place the paper in an envelope and seal it with wax. Then, together, we open our envelopes six months later, and, if it's appropriate, we share how we have done. It's a practical and accountable way of trying to follow the example of Jesus and to fulfil God's desire for us to be holy as he is.

A sculptor was once asked when he would be finishing the sculpture he was working on. He stopped filing and scraping, and as he polished the piece he said, 'I'll never finish it. I just keep refining it until they come and take it away.' We shall never finish refining our characters, and God doesn't expect us to. Our role is to set a strategy for change and stay in touch with the Spirit to achieve it, little by little, until he comes to take us away.

There was no need for it, no reason.
No one knew why or dared to ask.
Who could? Maybe somebody should have
but nobody did … and the plan went ahead.
There was no thread of meaning, no purpose.
Why not leave things alone instead?
He simply shook his head.
Everything was perfect before he did.
Nothing stirred the peace that reigned supreme.
But he went ahead and the world was spoilt.
All that he'd done was blown away
like fragile leaves on a stormy day.
The gold had turned to grey;
someone would have to pay
to right the wrong,
to change the darkness into day.

The Sun would have to shine again.
He simply said he would.

Why did he do it?
Why soil his hands?
I simply cannot understand
why he should stoop to create man.

Lord, I am a sinner whom you've made free.
I marvel at your love for me
that welcomes me in your family.
You're unique in all you are
and I want to be different for you.

Help me to be pure and holy and clean;
let Jesus be seen in me.

Questions for discussion

1. Since God is holy, how can we feel comfortable in his family? (Rom 8:1,34–39; 1 John 1:9)

2. What characteristics come to mind when you think of God as holy? (Exod 19:3; 1 Sam 2:2; Ps 77:13; Isa 5:16; 8:13; 40:25)

3. What does God's holiness reveal about his love for his people? (Deut 7:6; Eph 5:25–27; Col 1:22; Heb 13:12; 1 Pet 2:9)

4. How does the fact that God is holy encourage us to be prepared to trust him? (Isa 41:14; 43:15; 48:17)

5. What lessons for our lifestyle can we learn from the fact that God is holy? (Deut 23:14; Rom 12:1; 1 Cor 1:2; Eph 1:4; 5:3; 1 Thess 3:13; 4:4,7)

Questions to think about

1. Is it possible to feel spiritually clean in the presence of God?

2. Why did a holy God choose to save unholy humanity?

3. What difference should the fact that God is holy have on our lifestyles?

4. What targets can we set to reflect God's character in us?

9 He's in charge and we're safe

Have you ever wondered:

- whether God actually knows what I am doing now?
- whether accidents occur without God's permission?
- why bad things happen to good people?
- whether God is with me in my darkness?

A few years ago we had a family holiday in Orlando, Florida, where the Disney parks and an assortment of water parks are located. The latter are vast areas of entertainment, all involving water. One of the experiences on offer was a tall water slide with a 30-metre vertical drop, the base of which curves into a shallow receiving pool. My young son was intrigued, and I rashly volunteered to join him. It involved a steep climb up steps to a platform where a number of lifeguards supervised two queues of mainly young people and directed them towards two gates. At this point, though my brain shouted, 'Go back', my embarrassment at the thought of going down the steps between the ascending crowds of ardent devotees overcame my common sense. Those about to undertake 'the experience of their lives' sat in front of the gates, crossed their arms over their chests and crossed their ankles. At a word from the lifeguard, each person shuffled to the edge of the slide, their legs dangling over the vertical drop. At that point, it was too late to go back. I was no longer in control of my destiny; the people waiting behind me were! With my son on the adjacent slide, I had no option but to launch off into the unknown. With my life flashing before my eyes and my heart beating far too quickly for my age, off I went.

Being out of control makes us vulnerable. It can fill us with fear, panic and a sense of isolation. Not being in control is an unpleasant experience. Yet it happens to us all the time. Circumstances change; life throws something unexpected at us. It's scary because not only do we feel *we're* not in control of our lives, but sometimes it feels as if no one else is either. Sometimes it seems that not even God is. But he *is* in control.

Through the years I have affirmed two maxims that are based on the evidence of the Bible. They are:

- an increasing readiness to relax because God's *in charge*
- an increasing readiness to relax because *God's* in charge

Moses was safe because God was in charge

Let me take you back a few thousand years to consider a man who knew what it was like to feel vulnerable. God had asked Moses to fulfil a mission that would create many enemies. He was asked to confront the most powerful man in the world, who was also the head of the most powerful religion in the world, and to do it as the representative of a God he had never seen. In order to support Moses, God convinced him that he was more in control of the situation than Moses could ever imagine. God showed Moses that he was on his side by working miracles that demonstrated that Moses was not on his own. A superior force was with him and was acting as his support.

At the same time, God demonstrated that he was against anyone or anything that may have sought to impede Moses. Every miracle that filled Moses with hope struck fear into the demonic forces who were against Moses. God was holding Moses tight; tighter than Moses realised.

The plagues God sent on the Egyptians achieved two objectives. First, they demonstrated to Moses (and to Pharaoh) that God intended to fulfil his desires. Moses was secure despite his apparent weakness compared to Pharaoh with his armies and gods. Secondly, they opposed the various deities of Egypt. Many Egyptian gods and goddesses were believed to have earthly representatives who received worship on their behalf. A number of the plagues undermined this worship by being directed to those representatives (Exod 12:12; 18:11).

For instance, when God turned the Nile into blood it was not just his way of supporting Moses' claims in Pharaoh's eyes; it was also a statement against the god of the Nile. The Egyptians believed that the god infused the river. Pharaoh's daughter bathed in it, not because it was the cleanest water but because she believed that the deity of the river would permeate her being as she did so. Along the river were over a hundred shrines, and the city of Nilopolis was a major centre for the worship of the river god. By turning the water into blood, God transformed something that represented life and fertility so that it represented death and sterility.

Similarly, frogs were believed to be the earthly representatives of fertility gods. God made a mockery of these so-called gods by increasing the animals' birth rate to such an unprecedented degree that the people had to kill them and burn them. God belittled the god that apparently owned the power of birth by arranging a population explosion of ridiculous proportions.

The plague of lice was particularly disruptive to the worship of the pagan gods because they rendered the priests ceremonially unclean, so that they could not serve in the temples. Thus the gods received no service or worship.

The darkness God sent was frightening and interrupted normal life, and it too was another statement against the demonic forces that took advantage of the peoples' superstitious beliefs. The Egyptians believed that the most powerful god was the Sun god, Ra. All the other temples faced east, where the Sun rose, as it was assumed to be the most superior god. But this symbol of life and light God cast into shade for three days.

The message of these and the other plagues is clear. When God commissions someone to act on his behalf, he arranges protection and support against all who may seek to put a stop to that activity. God provided protection for Moses and put his enemies in their place. Knowing that God is determined to do the same for all believers helps us to put our own lives into perspective.

Paul was safe because God was in charge

Thousands of years later, God arranged for another of his messengers to stand before another ruler, the head of the most powerful empire in the world at that time, who lived in a city dominated by the worship of many gods including himself. Like Moses, the apostle Paul was to enter a hostile environment with a message of freedom for people in bondage, though there was little reason to believe that many people would accept it.

Since Paul was delegated by God to undertake this mission, it was to be expected that evil forces would seek to undermine his plans. However, the final two chapters of Acts record that, despite all the events that could have terminated the mission, Paul arrived safely at his destination and, for two years, engaged in the work that God had called him to do (Acts 28:17–28). The reason for this is clear. God was in charge of the mission. Luke does not record whether Paul met the emperor, whether he established churches in Rome, what happened to him during those two years, whether he returned to Antioch or whether he died in Rome. What Luke does record in great detail is the sea voyage from Israel to Rome. He does so for a singular purpose: to demonstrate that God, who directs the destinies of his people, is sovereign. He ensures that he achieves his will through them despite the obstacles in the way.

So Luke records at length the problems the travellers encountered (Acts 27:7 – 28:6): the wind that made it difficult to sail and slowed them down, the indecision and unwise action of the captain, the fierce storm and darkness, the danger of starvation, the attempt by some of the crew to abandon the ship, the shipwreck, the soldiers' plan to kill the prisoners to forestall their escape, and Paul's snakebite. None of these obstacles was sufficient to disrupt God's plans for Paul. Why? Paul stated that *God* had determined that he would stand before Caesar (Acts 23:11; 27:24). Therefore, Paul could encourage everyone else not to fear, because his God could be trusted

This story is particularly significant in the first-century context. We must not forget the danger the Mediterranean Sea meant to the ancients. Today's cruise liners and ferries, which sail with accurate maritime aids, are very different from the primitive boats which faced the dangerous conditions during the first century.

Two of the main books used in the schools of the era were the *Odyssey* (traditionally viewed as the work of Homer) and Virgil's *Aeneid*. Each was used as a textbook that pupils read, memorised and dramatised. In particular, these books identified principles of life and conduct that helped to teach children how to become model citizens. They told of heroes who battled against the odds to cross the Greek (Mediterranean) Sea, overcoming the strategies of gods, storms and natural enemies along the way, until they achieved their objective. In the *Aeneid*, the prize is viewed as Rome, where Aeneas and his Trojan companions settled. The supremacy of the gods supporting these heroes is proved by their ability to support their protégés against all the obstacles that faced them.

Luke wrote the book of Acts for mainly Gentile readers. They were familiar with such epics and the messages they presented. In his account of Paul's sea voyage, Luke demonstrates that the God who protects Paul is superior to all other gods because he shields him as he crosses the hazardous Greek Sea from Israel to Rome. His Christian readers can take heart that the God who protected Paul is committed to protecting them too. At the same time, those who don't trust God are encouraged to transfer their allegiance to the one whose authority is supreme. The last verse of the book of Acts emphasises this unprecedented authority: Paul is recorded as preaching the kingdom of God and teaching about the Lord Jesus Christ 'boldly and without hindrance'. The final word in the original Greek means 'unhindered'. Luke's last word on the life of Paul reminds the readers that God, who reigns in supreme power, was supervising Paul's destiny and nothing could obstruct him.

God overshadowed Paul, guiding him and controlling his destiny in even the most hostile circumstances. The same God controls the lives of every other believer. We may not always feel that we have a hold on God, but he always has a hold on us. Christ has ascended, but he is not absent.

When things go wrong, God is still in charge

When things go wrong, it isn't necessarily because we have sinned or stepped out of God's will or because the devil caused it. Often it occurs because we are part of a world that has not been right since sin slid into the Garden of Eden. Whatever the cause of our problems, God is not absent from us. The most evil act in history was the crucifixion of Jesus. There it appeared that God was not in control, but that wicked people, operating their own selfish agenda, were directing the destiny of Jesus. In reality, God was still in control, as Peter affirmed in his speech on the Day of Pentecost: '[Jesus] was handed over to you by God's set purpose and foreknowledge' (Acts 2:23).

We don't have the answers to many of life's problems and traumas. But what we do have is the certainty that God is still in charge. Safety and security are found not in the absence of danger but in the presence of God. The earliest days of the church saw a devastating catalogue of natural calamities including famines, earthquakes and plagues, as well as verbal and physical attacks on Christians, resulting in countless martyrdoms. Christians were not safeguarded from the events of that era. What they had to learn was that these events did not separate them from God. Most people of the time thought the gods were not interested in their situations, much less that they could be bothered to get involved in their lives. The message of the Bible is that God is so interested that he came into this world in the person of Jesus to show how much he wanted to infuse us with his presence and resources. His purpose is to make a difference in our lives and in the situations in which we find ourselves.

God holds our destiny in his hands, whatever it might be, whether life or death, a pension or martyrdom. He is in control and never out of control. There's never a panic in heaven. God is in control even when it feels as if no one is in control. He is looking after us even when it feels that no one is looking after us. He is determined to give us whatever is best for us and to fulfil his will in our lives. Because he has supreme authority he can do whatever he wants. The psalmist declares, 'The LORD does whatever pleases him, in the heavens and on the earth' (135:6). Paul affirms that God will ensure that the work he has started in our lives is completed (Phil 1:6), while Peter confirms that we are 'shielded by God's power' (1 Pet 1:5).

It is no surprise that many of God's names relate to his sovereignty. The first book of the Bible emphasises that he is God Most High (Gen 14:20), God Almighty (17:1) and Sovereign Lord (15:2). The final book of the Bible gives God similar titles, including Lord God Almighty (Rev 1:8) and God the Almighty (19:16), while the final chapter refers to God's throne (22:1). It is as if the writers want the readers to be assured from first to last that, whatever life and the future hold, God controls both, and it's easy for him. The more we fill our minds with these certain truths, the more our lives will radiate peace and security.

When he speaks, the earth shakes.
When he walks, creation watches.
When he looks, silence reigns.
Where he treads, he claims.

Where he lives, he reigns,
for he is King.

He has no foes who trouble him;
no enemy who causes stress or strain;
no force that makes him catch his breath
or struggle, slow down,
or even think of moving back again.

Like a noble lion, he moves, in serene
and awesome majesty
and wherever we, his cubs, are,
the Lion King is near.

He is our shade and strength,
our stream in the desert,
our nest in the thorn bush,
our pocket in the crush of life.

We are safe because we are in his palm
as is the world in which we are.
He breathes calm into our lives
and folds us into his love.
He whispers peace
and ripples stillness
into our storms
for he is in charge
of all we are.

Questions for discussion

1. What evidence is there that God supervises our lives?
   (1 Pet 5:1)

2. How should we think when life seems unfair? (Isa 45:17;
   Eph 1:11; James 1:2–4)

3. How does Psalm 23 show how God watches over and cares for us?

4. In what ways did God supervise Jesus in his life and ministry?

5. How does God's peace link with his authority? (Eph 2:14,15; Phil 4:9; 1 Thess 5:23)

Questions to think about

1. What difference does the fact that God is sovereign make to the way you face the future?

2. Why doesn't God demonstrate his sovereignty clearly in the world today?

3. How would you counsel a believer who is struggling to find God in his or her suffering?

4. Since he has the power to end all suffering, why doesn't he do so?

10 He knows all and we can trust him

Have you ever wondered:

- whether God knows the future?
- how involved God is in my destiny?
- whether God knows what will happen to me tomorrow?
- whether our prayers can affect the future if God already knows it?

The thing we can be most certain of is the past – it has happened and, though we might wish to change some of it, we can't. The thing we can be least certain about is what hasn't happened yet – the future. The future is an object of speculation. Are we going to pass or fail that exam, have two children or none, be in the same job in three years' time or not, be alive in five years' time or not? The future is exciting just because it is uncertain; changes that may be very positive can occur. However, it's also a little scary because the events it brings may turn hope to hopelessness. Would I choose to know the future if it was possible so to do? The fact is, I don't know what tomorrow holds, but God does.

God knows everything

It stretches my imagination to breaking-point when I try to understand that God knows everything. God doesn't need to learn; he has no need to engage in study or research, because he knows more than any number of encyclopedias can hold. Not only does he know every fact there is to know, but he also understands everything. He knows when a leaf falls in a forest, where it falls and why it falls. He knows how many stars exist and why; he even knows their names (Ps 147:4). I know that the clouds hang in the sky; God knows how they do so (Job 37:16). He knows that we are individually distinct from other people but he also knows why we are all different. Job declared that God 'sees everything under the heavens' (Job 28:24), while Psalm 147:5 states that 'his understanding has no limit'.

The fact that God knows everything brings many benefits to us as Christians:

First, we needn't fear that God loves us only because he can't see the sinful parts of our lives. He knows everything about us, the good, the bad and the ugly, and still remains committed to us. David came to the same conclusion when he acknowledged, 'Lord, you have searched me and you know me', and said such knowledge was too wonderful for him (Ps 139:1,6). Far from causing him embarrassment or fear, it delighted him because it combated his anxieties while at the same time enabling him to benefit from the Lord's knowledge of his progress (Ps 139:23,24).

This characteristic of God is very important, for it means we can accept that God loves us unconditionally. This is the greatest form of love; everyone wants to know they are loved no matter what. This is never completely possible between humans because no one can know someone else perfectly. But God does, and he loves us eternally despite what he knows about us. There is nothing in us that God doesn't already know. He's never surprised by our actions or thoughts. This doesn't mean he is indifferent to our sins, but it does mean that he is never going to come across something in us that takes him by surprise and stops him loving us.

Secondly, because he knows all our circumstances we are secure whatever they are. He does not function like the emergency services, who answer our call and have to find out where we are and what we need. He hears us before we breathe the words; they are recorded by him before we rehearse them in our minds. Jesus encourages his disciples by reminding them that 'even the very hairs of your head are all numbered' (Matt 10:30). He always knows what's around the corner. He reigns in calm tranquillity.

Thirdly, given that he knows everything, he can't possibly make a mistake. He cannot initiate any flawed activity. Error is not possible with God.

Fourthly, we don't need to remind him about anything. God does not need a shopping-list, memos or a diary. The angels are not his secretaries, reminding God of his appointments and daily agenda. Instead, they ensure that his sovereign, wise plans are carried out. We could never inform God of something he did not already know about. He knows all there is to know, now and for ever.

Finally, he is unique and we worship him as the Incomparable One (Isa 55:9).

God knows more than we do

Of course, saying that God knows more than we do is to state the obvious, but still it's helpful to do so. Change occurs so rapidly today that knowledge quickly gets outdated in all disciplines. I heard of a scientist who was asked how many subatomic particles had been discovered. Looking at his watch, he said, 'At this moment in time, the number of subatomic particles that have been discovered is ...' and then named a figure in the hundreds. He knew that technological advances were so rapid that the number could change very quickly. It helps us to be humble when we recognise that the more we know, the more we realise there is to know. The quest for knowledge can be fulfilling but also frustrating. However much the whole of humanity put together may know, there are enormous gaps in our knowledge. We only have to think of the enormity of space, the complexity of the human body or the mystery of life itself to know how true this is.

Job was drawn into a one-sided conversation with God in which God told him that many aspects of life were outside Job's knowledge (38:1–41). 'Where were you when I laid the earth's foundation?' he asked. 'Have you journeyed to the springs of the sea or walked in the recesses of the deep?' 'Do you know the laws of the heavens?' 'Who has the wisdom to count the clouds?'(vs 4,16,33,37).

God was seeking not to humiliate Job, but to remind him that his knowledge was limited. This fact helped Job by putting into perspective his own questions about his suffering. He did not understand or know why it was happening, but God revealed that *he* did. The one who gives orders to the morning, who knows how to limit the power of the sea and who fathers the rain would not allow Job to fall from his grip. Job concludes, 'My ears had heard of you but now my eyes have seen you' (42:5). When we catch a glimpse into the mind of God we wonder why we ever worried.

When our son Luke was a toddler and before he could talk, he taught us an important lesson. As we came home late one evening, he tried to get our attention by pointing to the dark skies. We couldn't determine what it was that had struck him so forcibly, but his excitement was contagious. Eventually, we realised it was the moon. Something we were used to was a miracle to him when he saw it for the first time. Since then, I have made it my aim to never lose the sense of wonder that comes from considering God's creation; a complex tapestry of unimaginable and breathtaking beauty in all its manifestations, making us gasp in admiration and awe at the excellence of such a wise God.

God knows everything about the future

The Bible is clear that God knows the future. Isaiah 42:9 tells us that God declares the future before it happens. Jesus knew that Judas would betray him and that Peter would deny him. God's complete knowledge of the future can be profoundly encouraging because it indicates that everything is under his control, even the things and situations that don't exist yet.

But the fact that God knows the future also raises serious questions. For example, if God knows the future, what's the point of praying? How can God know about things that haven't happened yet? Doesn't it mean that God predetermines the future and that therefore people have no free will?

First, although our explanations may be limited or even non-existent, we must let the Bible state the facts about God, however incompatible with our understanding they may be. Since God is incomparable, we do well to reflect on the words of Paul:

'Oh, the depth of the riches of the wisdom and knowledge
of God!
How unsearchable his judgments,
and his paths beyond tracing out!
"Who has known the mind of the Lord?
Or who has been his counsellor?"'

(Rom 11:33,34)

Although it is valuable to explore God, there comes a time when we have to acknowledge that 'mystery' is the best word to describe him. To admit that God is mysterious and therefore fundamentally unknowable in his entirety is to accept what the Bible says even when it does not fit with our wisdom.

Secondly, some have suggested that God is outside time; he knows what will occur in future time but does not determine the way people act. He knows what will occur without determining that it will occur., God knows what I will do next, but the fact that he knows this doesn't mean I am forced to do it. Indeed, if I did something different, that wouldn't make God wrong, because he would know that I was going to do something different. Perhaps God knows the future only partially? But that would place him at the mercy of the future, significantly undermining the security of Christians and making a nonsense of Paul's encouraging words to the church in Philippi: 'he who began a good work in you will carry it on to completion' (Phil 1:6).

Thirdly, the fact that God knows the future does not release individuals from taking responsibility for their actions. The Bible holds both these factors in tension and does not seek to resolve or explain the apparent paradox. Proverbs 16:9 states: 'In his heart a man plans his course, but the Lord determines his steps.' The Bible does not permit us to have a fatalistic approach to life, viewing God as making the future happen in a particular way, so that people feel powerless. Both God and individuals are responsible for the future. There is a mystery here, but it is better to acknowledge that mystery and live with the Bible's tension than to try to unravel it in a way that the Bible chooses not to do.

Similarly, the interaction between prayer and the will of God is a mystery, in part. On the one hand, it is very simple. Prayer is communication with God, but it is also God's way of communicating with us. It is not the only means; he speaks to us in the Bible and through the Spirit. But God can also make his will known to us in prayer. Prayer is not an opportunity for us to get God to change his mind or get him to do want we want, but an opportunity for God to help us pray as he would pray if he were praying with us. Prayer is valuable, not as a means of changing the future, but as a way to engage with God in bringing the future into reality in the present.

God is wise in the use of his knowledge

Not only does God know everything but, more importantly, he uses his knowledge carefully and wisely. The Bible's God is not a detached superbrain. Rather, he uses his knowledge for the benefit of his creation. The Bible often links God's knowledge with his wisdom (eg Rom 11:33). At the same time, wisdom is often associated with God's power. God knows the best course of action and has the power to take it. His wisdom may sometimes be recognised as such only when looking back and, in some cases, that will mean when we reach the other side of death. It was years after his brothers had sold him into slavery that Joseph was able to acknowledge that 'it was not you who sent me here, but God' (Gen 45:8).

God does what pleases him

Allied closely to his wisdom and power is the fact that God does only what pleases him (Isa 46:10). This flows logically from the fact that he knows everything and uses his knowledge wisely. But now it includes a personal dimension, that of pleasure. God is pleased to act in the way he does. The implications for believers are significant. God knows all about us (Ps 139:2–4). He chooses to develop our lives wisely (Eph 1:11) on the basis of his incomparable authority (Dan 4:35), but also is motivated to bring it to fruition because he is pleased to do so. Psalm 115:3 states that 'he does whatever pleases him'. These truths draw us to worship, as we recognise that the one who knows us intimately chooses to safeguard us for the eternal future that he has planned with us in mind.

> *I watched it uncertain, afraid to let go.*
> *It struggled to hold on, fluttering to and fro.*
> *The leaf held on with all its might.*
> *To the tree it held tight*
> *and all the while the wind softly caressed it and*
> *encouraged it to fly*
> *But it resisted the pull.*
> *It was safe where it was.*
> *Who knew where the wind would blow?*

*And all the while, the wind warmly caressed it and
encouraged it to fly.*

*One day it did. Tired of holding on, it let go
and prepared to flutter down
to the dirt below where it knew it would die.
But the wind that had gently plucked it from the tree
tucked it under its arm
and took it high, far higher than ever it had dreamed it
could go.
Once it was tied to the tree
but now it was free on the breeze.*

*Lord, I wish I was that leaf. I wish I could trust you so
completely, to know you hold me, and sense your peace.
But, I'm afraid Lord, afraid to let go. I fear the future;
where might I go? What if I fail? What will letting go entail,
Lord?*

*'Son, trust in my Spirit, the Breeze.
His love for you is what sets you free.
He says that he'll change you, but love is his mould.
He promises to hold you, but tight in his fold.
He promises to use you, but it's all in his love.
You'll fly – but remember your teacher's a dove.
And together you'll fly in peace on the breeze.
His love for you is what gives you peace.
For my will for you is not a sigh or a rod;
it's a song, to take you high, to me, your God.
My Spirit in you is all you need
to be assured that I love you;
for you belong to me.'*

Questions for discussion

1. What difference does the fact that God has perfect knowledge make to our present circumstances? (Ps 103:14; 139:2–4; John 10:14)
2. What difference does knowing that God has perfect knowledge make to your thoughts about the future? (Job 23:10; Dan 2:22; Isa 55:9)
3. How can we receive some of God's wisdom? (Ps 111:10; 119:99; Col 3:16)
4. What most impresses you about God's knowledge? (Ps 147:5; Isa 65:24; Acts 15:18)

Questions to think about

1. Does God determine our future or do we have a measure of free will?
2. If God knows the future, why should we pray about events to come?
3. Since God knows all about us, why does he still love us?
4. Does the fact that God knows everything concern, impress or please you? Why?

11 He never leaves us

Have you ever wondered:

- what it was like for Jesus to have been forsaken by his Father when dying on the cross?
- what it would be like to lose your family and friends?
- what it means when Jesus says he'll never leave us?
- where God is and how close he is to us?

It was 27 May, ten minutes to midnight. I was in a hospital corridor and Judy was in an adjoining ward. I was on the phone to my mother. My initial words to her were, 'It's a boy!' Our first child, Luke, was born. He had big brown eyes and soft blond curls. He grew to be a quiet, attentive child who never found it hard to say sorry; the kind of boy teachers loved to have in their classes. But along with this sensitivity went a gentleness and vulnerability. How would he cope with his first day in nursery, in school? Would he be able to handle disappointment, bullies, exams or all the other hurdles children have to overcome? Would he get through adolescence unscathed, or would he be marred for life? His early years were times of reflection (no different from those of many other parents) when we learned to recognise that Luke was not going anywhere on his own. Someone who loved him far more than even we could goes with him wherever he goes; God is with him. A few days after he went to university, he sent us the poem that concludes Chapter 3, in which he sought to describe something of his awareness and appreciation of God.

While we were wondering whether he would cope, we were learning that God was making sure he would. Since then, he has been on missions to the foothills of the Himalayas, the vast spaces of Kenya and the beautiful mountains of South Africa. All the time, we have been learning to recognise that Luke has never been on his own.

God has chosen never to leave us

To discover the incredible nature of the truth that God is always with us, we have to travel back in time to that moment when Jesus walked directly into sin's most concentrated radiation and allowed himself to be touched by its curse. By that act of self-sacrifice, he broke the chain reaction that was sending us headlong into an eternity away from God. He broke the power of sin over our lives. We came through into life because he went through into death. He who is unapproachable in majesty, in need of nothing and no one, uniquely self-sufficient and absolutely complete, dedicated himself to die for people who couldn't find him and who weren't even looking. The Christians in Rome, who knew what it was like to be alienated and made to feel unwanted, and who experienced the ferocity of the first persecutions, were reminded by Paul that it was impossible for them to be separated from God (Rom 8:38,39).

He who has already achieved so much for us will not give up on us now. Instead, he gives us the Spirit to stay with us to the end (Phil 1:6). He is in our lives not simply to keep us on the straight and narrow; not to act as a heavenly bouncer to keep us in line. He is not a policeman from paradise, a matron with attitude, a headmaster with a stick, a chain around our legs or a straitjacket to keep us holy. Rather, he is our bodyguard, our tour guide to get us to our destination and to make sure that we enjoy the journey. His role is not just to be there when we need him but to be there when we don't. He keeps us safe so that we shall receive our inheritance, a life with God for ever (Eph 1:14). But also he keeps us because we are God's inheritance (Eph 1:18).

God holds you tighter than you know

Some years ago, we went on holiday as a family to the Mediterranean. It was Luke who, as a young teenager, decided that we should have a go at paragliding. I wasn't so sure, but when he expressed such enthusiasm and so enjoyed the experience, I thought maybe I should follow his example. Judy had a go, so how could I not?

It was my first and last paragliding experience. Having given my life savings for 15 minutes of terror in the skies, I was harnessed to the gear by two bronzed young men who made my untanned body look unprepared for such a close brush with the sun.

A coil of rope joined me to a speedboat that was rapidly shrinking as it sped into the distance. At the same time, I stood on the deck and watched it become clouded by the spray that was churned up by its powerful double engines, while the coil of rope before my feet unravelled all too quickly. There was no turning back. Soon I would move to the end of the deck and be catapulted into space. Before I had time to cultivate a nonchalant air, I shot into the sky and into the future. Before I knew it, I was above the hotels, above the birds, above the world.

But I had a problem. I couldn't enjoy the experience because I couldn't remember whether I was to hold on to the harness or whether I could relax my grip. My brain said that I wasn't expected to hold on tightly to stop slipping through the harness but my heart wasn't so sure. So I held on. By the time I arrived back on solid ground, my fingers had to be prised from the harness, they had become welded to the rope. I had not needed to hang on so tightly. I could have relaxed, because the harness was holding me tight.

It is liberating to recognise that God is a secure harness who wraps himself around our lives and never lets us go. Of course, this does not mean that we are protected from problems and pain, but it does mean that we never go through them alone.

Empty promises

We live in a world that has grown accustomed to words that have no substance and tired of them, from the casual 'I'll phone you later' to government promises of millions of dollars for international aid. We have become sceptical if not cynical, because words such as 'trust' and 'faithfulness' are used with less and less integrity. The junk mail promises us a prize if only we ring a number or listen to a presentation or send for some information, but we know that if it sounds too good to be true it probably is. God is very different. His promises *do* sound too good to be true, and yet they *are* true. God has always been the exception. By definition, he is faithful and trustworthy (Deut 7:9).

Eternal promises

Over two thousand years ago a group of Christians, who had experienced only peace, joy and hope in their new faith, were beginning to struggle with emotions they had never faced before. They felt fear, anxiety and regret. A fog of fear was drifting into their days; they were strangers in their own streets, and it felt lonely. It was made worse by the fact that only a few years earlier Jesus had said he was coming back again, and they were still waiting. Now their friends were being arrested, imprisoned and rejected, and they were feeling abandoned, deserted and lost.

The book of Hebrews was written to these people, and the writer had a single message to encourage and stabilise them: Jesus was superior to anyone they can imagine, and God was always with them (Heb 13:5). God's promise, 'I will never leave you; never will I forsake you', is a quote from Deuteronomy 31:6. There, God made this promise to Moses and the Israelites before the people crossed the River Jordan and entered the land that God had promised them when he rescued them from slavery in Egypt. Moses, who had led them thus far, was not going to lead them into Israel. The people were inevitably concerned, since many battles lay ahead and they were going without Moses.

Joshua was to become their leader, but he was inexperienced and knew it. If *they* felt uncertain, how lonely did *he* feel? Maybe that's why God echoed the same promise to him (Deut 31:8). God gave them all the same message: 'I'm going with you.'

God makes the same promise to Christians today. He doesn't change, and neither do his promises.

The promise in Hebrews 13:5, 'God has said, "Never will I leave you; never will I forsake you"', is even more emphatic in its original language, Greek.

- It emphasises just who is making the promise: 'for he himself has said ...'
- The first part of the promise could be translated, 'I will never, never leave you.' It's not just that God promises never to leave us; he promises never to be unable to help us when we need him; He's failure proof.
- The final part of the promise could be translated, 'I will never, never, never forsake you.'
- The promise is made to each Christian individually rather than to the church as a whole; the word 'you' is singular, not plural. This is God's personal commitment to each of his people.

Guaranteed promises

For years I have noted all my appointments and lists of things to do in a diary. It is central to my working day, but I still forget to fulfil some functions. Either I forget to record something or I miss it on the page. Sometimes it means I break a promise. I haven't intended to break it; it's not that I didn't want to keep it; it's often just simple forgetfulness. But God *can't* break his promises. He is trustworthy, and his promises can bear all the weight we place on them.

A pastor visited a Christian in his nineties and found him very troubled. The problem soon tumbled out: the old man had been losing his memory. What distressed him most was that he couldn't remember the many Bible verses he had learnt over the years. The pastor's response was timely 'You may have forgotten God's promises, but God hasn't.'

Powerful personal promises

I was brought up to believe that my salvation and my growth as a Christian depended on me. 'Take one step to God and then he'll take two steps to you,' I was told. It took me many years to realise that God was more interested in my spiritual development than I was, and that he had given me the resources and constant support of the ever-present Spirit to enable me to grow.

For much of my life I was like a man shovelling coal into the boiler to provide the energy to keep the train going. He has no time to enjoy the journey; he's too busy ensuring that he gets to the end of the line. I am learning to recognise that power source is not my effort alone but external, like the trains that run on electricity. They don't need fuel; they need brakes. The electricity is pulsating, the energy is ready to be unleashed, the train is resourced from an energy base outside itself. That's what gets the train to the destination.

Charlton Heston was once practising for the chariot race in the epic film *Ben Hur*. He told the director, Cecil B de Mille, 'I'll never win the race. I can hardly stay on the chariot.' The great director said, 'You just get on the chariot and hang on; it's my job to make sure you win.' Our role is to start the journey; it's God's role to make sure we reach the destination.

When we recognise God's inexplicable commitment to us we surely feel deep gratitude. Rather than taking God for granted because he's always there, we are led to a deep sense of awe. God is awesome.

> *While the eagle's chicks squawked in the nest on the cliff*
> *the eagle would soar on the breeze and drift*
> *and when the time came for the chicks to fly*
> *despite their anxious fluttering cries*

they had nothing to fear
for the wings of the eagle were near.

In the storm that smashed into Galilee
were a frightened group of men.
They were powerless and helpless to fend
off the wind
but Jesus was with them right then.

When those fearful disciples heard Jesus say
'I want you to go; make disciples today',
their hearts began beating,
for each of them knew
they could not achieve it
unless he was there too.

The question for them and the one that we feel
is 'How do I know if he'll be there for me,
my companion, my song, my close harmony?'
For if it's really true that he'll be
my songmaker, my melody,
then no one and nothing can obstruct
his working out his will in me.

For you the past has gone
but some of it is stained
with memories you wish weren't there.
Don't let them restrict you or cause you fear
for the one who knows you always stands near,
not in the shadows on the edge of your life,
but as central to you as is husband to wife.

The God who made you,
put colour in your hair,
is the one who lovingly says,
'For ever, I care.'

Questions for discussion

1. How can we know that God can be trusted? (Deut 7:9;
    Ps 36:5; 89:8; Lam 3:22,23)

2. How does God show himself faithful in his relationship
    with us? (Ps 119:75; 145:3; 1 Cor 1:9; 10:13; 1 Thess 5:24)

3. How can the fact that God can be trusted make a difference
    to our concept of the future? (Ps 31:23; Phil 1:6; 2 Tim 1:12;
    1 Pet 4:19)

4. How does it change our lives when we grasp the truth that
    God is faithful to us? (2 Tim 2:13; 1 John 1:9)

Questions to think about

1. What impact does the fact that God is faithful have on our
    lives and futures?

2. In what ways can we reflect God's faithfulness in our
    behaviour?

3. What is God's greatest expression of faithfulness to you?

4. How can we increasingly appreciate God's faithfulness?

12 He's always saying 'Hello'

Have you ever wondered:

- how God is involved in prayer?
- whether prayer is one-way or two-way communication?
- whether God's role is to listen while I talk, or whether I am supposed to listen as well?
- how to listen to God?

I hate sermons on prayer. They fill me with guilt and drive me to despair. The preacher describes prayer as able to move mountains; as interaction with the Almighty; as the springboard to a God-anointed life. He reminds me that revivals are born in prayer.

I say 'Amen' to it all, but inwardly I cringe. Satan creeps on to my shoulder and whispers 'Fraud!', while my conscience reminds me that as a prayer warrior I'm a failure. My most common prayers are fairly short: 'Thank you' and 'Sorry'.

If the preacher asks me if I want to develop a better prayer life, or even a prayer life that has some hope of improvement, he can't lose. With prayer, I'm at my weakest. What does he want me to do? Come to the front, receive prayer, stand on my head? I'll do it, if only I can clamber over this prayer mountain, this hurdle that's too high – just so that next time he preaches on prayer I can look him in the eye and say, 'It's OK now. I've got this prayer problem under control.' If only!

My experiences so far have not always helped me. Three issues used to dominate my prayer life in my early years as a Christian – methods, the Bible and guilt. The Quiet Time was a part of my daily life – a time of reading the Bible and prayer. It was foundational to my development, but rarely an easy task. And that was the problem: it was a task, a discipline. In fact, when I thought of prayer, I quickly associated it with the word 'discipline'. Prayer was something one had to do; a discipline to be learnt; a practice to be worked at. Strangely enough, words like 'liberty', 'joy' or 'Wow!' did not come to my mind when I thought of prayer. I learnt how to engage in 'Seven Minutes with God' and other methods developed to help people like me through the tiresome battlefield of prayer. Don't misunderstand me – prayer wasn't always hard work, and neither is discipline (a word that should not be far from a disciple who is developing in prayer). The problem for me was that it was the *only* word I associated with prayer.

Prayer that didn't have a significant element of sacrifice about it was somehow questionable, deficient, if not counterfeit. Prayer that took place in the early hours when all my friends were asleep was worth more than the prayer offered during the lunch break. During my youth, a famous evangelist came to my city. He prayed at 6 am and he was a successful evangelist. His early prayer time was surely an important key to his effectiveness. Sure enough, even though he did not encourage anyone to follow his pattern for prayer, I got up at 6 am to pray. But I fell asleep somewhere in the middle of the prayer. The next morning I was determined to do better, but I didn't. The following morning I gave up. Maybe I should have persevered. There was another of my keywords when it came to prayer: perseverance. People who pray must be passionate and persevering, and too often I lacked both characteristics. I lived with the guilt of those failures for many years. Only later in my Christian journey did I realise that prayer is very personal, and that many of the burdens we carry concerning it are self-imposed.

We are often misled into trying to follow the agendas and guidelines that God has given to others, without first checking whether they are appropriate for us. If they are, we can learn from the experiences of those who are following a similar pattern. If they are not, we should discover the prayer pilgrimage that is appropriate for us and follow it faithfully, learning to develop it along the way. For some Christians, the morning is the best time to be with God; for others, the best time may be last thing at night. Others try to build time with God into the course of their day. Prayer is not a competition; it's a conversation, a way of life. That means it's very personal to each Christian.

Something else that increased my frustration with myself was what I read in the Bible. It shone its spotlight on me and what it showed up wasn't pleasant. Jesus spent whole nights in prayer! Now, I've done that in my time. I was a missionary for a year. Every Friday my team spent the night in prayer. But somehow Friday nights didn't seem to match up to the nights Jesus spent in prayer. Paul didn't help either; he told the Thessalonian Christians to pray continually (1 Thess 5:17), and they'd only been Christians for a few months! Paul was expecting them to do what I could only dream about – though it was more of a nightmare than a dream! What did Paul mean, anyway? How can anyone pray continually?

All this deepened my reservoir of guilt while my surface Christian face betrayed none of it. How could I share such failings with other Christians, who seemed not to experience my battles with prayer? Older Christians sometimes plunged me under the waters of guilt until I nearly drowned with such encouragements as these:

'If the Queen was here, your mind wouldn't wander!'

'Jesus died on the cross for you and you can't even stay awake for a few minutes to pray!'

'What do you think you're going to do in heaven if you don't pray now?'

The thought of heaven as one eternal prayer meeting didn't help me, until I began to rethink prayer.

And so began my journey as a prayer pilgrim. This chapter

shares some of the lessons I'm learning along the way.

Prayer is primarily an encounter with God

For most of my life, I've identified prayer with talking to God. Of course, that's part of prayer, and I endorse the importance of prayer meetings and personal conversational prayer. But I'm learning that talking to God is only a part of prayer. I am learning to define prayer as a God-conscious event; it's a time when I'm conscious of God, when heaven breaks into my life on earth, when the transcendent God who created the universe opens a window in my world and says, 'Hello, Keith.' God's interruption establishes an encounter with him and, in that encounter, a prayer is born. No words need to be spoken; it's enough that I have become aware of God. I am learning to define those encounters as prayers. It's not the only form of prayer, but it's still prayer, initiated by God. The psalmist appears to be speaking of a similar experience when he encourages his readers to be quiet and, in that stillness, to acknowledge the presence of God. 'Hush – God's here' (see Ps 46:10).

Sometimes I work at home. Picture the scene. I'm engrossed in my studies, but later in the day a key turns in the lock of our front door. My wife Judy has come home. I've not seen her yet; no words have been spoken but a range of emotions, thoughts and feelings have been sparked off within me. At that moment, words are not as important as the fact that I am conscious of her presence. An encounter has already taken place in my mind. I'm learning to see prayer like this, as encounters with God when he opens a door into my life and, without words, I'm aware that he's there. One of the most sobering verses in the Bible is Genesis 28:16, in which Jacob says, 'Surely the LORD is in this place, and I was not aware of it.' We need to learn not to miss God when he visits us.

A poor man sat in church. He'd been there for hours, just sitting. The minister came up to him and asked if he was all right.

He said that he was, and explained what he had been doing. 'I've been looking at God, God's been looking at me, and we're happy together.' He had learnt to encounter God without spoiling that intimacy with speech.

Prayer doesn't have to be frenetic or hard work. Prayer is the excitement of encountering God, of experiencing a God-conscious moment. It may involve words; it may not. This is what I'm learning.

Prayer is learning to encounter God in his world

I am learning to listen for the key in the lock when God opens a door into my life and says, 'Hello, it's me again.' It happens more times than we realise. I remember seeing my daughter sitting in church with her friends. As I saw her, I had an encounter with God. Anna-Marie was laughing, full of life, fresh, pretty, vivacious – and then she saw me looking at her through the ranks of people in church, and she smiled. It was a father–daughter moment and I felt proud, but I also felt God. It was as if he said, 'I've made her the girl she is; the person she's going to be.' It was a God-conscious moment; when God said 'Hello' and, in effect, 'Relax, I'm in charge.'

I think of times when my students and I have explored the Bible. We have asked questions and even perhaps discovered answers. Sometimes, the answers surprise and stimulate us. In those times, we are encountering God. We often respond to those encounters with words that don't seem to belong to prayer, such as 'Wow!' or 'That's remarkable!' or 'Mmm – I've never thought of that before.' God has opened his Word and said 'Hello', and we've replied 'Wow!'

With colleagues and students, I have often explored aspects of God and his dealings with us. In our creative probing we have tried to tap into the inexhaustible nature of God. As we do, before we know it we find that, while we are encountering each other as Christians in our quest of God, we are encountering God himself. We haven't prayed, and yet we have, for we have encountered God. We haven't stopped to pray, but he has stepped in to say 'Hello'.

One of my students came to our college from Korea. Before her arrival she had suffered a major accident that caused a severe loss of memory. Nevertheless, throughout her time as a student she was conscientious and caring, faithful in the smallest details, which few others noticed. I noticed. She now serves the Lord in an isolated region of Northern Ghana. When I think of In-Hee, God speaks to me and says 'Hello'.

I am learning to recognise that prayer is to encounter God and to listen for his 'Hello' in people around me, in circumstances good and bad (2 Cor 1:9; 1 Thess 2:2), in his creation, in his Word, and even in me. This is probably the kind of prayer-consciousness Paul had in mind when he encouraged his readers to be faithful in prayer (Rom 12:12).

Prayer means responding to God as well as speaking to God

In his book *Working the Angles*, Eugene Peterson speaks of 'the overwhelming previousness of God's speech to our prayers'. Prayer is not always a matter of me saying 'Hello' to God; it's often God who's the first to say 'Hello'. Many of my prayers do consist of me saying 'Hello', and, of course, that's fine. But how many times does God start the conversation and we just don't hear him?

When my daughter was very young, I was driving to the airport with her to pick up Judy. 'Why doesn't God speak to me?' Anna-Marie asked. I knew what she meant. As Christians, we talk about God speaking to us but we have very limited notions as to how he does so. Perhaps he will speak through a sermon, a prophecy or our personal Bible-reading. Few of us expect an audible voice or an angelic visitation. But the fact is, he's everywhere, and I'm learning the importance of identifying where he is so that I can respond to him, whatever he says, however he says it. Paul anticipated this when he wrote to the church in the bustling metropolis of Rome and reminded the believers that God whispers his presence throughout his creation (Rom 1:20).

I remember reading a book that offered many guidelines for getting God's attention. But we don't need to learn how to get God's attention. He's already perfectly attentive to us. Instead, I am learning how to listen for him.

You may have heard the old story of a group of radio operators turning up for an interview and being shown into a crowded waiting-room to await their turn. The call never came. After some uncertainty, one man jumped out of his chair and ran into the interview room, emerging a few minutes later to announce that he had been offered the job – to the astonishment of those present. He told them to listen and, sure enough, a message was being tapped out in Morse code, informing them that the first person who responded to it and came into the interview room would be offered the job. But only one man was listening.

I've often assumed that God is to be encountered in the magnificent, the extraordinary, the sensational and the atmospherically charged (and sometimes he is). But I'm learning that he is also encountered in the ordinary events of life.

Prayer is very personal

God loves us individually and perfectly. He loves us uniquely and differently. He therefore encounters each of us differently. He says 'Hello' to each of us, countless times every day. But he does so in different ways, depending on who we are and how we are. That's the way a good father relates to his children, and God is the best father there is.

So rejoice in your individuality. Refuse to be driven to feel that you have to relate to God in any way other than that which he has chosen for you. Don't let God's agenda for others burden you. Be true to yourself as the person God is making you. Listen out for God, for he speaks to us in our own accents so that we can recognise him.

The Bible reflects a remarkable variety of forms of prayer, depending on who is praying and what the circumstances are (1 Kings 8:54; Ps 35:13; Matt 26:39). Some of us encounter God in loud worship, others in silence; some in the magnificent, others in the ordinary; some in written prayers, others with songs of praise, and yet others with tears. Be aware of who you are and listen for God to speak to you in ways that he knows are appropriate for you. Then be creative in your response to him.

Have you ever wondered whether we'll pray in heaven? We'll certainly encounter God there – in each other, in the angels, in our conversations, our excitement, our humour, our discussions, our plans, our memories and our dreams. Everything will reflect God. In heaven he will be reflected perfectly, but even in this dark world he's still God and it's still his world and he still sparkles in it. At times, his light rushes towards us like a searchlight; at other times, it's like a candle beckoning us softly to follow. In all these ways God is saying, 'Here I am; I've just called to say "Hello".' And when we say 'Hello' to God in response, a prayer is born as we encounter him in our lives.

I can't begin to imagine what God's got in store in heaven for me,
but it'll keep me content for eternity
for God will be in it, I'm sure.

I want to explore and gaze at the places I've never been to before.
I want to climb the mountains on the moon and paddle to the distant shore
of a desert island, and then explore some more,
and all I see will reflect God, I'm sure.

I want to talk to Paul and James and talk and talk some more.

*I want to speak with the angels, put my cheek to a lion's
paw,
and watch the films of the exodus and the flood
from the heavenly video store.
I want to see how creation occurred, and yet there's so
much more;
and in it all, I'll encounter God; of that one thing I'm sure.*

*But will I have time for prayer in heaven? Surely that's the
reason I'm there.
Yet, there's so much to do, I'm not sure I'll have time to
spare.
But still, I should pray. There must be a time to stop and
say
a few words to the Lord in prayer.*

*But I sense him saying that my whole life there
will be one big encounter with him.
Wherever I go, he'll have been there
before, and his perfume will fill every place,
and the people I see and talk to will reflect all the time his
grace
and although I'll not see his face, God will still embrace me
and trace
within my heart and mind the finger of love, the finger of
grace.*

*I won't need to pray in heaven. Prayer won't bring me to
God.
He'll be in everyone, everything, every sight, every song
that I sing.
He'll be there in the acts and the deeds.
He'll be there in the sights that I see.
He'll be there in the plans that I have for the future,
the talks that I have about the past.
The places I'll go to, he's been to, and he'll be in the bits in*

between.
Everywhere I go, God will say 'Hello'.
I'll encounter him without trying.
Without prayer, he'll still be there;
the consciousness of God will be like the air.

Maybe there'll be no prayer meetings in heaven
but prayer as it was meant to be;
responding to God in encounters he's planned
with me in mind, a mere speck in the sand.

For all eternity, he'll be whispering 'Hello'
in everyone around me and everywhere I go.

Questions for discussion

1. Does God enjoy it when we pray to him? (Deut 4:7; Job 33:26; Acts 10:4; 1 Pet 3:12)

2. Can we change God's mind when we pray? (Matt 26:39,42; 1 John 5:14)

3. What are some of the purposes of prayer? (Ps 32:6,7; Jer 42:3; Dan 6:11; 9:4,5; Acts 1:24; 6:6; 28:8; Phil 1:9–11; Col 4:3,4; James 5:16; 1 John 1:9)

4. What kinds of prayer does God appreciate? (1 Chron 5:20; Prov 15:8,29; James 5:16)

5. Where is God speaking today? (Ps 19:1–4)

Questions to think about

1. Should we pray to the Father, to Jesus, or to the Spirit, or doesn't it matter?

2. Why is prayer important for Christians?

3. Does it matter how long we pray or when we pray?

4. Is praying together more significant than praying on your own?

5. How should Christians listen for God in prayer?

13 Where do we go from here?

Things to remember:

- God is unimaginable, but he has invited you to explore him
- He wants you to know him more deeply than you ever thought possible
- Knowing God is potentially the most enjoyable quest in life
- We shall be exploring God for all eternity. Start now!
- Contemplating God will change you
- As you reflect on God, he will be reflected through you
- God has provided you with conversational partners in this exploration. Use all the resources they offer:
  The Holy Spirit
  The Bible
  Church leaders
  Friends
  Creation
  Your imagination and creative skills
  Life's experiences
  Art
  Poetry

Things to do:

Ask God to help you to explore him.

- Every day, thank him for a different aspect of his character
- Read a book about God
- Write a poem about God or his relationship with you
- Meditate on a Bible verse that describes God
- Slowly read aloud some Bible verses that explore aspects of God
- Enrol on a course exploring God
- Think about God for two or three minutes at a time
- Ask a friend: 'What is the most important aspect about God to you, and why?'
- Study one aspect of God that intrigues you
- Use a concordance to look at every verse in the Bible that records a particular aspect of God
- Try to discover the depth of meaning in God's love, holiness and power
- In conversation with some friends, complete the statement, 'God is ...'
- Express an aspect of God in a painting or drawing
- Compose a song about a characteristic of God
- Imagine a world without God
- Learn to listen for God in life
- Try to describe God as if you were speaking to these different people: a child, someone who has no concept of God, someone who has lost hope, and someone who is starting the journey
- Ask some older Christians: 'What are the three most important aspects of God to you?'
- Read some hymns that ponder the person of God
- Learn to wonder about God by asking questions like these:
  Could God be better?
  Where is God?
  How endless is his love?

How is God reflected in a leaf, a storm, the night, death?

When Jesus died, abandoned by all he'd known and loved,
his life had crashed to oblivion, it seemed, ignored by
heaven above.
The words on the lips of his followers as they gazed on his
cross on high
were words of sorrow that Good Friday; they whispered to
him, 'Goodbye.'

His mission at that moment had ended; a dirge seemed the
appropriate song
for all he'd lived and planned and dreamed; all of it had
gone.
But you and I know that not all was lost; his critics were
proved wrong
for when he died, Jesus Christ was simply passing on.

He moved; changed place, location; from Saviour to High
Priest.
His time on earth had finished; the star had moved from
the East
and followed him in all his life, in all his deeds had shone;
but now he's the Son in the heavens, for the Father has
moved him on.

He came to live, to love, to loose,
He came to fight and to win.
He came to feel for the pain of mankind,
to be spoiled with the stain of our sin.
And he came to show us the Father
for he was the Father's Son
and to say to us in his life and his death
that the Father was moving him on.

And in all you do, wherever you go,
when life's good and when it goes wrong;
whatever the valley, whatever the joy,
whatever the tune of your song,
the One who's in charge of this world and you
is the one who looked after his Son
and the pathway in life for all children of his
is always to be moving on.
With God, moving back is a feature
that does not fit into his plan.
He's much more concerned with the future,
with the lie and the range of the land that's ahead.
The past you've walked in – it's gone.
To the Father of Jesus you belong.

As you say goodbye to the present and past,
even to dreams that you thought would last,
and as people are saying goodbye, then they're gone
and you're left alone, very much on your own,
listen to the voice of the one who's been there
as he speaks with a heart that is filled with his care:
'Come with me; we're on our way.
Your future is born.
We're passing from this place;
I'm moving you on.'

Unravelling The Threads.
A True Story
Leila Merriman.

To Edi·

Love

Leila.

x

A catalogue record for this book is available from the British
Library
Published by L.M. Publications
8 Weybourne Gardens
Southend on Sea Essex SS2 4AU
Printed by 4edge Printers, Hockley Essex
Unravelling the Threads is a re-write of Twisted Threads first
published in 2004.

About the author

Born in Upminster, Essex in 1934 to a single Irish girl. Leila Merriman grew up in County Westmeath, Ireland with her grandparents.   Returning to Upminster after the war she went to St Mary's Convent School, moving to Southend in 1947. She loved sport and was a champion swimmer. In 1956 she married and had two children, but was divorced ten years later. She became very involved in local politics, was Mayoress of Southend 1987_88 and a County Councillor for ten years..

She married for the second time in 1987. Now retired, she continues her work for Breakthrough Breast cancer and enjoys gardening, her grandchildren and writing..

Thank you's

My Mum, thanks for giving me life; without you the story couldn't be told.

Maggie Smith, University of the Third Age, thank you for your friendship and advice.

Author's notes.

This book, is the story of my life so far, was originally published in 2004 as "Twisted Threads." I have researched as much as possible and the facts are true, but parts, including others behaviour and thoughts when apart from me, have to be imaginary. The main thread is the story of my Mother and me. Concern for my two children led me to gloss over the ten years of my first marriage, but those ten years are a very important part of my life. What happened to me then made me what I am to-day, proud of the journey I have made, proud of what I have achieved and proud of how far I have come. Recently I uncovered information which enabled me to unravel yet another thread. The original book has been rewritten and re-titled, with an added chapter which brings closure to the story.

Chapter 1

My Grandparents may have been christened Michael and Elizabeth, but few called them anything but Mick and Lizzie.

Lizzie was born in Donneybrook, Dublin in 1874. Mick in Delvin a year earlier, both into working class families.

A handsome man, cheeks hollow in his thin face, straight black hair combed over his forehead. His strong wiry body always carried the smell of the land, a good earthy smell. There was no doubt he had kissed the Blarney Stone. He could tell a tale like the best. But he had a very tough, almost cruel, streak in him. A very generous man he trusted everyone except perhaps the village gardia

As soon as he could walk he could take care of himself and keep up with his peers. You had to in those days in Ireland. He became an expert at hunting, snaring, shooting and fishing - skills that were to serve him well in later years. It would provide him with a job and provide little extras for the seventeen children he and Lizzie raised. Those skills were a godsend. There is nothing like a nice fat rabbit, a fresh trout or pike from the river, a plump bird shot from the sky when there are so many mouths to feed. When it came to feeding the family they were always rich beyond words. In other areas, they were as poor as church mice.

As a young man, his activities did get him into trouble, and he served a short prison sentence. While out shooting in the woods one day with his friend, Charlie, the gamekeeper from a nearby estate caught them.

Luckily for Mick the pals had time to separate. In those days there was no messing about, if you were caught poaching you were shot on sight and Charlie got shot in the leg. Even so Charlie was the one who got away. He couldn't afford medical treatment and when he died in his eighties the lead was still in his leg. That episode was Mick's only brush with the law, basically because he never got caught, or if he did he talked his way out of it.

Mick and Lizzie were destined to meet. He was born very near the Castle where she worked and they would both be at Mass on a Sunday or if they took a walk down Delvins little High Street they

1

couldn't miss each other.

Lizzie was a beauty, quite small and solidly built. Her jet-black hair, parted in the centre and brushed back into a bun at the back of her neck, looked fluffy as it framed a round face. She had the deepest blue eyes, with a tiny nose and small lips, all in a perfectly formed angelic face. Lizzie went straight into service from school; even if girls had the brains to be scientists, surgeons or doctors, if they came from poor families they had no chance. Parents couldn't afford to feed and clothe them and looked on them working to help them care for their siblings. Leaving home was a great culture shock for these shy, naïve youngsters. There wasn't much choice of jobs and most of them ended up in service on large estates, a daunting experience, and a strict, hard life. They were forbidden to speak to the Master or Mistress unless they were spoken too. They then had to make sure they address them correctly. They couldn't speak to anyone in a position above them, they wouldn't dare. Then they did speak it had to be quietly. The Master and Mistress didn't want to be disturbed by the sound of voices. Lizzie went into service with Lord Greville and Lady Rosa at Cloyne Castle, Delvin. It was completed in 1877, at one time Oliver Cromwell had designs on it for himself, so the then owner Richard Nugent burnt it to the ground.

The days duties in the castle started early, 5.30 the kitchen grates had to be brushed down and cleaned out and the hot water organised. From then on the day ran like clockwork. If breakfast was at eight o'clock, it was 8'clock on the dot. Beds would be started at 10 o'clock and so on right throughout the day. Lizzie had one afternoon off each week. She would take a walk down Delvin's little antique High Street, calling in at Tierneys to buy paper and envelopes or cards to write home to family and friends. One essential item on her shopping list would be a bottle of vinegar from the little grocery store. She would always add a few tablespoons of it to the final rinsing water when washing her hair, ensuring her glorious jet black hair kept its shine

When they did meet Mick was completely captivated by her beauty and she couldn't resist those laughing blue Irish eyes. It was love at first sight. They married in Donnybrook, Dublin, Lizzie's birthplace, in 1894.

On her wedding day, Lizzie wore the deepest blue blouse to bring out the colour of her eyes. The blouse had very full sleeves, the

2

skirt very plain and flared with a thick belt round her waist, bustles were out of fashion in 1894. Her stockings were wool and silk with calf length lace-up boots. Her beautiful long black hair, worn in a bun, had been brushed until it shone more than ever. Her only jewellery was her wedding ring. In those days, working class girls didn't wear jewellery. Only wealthy folk wore jewellery, but she had an extra ingredient. She didn't need jewellery to make her shine, whether Mick knew or not she was blooming because she was carrying twins.

Mick stood tall, very smart in his knickerbockers. His jacket was tweed and loose fitting. His leather boots lace-up, ending above the ankle, showing of his thick woollen socks, a garter made him look very dashing. For his special occasion he wore a tweed hat with a narrow turned-down brim. They began there great adventure of life together not with a honeymoon but went straight back to work.

During his late teens Mick was employed on the construction of the tram lines in Dublin. Now he had a bride and the responsibility of providing a home, he had changed jobs, and found a position as a gamekeeper, something that went back to his very roots. He knew and understood everything about the land, and what the work entailed, he had grown up with it since he could walk. His first job was at a large estate at Kello, County Longford. A cottage came with the position and it was there the twins were born – a boy and a girl. It was quite usual in Victorian times for a young Mother to farm her babies out, and the baby girl was given to an Aunt to bring up. Babies would be given to Grandparents, maiden aunts, childless couples or any family member who wanted to look after another little soul.

Mick moved on to the Charterville Estate, Tullamore, County Offey, where another boy was born. He was passed on to his Grandparents in Dublin.

One night Mick came across two local brothers poaching. There was an argument and Mick jammed his gun in one of the men's faces. Luckily the two decided to make a run for it and they both got away, before Mick could really hurt them, and even without a gun Mick was ready to tackle anyone. It was an absolutely freezing night and perhaps it was the extreme cold, but the next morning when Mick was cleaning his gun he couldn't run the rod down the barrel. He found the poachers eyebrow still frozen to the inside. And marched with the gun and the eyebrow to the police station.

"Can you give me a description of these men?" asked the officer.

"Find someone without this" Mick held out the eyebrow. The brothers were found – one minus his eyebrow – and charged with poaching, receiving long prison sentences.

Whether the incident had anything to do with events, Mick didn't stay in that job much longer. He moved on to the Hill of Tara at Lismullan, the Estate of Sir John Dillon. Mick liked to tell the story about the day Lady Dillon decided to watch the hay making. Ladies at the turn of the century wore very long clothes and on this particular day a wee mouse found its way up the inside of Lady Dillons skirt. She screamed non stop and all the staff ran to her aid. But she would trust only one and Mick was called for. Recalling the incident, he liked to boast

"I'm the only member of staff who's had me hand up her ladyship's skirt"

By 1906 there were another seven babies; Lizzie nursed all of them, including a second set of twins, who to her great grief, died in infancy. With his family growing at such an alarming rate, Mick decided to quit his dangerous and ever more hazardous job as gamekeeper..

Poaching was the only means a lot of people had to feed their starving families. Mick well understood how hungry little mouths can make men desperate. The gentry loved hunting, shooting and fishing for pleasure and were slowly taking over the land, as lake, rivers and woods were reserved for them. So the poor who desperately needed to feed their families were getting shut out completely.

Mick was forced to do his share of poaching to feed his own family. At night while on patrol he would sneak a couple of trout from the river, creeping off with his ill-gotten goods under his coat. With luck the boss was asleep and wouldn't catch him. By day he had to help his boss by catching the poachers, but as Mick himself was often the culprit, he busied himself covering up.

One night Mick took a pal with him to do some serious poaching. They were loaded with game, fish and rabbits tied round and round their waists with rope, when they heard a sound in the bushes

"We're well and truly caught, Mick what....."

"They'll not put me away"

Mick spoke more confidently than he felt.

Poaching carried a jail sentence, and for the amount they were carrying it would probably be a life sentence.

"What are we going to do?"

"There's only one thing we can do," replied Mick.

Raising his gun he fired both barrels in the direction of the bushes. There was an almighty crash, the crack of breaking branches as the body fell to the ground. Mick ran forward in the dark, heart pounding, expecting to find the body of Sir John Dillon. Instead, he discovered he had killed a horse

"I can't believe I did that" he said.

"We were lucky this time."

His pal was relieved. Not so Mick – he was no murderer and game keeping was no longer a job for him if he'd become so desperate he almost killed someone. He was going to quit.

Next morning, Sir John was incensed.

Those bloody poachers. Not only did they walk off with some of his best birds, they had shot his horse.

Mick promised to find the men and make sure they were put on trial.

"If I get my hands on them," ranted Sir John, "I'll shoot the buggers myself. They won't need a trial."

It was a difficult day for Mick, who knew he must do something immediately. He would apply for a cottage from Westmeath County Council.

Chapter 2.

Westmeath County Council found them the ideal site at Cullys Farm, three miles from Delvin and only one and a half miles from where Mick was born. One acre of land went with the cottage, enough ground for Mick to grow fruit and vegetables to feed his large family. The surveyor arrived to do the measuring and stake the ground. All was ready for the workers to dig the ditch, plant the trees and the privet hedge. Mick stood watching the activities with interest. He felt he could do with just a little more land. An honest rogue he waited for the workmen to go to lunch, then quickly moved the stakes back giving himself another half acre. When the mistake was found out, there were some very displeased people but it was too late to do anything about it. So it was that Lizzie and Mick moved into their cottage, the first and last home of their own. They were to have seven more babies and finally to die there in that four roomed cottage in Moortown.

The cottage was a plain square building, with a wooden door right in the middle at the front, a window on either side. The front door led straight into the living room, with a window at the far end looking out over the two barns and a chicken shed. Along the wall on the left was a vast inglenook fireplace with an iron arm to support various pots and pans. On the floor in front of it a large straw basket held the wood and sods of turf to keep the fire going.

A comfortable elderly armchair heaped with cushions stood on either side of the fireplace, and along the opposite wall was a long oak table, with benches either side, and at each end chairs with arms. Cupboards and shelves filled the wall above the table, while another table cluttered with bits and pieces stood in front of the window – It held mending and knitting, books, sewing, odds and ends. A door next to the fireplace led into a long room the length of the cottage. Lizzie and the girls slept there in one huge bed, sometimes six at a time, three up top and three down the bottom, perhaps a baby in a basket and another one in a cot. On the other side of the cottage were two smaller rooms, where Mick and the boys slept.

Lizzie insisted on having a statue of the baby Jesus in every room and there would be Holy pictures on the walls, especially the Virgin Mary, St. Patrick and a Rosary beads would be hanging up somewhere. By the front door was a font with Holy Water, so all visitor could bless themselves as they came and went.

When darkness fell, the oil lamp, the only means of lighting apart from candles, shone on the big table – no electricity, gas or running water had as yet reached the homes of the poor in Ireland.

How Lizzie coped God only knows, but even giving birth to her six girls and eleven boys, not to mention the six miscarriages, she was still beautiful and her cheeks were always rosy. It seemed she was never without an apron, even when she went out. Her day started very early, she was always first up to do the breakfast bake. She would place flattened bread dough in a heavy cast iron pot, swing the pot over the hot turfs, using the tongs to put the lid on, then cover it with red hot turfs. In no time those lovely home made loaves were ready. It was funny, that was one thing in the home Mick could help her with if she was pushed to the limit. He actually baked better bread than she did and he was known for his light touch.

Mornings in that small cottage was bedlam, all those going to work or school got themselves up. No queuing for the bathroom, everyone would dash outdoors and find a bush or tree to squat and leaves would act as toilet paper. Then a quick splash of water over the face from the pump in front of the house and they were ready.

The smell of the freshly baked bread made them want to get up and tuck in. A couple of loaves would have been cut in chunks and placed on the table with a pot of newly churned butter and a jug of milk. The big iron frying pan would be balancing on some red hot turfs and their own home produced rashers of bacon, their own home made sausages and black puddings would be sizzling. One of the boys would have been down to the meadow and picked dewy fresh mushrooms. The smell coming from the frying pan was nectar and caressing the nostrils and it would drift through the whole cottage. As many eggs as her large brood could eat were cracked and dropped into the hot fat. Then the kids would fight to dip their bread in the pan and gather up all the lovely juices. They would run their bread round the pan until every drop was mopped up.

The younger members rose in their own time to join their big brothers and sisters. There was always someone free to help them get dressed, help them with their food or give the latest baby it's bottle.

After breakfast everyone would have their chores before work or school. Logs would have to be cut with the two handled saw. Mick would be delighted if during the day he came across a really large tree uprooted, he would get his old cart and with a little smile to himself, say "That's the wood for a while," The first born, Christy, was the strongest of them all and the one Mick called on when the awkward jobs came up. Like cleaning the chimney. Mick would send Christy up on the roof, then tie a bundle of prickly branches like Holy half way up a rope. Then standing in the fireplace, he and Christy would pull it up and down. Michael, who came sixth in the family, had a very sensitive touch with the animals. He would be the one to help Mick with the milking and would probably be responsible for the large jug of milk on the table at meal times. Michael would put the milk from the evening in a big urn for Lizzie to use for domestic purposes. The milk from the morning would be kept separate because it was creamier and that was used to make butter. Enough turf to last the day would be put in the basket. The girls would be busy feeding the chickens and ducks and collecting the eggs.

While everyone was busy Lizzie would be preparing the lunch boxes for those going to school. It was a three mile walk to Ballinvalley School and the children had big appetites, so enough food had to be packed to sustain them all day. Lizzie would have another bake the night before, everything was home-baked, bread, cakes, meat and fruit pies. What ever was available would be placed in the boxes with the bread. A piece of cheese, slices of home cooked ham, cold sausages, hard boiled eggs or jam. If Lizzie found herself with nothing she would sprinkle sugar on the bread and butter. Always a slice of her home made cake would be added. In the cold weather it would be a bottle of milk to drink but in the hot weather Lizzie made her own drinks using rose hip, elderflower, or whatever berry were in her garden. She would boil the berries producing the sweetest smells, add the sugar and then drain through a muslin cloth. The kids loved her home made brew.

For dinner Lizzie would often go into the yard armed with a large carving knife; grabbing the chosen chickens she would cut of their heads and add them to the vegetables and potatoes which filled the pigs pot. Fruit pies, with a jug of cream followed, with plenty of her non-alcoholic brew for the youngsters, a few beers for the bigger ones. When everyone was full, leftovers and bits would be added and the pigs fed. Dinner time was often boisterous to the point where Mick lost his temper.

"Quieten down, the lot of you"

Sometimes he would really mean it and wouldn't think twice about using his stick. The children usually knew how far they could go before they felt the sting of their fathers discipline.

Friday nights was bath night for the younger children. Lizzie washed out the pigs pot and half filled it with hot water, in turn they got in and had a thorough wash. The unlucky last ones would find the water somewhat scummy. On cold winter nights they would each wrap themselves in a towel and dry off in front of the dancing flames of the fire. If Mick had managed to find a fallen apple tree the burning logs scented the whole room.

Mick was the very best story teller: he would have the little ones spell bound with his stories of the little people, fairies and leprechauns, myths and legends of old Ireland. What he did not already know he make up as he went along. The bigger boys who had grown out of stories spend the evening trying to beat each other at cards, while the girls would be busy making things.

If Lizzie or Mick had been lucky enough to come across a sack, the girls would turn it into a rug. Everything was saved, odd wool and pieces of rag which the girls would cut into neat little pieces to be woven into the sack to make a pretty floor piece. They used their scraps to make bed covers too. As this is Ireland, many an evening passed with the deafening noise of music as they played and sang all the songs of old Ireland.

When God gave Lizzie all those beautiful children he gifted her with the patience of a Saint and she took all the hard work in her stride. As if there were not enough washing to do for her own brood, she took in more. Before she could begin she must fetch water from the pump, then lift the heavy pigs pot on and off the arm of the fire. All the washing was done by hand, rinsed, starched and put through the wringer. There was no clothes line and the washing was thrown over the bushes to dry. With all the material in the petticoats ironing was long and hot work. Lizzie would build up the fire then bandage her hands with rags, to protect them from the red hot handle before setting the iron on the hot turfs. She would be only halfway through ironing an item when the iron was cold and the process of heating must begin again. The little ones would amuse themselves while she

9

worked; there was little harm they could come to, the river and lakes were a safe distance away. On wet days they drove her mad, getting themselves filthy making mud pies. On those days the barn came into its own, as the bushes for drying the clothes were replaced by the stacks of hay Mick gathered in during the summer.

To earn even more pennies Lizzie scrubbed stone floors for the Barrys, their wealthy neighbours. *Mrs. Barry was Headmistress of the school all the girls attended. Ballinvalley Girls School.* The drive up to their front door was long and windy, with flower borders on both sides; Lizzies favourites were the rows of glorious chrysanthemums in the early Autumn. There seemed always to be a baby in Lizzies belly yet, lugging a heavy bucket of water she would go down on her hands and knees on the hard stone floor.

On the days Lizzie was away from home Mick usually planned to go fishing on Moortowns thirty five acre Lake Dysart, taking the little ones on the boat with him. If they didn't behave they would fall in. If there was a baby he would put it in his fishing bag he carried over his shoulder.

Christianity first started in Ireland in Moortown, Dysart Tola created the first of many clusters of settlements in St. Patrick's name he was later canonised St. Tola, so Moortown has it's own Saint.

The Barry's were very interested in Greyhounds and Mick longed to own one, finally acquiring one, how nobody knows. He had great hopes it was at least going to win the Greyhound Derby. He took the dog to Dublin for trials and what happened was unbelievable, the dog ran the wrong way around the track. Mick was furious with it and on the way home, he threw it in the River Liffy and it drowned. Remember this is about 1910 and times were very hard in Ireland and anything that wasn't of use couldn't be kept.

Work may have been soul destroying but there was rent to pay and things to buy that Lizzie and Mick couldn't produce for themselves. Flour and soap, oil for the lamp and candles, the leather to mend al those boots to last through the winter and an essential reserve for medicines, doctor or dentist would refuse to call without payment.

Then there was the priest. Unless you wanted to rot in hell you wouldn't dare refuse the priest. They may have preached charity but they certainly didn't practice it. With the vast wealth of the Catholic Church the priest, amazingly, would take your last penny. The Church

10

ruled by fear, blackmailed it's parishioners into submission. Lizzie would walk three miles to Church Sunday mornings, returning in the evening for Benediction; on weekday evenings there was the Stations of the Cross and Saturday night, it was confession time.

Why would this woman who had spent most of her life child-bearing, who never had a cross word to say to anyone, who was always the first to help a neighbour, never turned a stranger from the door but always offered a piece of bread and cheese and a drink, need to go out on a Saturday night in all weathers to confess? Confess what for God's sake?

A more charitable Priest could have said something like. -

"Look Mrs. Merriman, I've had a word with God. He says you're to rest for a year."

Lizzie would probably have answered

"Father, I couldn't. I am a sinner"

Rather was she an addict, desperately needing her fix of religion but then the priest would never offer such kindness. Without an iron fist how could you keep the pheasants down.

However often Lizzie went in a week, the collecting plate was always passed round, with neighbours watching to see how much was put in. "God will provide" the poor were always told. Will he provide the leather to mend all these boots, give Lizzie the strength to keep on her knees, scrubbing floors, not praying.

Like Lizzie, Mick too worked hard. He would be out daily, snaring or shooting something for the pot. With just a spade and fork he cultivated every inch of the acre and a half, growing every possible fruit and vegetables. There were rows and rows of potatoes, peas and cabbages, rhubarb, blackcurrant, redcurrant, raspberry and gooseberry bushes for Lizzies jams and fruit pies. He had no grazing land, but his neighbours turned a blind eye to his cows on their land. With these and his goats Mick provided the family with milk, butter and cheese. In return he would drop in a couple of nice fish to the neighbours on his way home from fishing.

He kept, pigs, ducks and chickens for meat, sausages and black puddings. The chickens and ducks provided the eggs and there was always a calf or foal to sell locally to raise a few pounds to buy what he couldn't grow.

Mick preferred to work outside and was always in charge of the preparation of the birds for the pheasant shoot at Cloyne Castle. For two weeks every year he was head man at the hare coursing at Loughnea and did the same job when they had the coursing at the black meadow at Moortown.

Prepared to tackle any task that came his way he was once hired by a neighbour from a near by village to plant out a field of potatoes. Knowing it was hot and thirsty work, the neighbour, a kindly man, hid twelve bottles of stout in the hay stack for Mick. The neighbour's wife despised drinking, somehow found out about the hidden bottles and smashed every one. A furious Mick went to great lengths to get his revenge by planting every single potato, having been chitted upside down, but his plan backfired because it was a bumper crop.

Having to fight every day for all the kid's survival made Mick tough and often short-tempered. One day, walking home from Delvin, he decided to sit on a neighbours bench to cut a bit of baccy. The neighbours dog, a vicious collie most people were afraid of, leapt across the fence to attack Mick, he grabbed it by the scruff of it's neck and cut it's throat with the hunting knife he was using.

One of the most important jobs each year was hay-making. Mick would be invited into a field, neighbour would help neighbour all hands pulling together until everyone had enough feed in their barns to last their animals through out the year. Mick scored, as children had time off from school to join in and he would arrive each day with his own Army of helpers.

To add a little more to her income.

Lizzie kept pigs and turkeys. She had a sow, which she alone looked after, delivering the piglets herself. If there were too many for the sow to feed, Lizzie would take them indoors and bottle feed them, selling them after twelve weeks. No push over, Lizzie would haggle over a sixpence. One pig would be kept for killing, to provide the family with bacon for the winter. Half would be covered in salt and wrapped in straw and placed on the floor under the table. When Lizzie needed a joint of bacon, she just lifted the corner of straw and cut a piece off.

To ensure her family had a good Christmas she raised a few turkeys to sell. Their reputation was known for miles around, the flavoursome turkeys were very much sought after.

Christmas was a magical time, the children talked about nothing else for weeks, wondering if Father Christmas had got their letters and would remember to call. On Christmas Eve they would hang up their stockings, each of which Lizzie, making sure no-one was disappointed, would fill with an orange, sweets, nuts, perhaps a ruler or a rubber, some wax crayons and a colouring book, some marbles, ribbons for the girls hair, a comb, hankies, all sorts of bits and pieces.

Christmas morning everyone was up early clamouring to go to the first Mass, stockings couldn't be taken down until they got home. The shouts of excitement as they looked to see what Father Christmas had brought them and uncovered the treasures raised the roof.

Next day was like carol singing in England but for just the one day as the children went round with the "Wren" They would walk miles to far-flung neighbours, singing all the carols and be rewarded with perhaps a drink and a penny or some fruit. They arrived home after their day out with their pockets bulging with goodies.

Life was not all Christmas and Mick was often irritable. At one particular noisy breakfast the children had got to him and he had whacked a couple of backsides. There were more arguments outside, between Mick and Jack, their fifth born, now a young man of seventeen. Mick thought nothing of beating his boys with a stick. Jack was furious.

"Right, father or not, that's one hiding too many"

"I'll not have you talk to me like that, boy"

Jack considered himself a man now.

"Then you won't have too. I'm off – I'll join the Army"

Next day Lizzie was distraught to find Jack had gone.

"Won't do him any harm" said Mick.

A few weeks later Mick had to ride into Delvin for supplies returning with a newspaper and baccy to relax on his favourite spot. Lizzie was busy with her chores and the little ones were getting under her feet as she swept the concrete floor with her hand-made witches broom. Mick was sitting on the step legs outstretched, reading, his old baccy pouch bulging in his pocket and his pipe full of baccy. He was always content when he got a few moments like that to himself.

Stopping and leaning on her broom Lizzie gazed tenderly at the man who had given her all those wonderful children.

"He's a good man" she thought. "He has a heart of gold and he's a terrific provider.

Sighing, she said aloud

"I wish you wouldn't argue with the children so much"

Mick grunted and carried on reading. Carrying on with her sweeping Lizzie shooed him off the step. He'd snared some rabbits and could skin and prepare them for the pot in minutes. If any of the kids were around they would wait wide eyed for Mick to get the chopper and chop off the lucky foot, they took it in turns to bag the prize. Topped up with vegetables the rabbits were soon slowly cooking for dinner.

Lizzie stood in the doorway and watched the delivery boy peddling fast along the lane, surprised when the bike came to a dead stop outside their gate. The boy jumped off and was up her path in seconds. Lizzie had no time to wonder who was sending her the telegram he handed her. Her heart sank as she read it.

"Gone to England to join the Army. Will write. Love, Jack"

Only a few weeks later, days after Jacks eighteenth birthday. Mick came home to find Lizzie almost in a state of collapse

"He was no more than a child" she sobbed. "If you weren't so bad-tempered he would still be with us"

Mick was at a loss. Then he spotted the telegram lying on the table. Jack had lost his life in France, fighting at Annes.

"I don't think I can stand this pain I'll never forgive you" Lizzie sobbed

This may have been the only unkind thing she did in her life. Though Lizzies heart was heavy, when morning came the daily grind started all over.

Towards the end of the first war there was an important event in Delvin's history, which lizzie and Mick were part off. In 1918 a book was written by the Headmaster of Ballinvalley's boys school, James Weldon's son. The novel "The Valley of the Squinting Windows" became a best seller, but the people of Delvin recognised themselves in the book of supposed fiction and there was outrage. It was said to be a fact that Jim Growney, who carried game for Mick when he had his shooting parties, supplied the author with most of the material. George Bernard Shaw was involved and it resulted in a High Court case in Dublin, with Lizzie a witness against Mr. Weldon..

It was easy to work out why Lizzie was so much against Mr. Weldon. One of her sons had a problem with his teacher, Henry Healy, who got physical with the boy and a fight developed. The teacher received a broken nose and went to the parish priest to lodge a complaint against the boy. Father James Flynn told him he should be ashamed of himself, admitting he couldn't handle Mick's son.

Even to-day Delvin is known as "The Valley of the Squinting Windows"

Chapter 3

Ten years passed and though the grief remained, it lessened. It may have been a hard life, but Lizzie felt blessed, the rest of her family was thriving. These days she had time to spare, a chance to catch up with a bit of gossip in Delvin, gossip which one day shocked her beyond words and she rushed home.

"Mick" she shrieked, frantically hitching up the horse and cart. "Get in, get in."

Mick in no hurry, dithered.

"What's going on"

"Get in, for Gods sake, just get in, there is a young girl in trouble in Mullingar Hospital and our son is supposed to be responsible"

"God help us"

As Lizzie urged the horse to go faster Mick knew what was coming next. He was right.

"I'll know straight away if that baby is a Merriman. If it is it will be coming home with us."

At the hospital the girl lay silent as lizzie picked the baby up. He was unmistakably a Merriman and as long as there was breath in her body she would love and cherish him. She cradled him in her arms as she and Mick made the return journey, the horse allowed to trot gently now. He was to be called Brendan.

It was a disgrace for a young girl to have a baby out of wedlock, as for the young man, his mates would give him a pat on the back and buy him a drink.

Brendan's mother never married, denied on her death bed that this baby ever happened, although Brendan was at her funeral. He had never heard from her the one word he always wanted to hear,

"Son"

I can understand exactly how he felt.

Lizzie and Mick had been married for thirty-five years. One son, Michael, was still at home and young Brendan was growing fast. Three of their children had settled not a spit away and two more were in Dublin, all with families of their own now so Brendan had plenty of cousins to play with.

Mick and Lizzie embraced their new role as Granddad and Grandma, their home always full of grandchildren. There were eventually dozens of them, some of whom they never met, as time passed and Merriman's scattered as far as Canada, America and Australia.

Lily, the tenth born, had been the first to break the mould and emigrate to England, and Lizzie, saddened by every farewell, a constant reminder of her grief for Jack, was forced to watch her next three daughters rush to join their big sister

Like the rest of the family, Lily was prepared to work till she dropped. Small, totally without any grace or charm and almost completely colourless, she had a pale skin, light blue eyes and mousy frizzy hair. Then there was her appalling stammer, the bottom half of her mouth and chin would jot out and going around in circles as she struggled to get a word out. Despite this Lily swore like a trooper and was never afraid to speak her mind, not caring whether she pleased or offended. To add to the charm there was always a hand rolled fag (you couldn't describe it as a cigarette) sticking to her bottom lip. It would circle round in unison with her chin, and she would frequently be forced to take it out before it choked her.

Lily still managed to find a man to marry, a vital priority in those times. It didn't matter if he was Mr. Right or Mr. Wrong, as long as a woman wasn't left on the shelf to become an old maid. Bill, her husband, was a big man, an Army Captain, red-blooded and manly, who liked his sex. Love didn't come into relationships – women married for security and men to get their washing done and other possible motives. Unfortunately Bill found out after the wedding that Lily thought sex was purely to beget a child. She wasn't going to be like her Mother, so after she had one baby she shut up shop, which led to a very violent marriage for both Lily and the child, who Lily named Sheila, after her sister.

With the support of Bills family Lily opened a haberdashery shop with living accommodation above, at Barkingside, just outside London. Times were hard for small business, England was between wars and the recession was still biting, the big stores were beginning to raise their ugly head, taking trade away from the little shops. Bill was away in the Army, but Lily felt supported by her sisters who lived nearby.

When the fifteen year old Sheila arrived from Ireland to stay the days were simpler as she could help out, but even so Lily eventually went bankrupt. A year or so later Una joined them. Sheila and Una, the youngest of the Merriman girls, were blessed with their Mothers good looks, the chiseled bones and white skinned face, the same deep set dark blue eyes and jet black hair. Sheila wore hers loose, halfway down her back.

Deeply indoctrinated with the Catholic faith and straight over from Ireland, all the girls looked for support and comfort to the church.

When the shop shut the four Merriman siblings would meet, get the cards out and play most of the night. One or two of them might take themselves to the church dance on a Saturday, but not Sheila. She didn't have a musical bone in her body but if the church had organized a whist drive or another card game she wouldn't miss that

By the time she was eighteen, although still shy and somewhat naïve, Sheila was beginning to feel grown up and was enjoying her new life. Then came the month her period was late. In despair from the first moment she realized it wasn't going to arrive at all, she prayed daily for a miracle, that things would be all right, but God wasn't listening. She had disgraced her family with the biggest sin a girl could commit.

Every member of the family, parents, brothers and sisters, no one escaped the public humiliation.

Lily was furious. Stammering worse than ever, she laid into her sister.

"You stupid little.......who did this"

Sheila was silent

"You will have to go away to have the bastard, you wicked........ There's a place for wicked girls like you. The nuns will teach you not to do it again"

Head bowed in shame and misery, Sheila arrived at the Convent for fallen girls. This monster in her belly that wouldn't go away. A devout Catholic, she was grateful to be allowed in, she felt she had come home. Like her Mother, if anyone said a bad word about a nun or a priest, she would have cut their tongue out.

On her arrival she was hurriedly shown into a small room and told to sit down by the nun who accompanied her. They sat in silence

18

and shortly two more nuns arrived, one holding a large pair of scissors and the second standing with her hands behind her back. Without saying a word to Sheila the nun with the scissors grabbed a handful of Sheilas long hair and started to hack it off. Sheila screamed, lashing out to prevent them from touching her. A thick leather strap rained down on her arms and in total shock she gave up the fight. Next she was forced to change into a dull brown sack-like dress and immediately put to work.

These girls had to earn their keep, normal life was over the day a girl entered the convent.

At six a.m. the rising bell rang for Mass, confessions, penance, and prayers, a ritual observed periodically right through the day. With no relief from this, day in and day out, even as devout a Catholic as Sheila found it hard to cope with the endless routine, especially in her troubled state of mind. She seemed to be forever on her knees asking God to forgive her sins.

Breakfast was at 8, never varied, lukewarm lumpy porridge with either sugar or milk but never both and cocoa.

Then to work, which meant either scrubbing the vast area of floor or being in the laundry. On floor duty the heavy buckets of water had to be carried along endless passages and wringing out the large cloths hurt hands and wrists. If you were lucky, a young girl might loose her baby with such hard work. Luck was not with Sheila.

All this work was accompanied by verbal abuse from the nuns, who walked around, pious in their habits, hands together in prayer, defying the girls to hesitate in their work for a moment.

"You miss, no talking"

Talking was out of bounds, but however hard the nuns tried there were girls whose spirits couldn't be broken. Sheila wasn't one of them, yet it seemed to her that the nuns treated her timidity as badly if not worse. She found it impossible to cope with the shame, but a quiet moan of despair when a nun was within earshot and Sheila would feel the toe of a boot on her body. As nuns passed they would whisper,

"Dirty, disgusting person"

For the midday meal the nuns boiled the potatoes in the dirt they were dug up in, meat was always something that looked like vomit and if it was soup for a change, the smell alone turned her stomach. The only good thing about the meal was the chance to sit down. Sheila preferred doing the floors than working in the laundry, where she had to lean over the tubs all day. The large houses in the area sent their washing to the convent to provide employment for the fallen women. With her big tummy it gave her backache like crazy. Concentrating on not letting the hot water burn her hands left little time to think

Tea time offered another chance to sit down. Most of the girls were too exhausted to say a word and as talking was not encouraged at the table it was a silent as well as a meager meal. Bread and butter and a pot of tea. On Sundays, for a treat it was bread and jam – but no butter. Night times it was a relief to get to bed, just to have a lie down. When she had enough energy, Sheila's mind went back to that little cottage in Moortown. Her happy childhood seemed only yesterday. Thinking about the friends she had left behind to seek this great life in London, the boys who had chased her around the playground and wondered what each and every one of them was doing now. If they knew the state she was in they would be ashamed to know her, would not want to own up to once having being her friend..

How she wished she could put the clock back, sit by the grand fire with her Mum and Dad and have a cuddle. Life would never be the same again, the shame would stay with her all the days of her life. Utter exhaustion brought on sleep, but however deeply she slept, as soon as she opened her eyes in the morning the lump was still there and it was getting bigger.

One morning in March, after a cold winter, it was Sheila's turn to get up ten minutes before the others and fetch the water to fill six jugs and place them by the wash bowls for the other girl in her room. She switched the light on and made her way along the long hallway. As she pushed the kitchen door open and switched the light on there, the floor change colour as the cockroaches darted between the floorboards. Could she bear this any longer. One of the nuns called her over,

"You have a visitor. In the hall"

A visitor. Who could that be?

It was now 1934, Lizzie and Mick could take life a lot more easily, only Michael and Brendan were at home. No more scrubbing floors or taking in washing for Lizzie, she made do with her turkeys and her piglets. They still missed Jack but one or other of her children was always home, which was a blessing to Lizzie. They never failed to write and would sometimes enclose a ten shilling note, which pleased old Mick to bits. Sometimes if times were good it would stretch to a whiskey in the pub.

"Not a lot to ask, Lizzie love" he would say

"You deserve it, off you go"

Lizzie never begrudged him his evenings out, he'd always worked hard.

There was always post from the family but on particular letter brought Lizzie a day she would never forget. She read it once, couldn't grasp what it was saying, read it again.

Once again it was time to get her coat.

"Mick, I have to go to England, it's Sheila"

"What's wrong, is she ill"

Mick's lovely Sheila, the bright one they expected so much from, could have done nothing wrong.

"Not ill exactly"

Lizzie couldn't tell him, not yet. She made the long weary journey to England alone. There was family to meet her in London and guide her on her way. Her sister Winifred, sent along her son Pat to help. Lizzie made her way to the convent in Upminster where Sheila was to have the baby. Glad to have a few days with Sheila before the event she knew her love for her daughter would not alter; she loved the bones of every one of her children and wouldn't show her bitter disappointment Lizzie hugged Sheila, they both wept. She found her daughter very frightened by the endless stories the lay workers fed them daily. The nuns had customers for the babies: they'll tell you the baby died.

"They never would" Lizzie's faith in the nuns was unshakeable.

"Mum. They say if the nuns don't like you they will let you suffer more when the baby comes"

"Nonsense"

"And they told us the nuns have babies by the priests. They get their breath snuffed out of them and they bury them in the garden"

"What wicked lies. These dreadful liars should be punished"

Upset by the stories, Sheila was glad to have her Mother contradict them. Lizzie quietly reassured her daughter, not realizing the rough time she had experienced at the Convent.

Sheila had changed, as if the very heart, soul and spirit had

21

been ripped out of her. Lizzie would never want to know or believe the dark side of the nuns and priests. In Lizzie's simple faith, if such a thought crossed her mind she would rot in hell for eternity.

But it would be over Lizzie's dead body if anything happens to a grandchild of hers.

I finally made my entrance into this big world on March 14th 1934, at ten past one on a Wednesday morning, after a very difficult two days. I wasn't weighed so I have no idea if I was a big or a small baby. Uncle Pat arrived first thing, probably as much to give Lizzie his support as to see Sheila or me.

For Sheila this episode of her life was over and would never again be referred to. Weeping, Lizzie hugged her as she said,

"I wish with all my heart that you had not done this, but you are still my daughter and I will always love and pray for you"

After a couple of days, just as she had done with Brendan six years before, Lizzie wrapped me up and took me home with her. Like him.

I had no Mother and that was the way it was always going to be. When Sheila came home to see her family and friends I would be ignored: other than at those times our paths need never cross. I still didn't have a name, but as my Grandma reached the door with me safely in her arms, Sheila her head turned towards the wall, called out,

"Call her Leila."

Chapter 4

Knowing she must get on with her life Sheila set about job hunting. Though still providing a roof over her head, Lily was most uncharitable about what had happened. Stuttering worse than usual she finally got the words out.

"I hope someone has drowned that fucking bastard."

"Bastard" – Sheila could not allow herself to think of that word. No-one in her large family, except possibly her Mother, could understand her despair during the months of carrying that baby, how her young life had been ruined. If any of them asked, she said she was no longer a Catholic. She would never forgive her treatment by the priests and the nuns and renounced the faith, a move which made her an outcast with some of them. To this day I am convinced that, although she had made up her mind never to think about and certainly never to mention any part of the whole episode, like any woman who gives away a baby she must surely have felt that part of her was missing

Sheila settled for a job as a live in barmaid at the Beehive Hotel in Gant's Hill, where she spent the next ten years. The owners Solly and May Jacobs had been in the Hotel and pub life since they married as teenagers. Now in the last decade of their working life they were comfortably off, mainly due to May's ability to handle cash; she knew every corner to cut to save a penny. A life spent in the trade had made her tough, worldly, a no nonsense woman.

May was probably just the right person for Sheila at that time. She and Solly had no children, so there was no difficult conversation to bring unpleasant memories. They took Sheila under their wing and gave her a pleasant room. With a pay packet every Friday she could start to buy herself some bits and pieces. May would tease her out of her shyness with her blunt talk and tales of pub life.

One evening May went into the gent's to close a window. A poor man was spending a penny, he creased up but May never batted an eye lid. She told him she had seen thousands – he still jumped.

It made Sheila jump too – and blush. May grinned at her as she relayed the story,

"Don't worry" she told Sheila, I put him right, told him I meant,

"I've seen one thousands of times"

Times like that put Sheila at her ease. She soon made friends and enjoyed the camaraderie of the clientele. One young girl around her age became a special friend and would pop in every evening for a stiff drink before starting her shift. Although she was a "lady of the night" Sheila in some ways was always envies of her. A very pretty blue eyed blonde, she had the loveliest of smiles and always smelt divine. A conservative dresser, Sheila was fascinated by the girls flamboyant attire. There was always a feather, buckle, belt or beads, long or short, bits of fluff or fur attached somewhere.

One evening she popped herself up on the bar stool, placed her elbows on the counter, chin in her hands, chatted away to Sheila in what they both thought was a private conversation.

"I'm absolutely pissed off to-night" she said, "I've had to see to a Catholic priest this afternoon, he got on my f-ing nerves fiddling with his dress coat, I thought he was never going to get it out. All the Catholic priest I service are the same, they piss me about.."

Unbeknown to the girls an earwigging customer was so appalled by the suggestion that a Catholic priest would use the services of a prostitute that he went straight to the police and the girl was chased out of town. Having experienced the dark side of the Catholic Church Sheila knew what the priest's and nun's were capable of and believed her friend, but kept quiet. She had much to loose and knew she was no match for either the Church or the police.

It was five months since Sheila left the convent and four since she started her job. Now that she had only herself to worry about, never again would she be stupid enough to let anyone pull the wool over her eyes, she was determined to have a good life. Among the people she worked with she was acquiring a touch of class and felt she was as good as the rest, if not better and saw no reason why she shouldn't be successful. She was blessed with her Mother's looks but she was still distraught at the state of her hair even all these months after it had been so cruelly cut. It was unbelievable how long it was taking to grow back to what Sheila considered a respectable length.

A few months later came an event that changed her life. Jack, one of Sollys two brothers, owned a greengrocers near where Solly and May lived. He was married with a four year old daughter, Elizabeth and another baby due any day. They were all shocked by the awful news that Jack's wife had died in child birth. The whole family supported the devastated Jack and eventually he decided to farm Elizabeth out to his sister in Westcliff.

"Give up your business and come in with us, Jack" the concerned Solly invited. "We could do with your help and there's plenty of room here. May can help look after baby John"

So Jack moved in. Almost thirty years older than Sheila and weighing over sixteen stone, his larger than life personality was irresistible. He was very sophisticated, utterly charming, gentle and kind, with a passion for racing, both greyhounds and horses. Eighteen months after his wife's death they were married and came to Ireland for their honeymoon where Sheila proudly introduced her husband to her parents, unaware how shocked Lizzie and Mick were, not only by his age – Jack was barely five years younger than Mick – but in this devout Catholic family, for their daughter to have married a Jew caused considerable distress. Sheila, enraptured by the man paraded him around like the cat who had been at the cream, showing him off to all her family and friends. Jack took Mick to the races and there were drinks all round at the pub. By the time the holiday was drawing to a close Jack's silver tongue had won everyone over. I of course, a two year old, was there, but I was treated as just one of the many children around. When they left, Grandma said,

"Say goodbye to your Auntie Sheila and Uncle Jack"

Sheila's one ambition now was to be a good wife; she was never going to be the wicked stepmother. She adored Jack's son John, loving him as her own satisfied her material instincts Between them – Sheila, Jack, Solly and May he became one spoiled little boy.

When the war began in 1939 Sheila was in her mid-twenties and had been at the Beehive for five years. A stunningly good-looking woman, taller than her Mother, her jet black hair once again hung almost to her waist. It didn't matter who came into the Hotel, what part of the world they came from, Sheila had the gift of knowing how to talk to them, no matter what there race, religion or customs, she would know about their backgrounds. She had an air of class, could put on the voice and act of a lady to perfection. Her fairly small wardrobe was of the best quality and she would only shop in Jewish establishments. Despite her very strict Catholic upbringing she was pro-Jewish and defended them on every corner.

She and Jack had become a very glamorous couple. No doubt life behind the bar was hard work, but ably assisted by Jack she played even harder and became even more involved in gambling than he was. On their days off they would often take a taxi from Gant's Hill to Bray, where Lily now lived. Sheila would visit the hairdressers, then the taxi would continue to Ascot for a day's racing. After dinner it was home by taxi. When it came to drink Sheila could hold her own with the best of them, there was always a Gin and Tonic in her hand. Other afternoons off might involve a theatre trip to the West End.

The first really bad news of the war come in 1940, Sheila was devastated to learn of the death of her brother, Brendan's father. After that Sheila and Jack became concerned by the progress of the war and were getting increasingly worried for the safety of young John.

.

Chapter 5

Uncle Pat had come to the Convent to support Lizzie on behalf of the family and to see her to the boat at Dun-laoghaire.

"Take care of yourself, you're a good woman" he said as he hugged her in farewell on the quay.

"This is my grandchild, this is a Merriman" was Lizzie's reply.

Huge waves in the Irish Sea pounded the sides of the boat. On board the passengers froze or were sick, mostly both. Lizzie, no longer young was totally exhausted., When she reached Delvin, it was very late, she knew she must take a taxi out to the cottage. Mick was inside sharing a jar with another uncle, Tom. It was Tom who took me out of poor Lizzies arms,

"What have we got here then?" he asked. Tom told me years later that I was blue with the cold and he spent most of the night pacing up and down with me but nothing would comfort me.

Lizzie was glad to sit down and relax after the strain of the last week, and the whole sad story came out. Mick who always supported Lizzie in any decision she made, said little other than,

"You're back now. I'll put the kettle on straight away. Let's have a look at the little one" He wasn't in the least bit put out by the new arrival, even when he knew what Sheila had done and said.

It was Mick, wise old owl, who shut me up in the end.

"Here, give her this" He opened his bottle of Guinness and added a few drops to a bottle with milk. Soon I slept, wrapped up warmly and laid in a drawer. I like to think I was sweet, soft and just a little loved New born babies are usually cherished by families filled with pride and joy. I could have had no idea, as I slept soundly by the glow of the turf fire of the feelings of hate, the shame and disgrace my birth had brought on my family. All my Aunts and Uncles wished something awful would happened to me. Lizzie cared not an iota for their gossips, nor for that matter her neighbours. As she was doing with Brendan, she would love and protect me, as long as there was breath in her body.

It was unthinkable not to take a baby to Church within days of it's birth. If that baby died without being baptized it would never go to heaven, it would linger forever in Limbo. What kind of a religion is that? To punish, not so much the baby but the parents who have to live with that trauma on their soul for the rest of their life. One would think the baby was a mass murderer or something equally sinister. But we are in Ireland in the 1930's when peasants, people like Mick and Lizzie were kept at heel by fear. The christening arrangements offered Lizzie and Mick a dilemma.

"Sheila had said she wanted 'Leila'" so I would always be known as 'Leila' but Lizzie wondered if in fact it was a real name and thought it would look odd on a birth certificate. She decided to give me her name, Elizabeth Winifred Merriman.

"It's a good name" she said to Mick, "A life has been lived in that name."

To me she whispered

"Leila. I'm giving you the most precious possession I have. Wear my name well, have a good life."

Placing a kiss on my wrinkled little face and giving me that unwanted scrap of humanity, a loving hug, she added, "You will be dearly loved, with me always beside you."

This was one christening that was not the occasion for a family celebration, almost none of my relatives came.

My Grandparents agreed I was a true Merriman, one half of me certainly was, but as for the other half would that ever be known – would anyone care. What made Sheila call me Leila. Had she in the later stages of carrying me had some feelings, would she have liked to have kept me. I did not know then and now I will never know. The Merrimans were known for their pale complexions, their almost porcelain skin, all had the same blue eyes the women straight black hair. I had a mop of curls, deep hazel eyes, rosy cheeks and skin that went golden when the sun shone. When any of the family discussed me and I'm sure they rarely stopped wondering about me, they would say I was definitely from a Mediterranean country.

I soon became Granddads little darling. Mick now had more time for children than he could spare as a young man when babies were born almost every year and he was stretched to his limits trying to feed them. When I got to walking I would waddle along to where he was, he would put his big rough hand down and reaching up as far as I could I would hold it and he would walk along at my pace. Although he was a bachelor and had no interest in kids, Michael didn't mind the disruption Brendan and I made and I found life wonderful. There were plenty of cousins to play with. I loved going to Aunt Maggie's, Grandma's second eldest daughter. It was a short walk to the crossroads, then turn left and walk about three miles along the country lane, they had plenty of land and animals and four children, but sadly Aunt Maggie died early of Cancer. If you turn right at the crossroads it was less than a quarter of a mile to where Uncle Tom and his wife, another Maggie, lived with their three boys, Michael, Sean and Tommy. Further along the lane was Christy with his wife Nancy and their two children. I was closest to Uncle Tom, who later played a major part in my life. When I met him on the road there was always a halfpenny for sweets.

I grew up very fast and soon learned many of my Granddad skills. When he went to the river Deel to fish, it was my job to hold the special net he used to catch minnows. Six feet deep, the river was wide and fast flowing. There was an abundance of fish; perch, pike, trout, salmon, tench, roach and eel. Granddad chiseled out three holes in the large stone bridge over the river to make steps so I could climb up. Holding on tight I could look over and watch the river flowing and the swans or ducks swimming. When I was older I could catch the eels myself, I would make a cut right round their throat, rub salt in the cut, so it was easy to slide the skin off. The skins would be hung up to dry and be used as shoe laces. I would cut the eel in pieces and, pop them in the pan on the turfs, they were delicious when, freshly caught. I wouldn't be able to say which was my favourite time, fishing in the Deel or out on the lake.

Lake Dysart covered thirty five acres.

I would rush along the path between the bracken, through the wood and scrambling into the boat ahead of Granddad, usually on a sunny day with a breeze. We would be out there for hours and I would watch the way the sun danced on the water, making patterns with beautiful colours. In the distance the water held strips of gold intertwining with aquamarine. When I grew a little I would sit beside Granddad and take an oar

Grandma was the main person in my life, but when Granddad took off I was there. One day he had errands to do in Delvin. He took the big horse, with me up in front of him for a ride. As often happened he got led astray, stopping to have a few jars with his mates in the pub. He put me up on the horses back, my little legs just long enough to cover it's broad back.

Then "Get" he said, giving the horse a smack and it set off home. I had to lie flat to reach its mane so I could hold on. Grandma was not amused. Granddad would bring home a bottle of Guinness in each pocket for later. When he did open one he would get my cup, pour a little in, filling the cup up with milk he would say, "Best drink you'll ever drink, Guinness and milk, puts hairs on your chest" I wasn't sure if a little girl would want a hairy chest.

Every one, man, woman and child had to help with the harvest. My very important job was to walk after the harvester to rescue all the baby mice and their nests that were disturbed by the big machine. At the end of the day I had hundreds of mice in an old tin bucket, which I loving and very carefully handed over to Granddad who knew a place where they would be safe. The innocence of childhood. I would have been heartbroken if I had known what happened to them.

There were great summer days spent in the bog cutting the turf. The pigs pot full of colcannon, would be put on the cart for dinner, no plates would be packed. My job was to fill Grandma's baskets with fraocan berries, and when that was done I could play. All the kids for miles around were there, all we had were some sticks for bats, a ball and our skipping ropes. If they had time, a couple of the grown ups would get out a long thick rope and turn it for us, possibly with as many as eight of us in the rope at the same time. It was just great fun, running, jumping over the holes where the turf was.

When it was dinner time, Granddad, Grandma, Brendan and I sat around the pot and with only a spoon, dug in to the delicious food and eat until we burst. Tea was served in jam jars with string tied around the neck and made into a handle. That was really glamorous when you are a kid, something you remember all your life.

Granddad had a still in the bog where he brewed his own poteen. On one occasion it sprang a leak and the wild geese got to it. They were rolling around on the ground legless.

Christmas was an even more magical time of the year for me. It was my job to stone the currants, sultanas and raisins,, I wouldn't pop even one into my mouth. That would be naughty. I was never naughty, I liked grandma being able to trust me. The cooking was exciting. Grandma make a big cake, all the grandchildren had a stir, made a wish and fought over who could lick the bowl out. The puddings created as much interest as we all watched in awe as the silver threepenny pieces were added and make a secret wish that we would get one of the silver goodies on Christmas day. Brendan was an amazing singer and played the accordion so we always had music in the cottage, Christmas didn't add to the music, in Ireland there were no carol singers, it was a time to prepare for the birth of Christ. Coupled with our own preparations, like writing to Santa Claus and making sure we had a big enough stocking. The family always remembered me, especially Uncle Tom, he never forgot, he bought three of everything for his three sons and the same for me. I was the little girl he never had.

As soon as I was big enough to reach the handle of the milk churn I would help Grandma make the butter. She patted it into about half pounds, then I would run out to the rhubarb patch and pick the biggest leaves, the butter would be wrapped in the leaves and stored.

One event that really upset me every year was Granddad killing the pig. He would give it a bang on the forehead to knock it out and then cut it's throat. I hated the noise it made. Every bowl Grandma owned was put on the ground to catch the blood. That would make the black puddings to feed the family, the guts was washed to provide the skins for the puddings and sausages. One half of the pig was wrapped in salt and straw and stored under the big table. When you sat down to eat or play at the table, your feet rested on the pig. I would watch Grandma lift the straw and cut off a lump of bacon when she needed it.

I had nothing to do but play. The acre and a half was my dolls house. I would be outside all day, amusing myself, making up games, lost in my own wonderful world. I just loved my doll's pram, it had no wheels, it was a wooden box with a handle and I could pull it along. I don't remember ever owning a doll, but I would dress up all sorts of things, a piece of bark from a tree, a funny shaped stone, a piece of wood that looked like it had arms and legs. My dolls clothes were rags. I would make up all sorts of stories about the inhabitants of my doll's pram. I was one happy contented little girl who had the whole world in that pram.

One day I went rushing into the cottage, "Granny, Granny, Granny, the cats had three kittens and the next one wont come out." Grandma wiped her hands on her apron,

"What are you up to now "she asked and came with me to have

a look. There was the cat trying to give birth to the fourth kitten and all was well.

"Where are the other kittens?" asked Grandma. Very proudly I said, "They're here, Grandma"

I had taken each kitten as it was born, dressed it in my dolls clothes and put it in my pram ready to take them for a walk but I was being held up by this last one. Picking each little new born kitten up Grandma unwrapped it and put it back with its mother.

"You mustn't ever take a baby away from it's Mother, it might die."

"Sorry, Grandma"

"I know you are being good and caring for them. Don't worry,"

"Can't I just look at them"

Peep in quietly, but not too often. And don't disturb the Mother. I expect they would love a ride when they are bigger.

Grandma was never cross. I was too young to wonder about a Mother for me.

At weekends Grandma sometimes went to visit her sons and daughters. I think she liked to go to Maggie's best. I loved it there and we seemed to go often. We would stay very late and the walk home in the dark was exciting with only the stars and the moon to light the way home along the country lane. Grandma would tell me stories about the little people, and the fairies people had at the bottom of the garden. One night we had stopped walking to listen to the sounds of the night, the moon was very bright and I glanced down just in time to see a little Leprechaun, run over my feet, quick as a flash – really I did. I don't think Granddad had put any Guinness in my milk that day.

Chapter 6

I started school September 1939 in the week the second World War began. Hitching up the horse and cart to take me to school on my first day, Grandma put aside her worries over her family, whose safety she prayer for daily. Joe, her baby, was a regular soldier, Uncle Gerald and Tom had joined up along with her nephew Pat, who had married Auntie Una.

Grandma placed a plank across the cart and we sat side by side. Grandma very straight with head held high. I hate to think that wonderful lady felt ashamed, no child could have been better loved or cared for. It had been a wonderful five years for me, Good as gold. I had never had a smack and was as contented as the day was long. The staff knew Grandma well, fifteen of her children had gone to that school, her grandchildren were there now. On my first day I sat on the floor behind the blackboard all day and cried. Why behind the blackboard? Perhaps I thought no one could see me there.

Balllinvalley School was built in 1900. Two storey's high, it had a large yard and resting in a few acres of grounds.. The upstairs two rooms were for the boys, downstairs for the girls. The years were split in two with one teacher in each room. One class would go to the front, teacher gave them their work, they would go to the back, sit down and get on with it. The next class would step forward, that routine went on until everyone had work to do. There was no doubt I was a very clever child. I'm not saying this to be big headed, rather get the story right. I soon settled down and was well behaved.

Walking three miles to school every day was no problem as I had family to keep me company. In the summer we went barefoot as there wasn't money for shoes. The only time I knew fear, when I came across tinkers camping on the roadside. I would walk past quickly, pressing myself as close as possible to the far hedge, mindful of stories I'd heard that they would take me away and keep me. I was relieved when I got past without being snatched.

Grandma was close to her second son who'd been given to her parents and she liked to make a trip to Dublin from time to time. Sometimes she took me with her; we would catch the bus in Delvin and travelled the fifty miles to Dublin. Once, walking along O'Connell Street she said to me, "You know Leila, nowhere in the world will you find girls as pretty as here in Dublin" and she sang sweetly.

> In Dublin's fair City
> Where the girls are so pretty
> I first set my eyes on sweet Mollie Malone
> As she wheels her wheelbarrow
> Through streets broad and narrow
> Crying, cockles and mussels alive, alive O!

On the street corners ladies stood with broad leather straps around their necks supporting baskets full of oranges on their fronts. They would cry I wish this was a talking page, their accents were glorious)

"Lovely juicy oranges, tuppence each, the oranges. Come on Missus, buy an orange"

I never had an orange, two pence was a lot of money but I did climb to the top of Nelson's Column. It isn't there now, it was blown up which is a pity, because from the top when you are six you can see the whole world.

Even in such a small spot on the map as Moortown, the war was never far from peoples minds and as early as 1940 Lizzie and Mick received another dreaded telegram. This time it was Gerald who had been killed and again Lizzie was heartbroken. Gazing at his son Brendan, the boy she had rescued from Mullingar Hospital, she held him tight

"Thank God we've got him, Mick" she said, "He's doubly precious now"

"Sure" Mick too was deeply upset. "There'll always be a part of our Gerald around while young Brendan stays"

"I'll never get over this one" Lizzie said, "my heart is truly broken" She had said that about Jack too, killed in the first war and it was true, she never did.

Like millions of parents still in London, Una was concerned for the safety of her only child and brought her daughter Maureen over to Grandma. My cousin Maureen was four years younger than me, and seemed such a little tot but we became the very best of friends. Much later she was my bridesmaid and she is Godmother to both my children. Right then we were just two little girls, one with a Mummy and Daddy and one without.

Granddad and Grandma had three of us now so I was never without a playmate. With his jet black hair, piercing blue eyes and engaging smile, Brendan was a typical Merriman. A tall well built teenager now, he had hands the size of a large bat and a rough, almost flaky skin. He was a talented boxer, really good and was always shunting around on his feet, sniffing and punching the air. As the two outcasts we'd bonded; I loved him to bits and would follow him around like a puppy.

I was seven when he suggested I go into the barn with him and practice sparing. As always, I was more than happy to tag along, but as soon as we got inside he got his thing out and filled a cup up with wee.

"Drink this" he demanded, handing the cup to me.

I was mortified.

"No, that's wee" I said, "It's still steaming"

"Drink it or I'll use your head as a punch bag"

I drank every drop without being physically sick, but for years the taste stayed in my mouth. From then on I hated him and wished him in hell.

It was time for a major event in my life, my first Holy Communion. Like most people in Ireland in those days I absolutely adored the Catholic faith, I had been totally indoctrinated, knew practically every word of the bible and would read it as often as I could. I found the preparation for the big day easy: we had to pass an exam to prove we were ready. Like other members of my class, I got a hundred percent pass which meant we would wear a different coloured sash from the other girls. In class we had to practice making our confession, by kneeing down on a box, in front of a small window with a net through which you could see the outline of the priest, side faced on. We made the sign of the cross and say,

"Bless me Father for I have sinned, I confess to you Father and to Almighty God that I have sinned exceedingly in thought, word and deed. Through my fault through my fault, through my most grievous fault"

What a load of rubbish for a seven year old. We were trained to think it was the most humbling experience to get down on our knees in front of another human being and cleanse our soul

When the day came for me to make my first confession, I was totally in awe of the priest. It is impossible to explain the sheer reverence of the occasion and when I knelt before him I thought it would be alright to ask a question. I wasn't sure what a sin was and with Brendan in mind I asked,

"Is it a sin to hate someone and wish them in hell"

What I didn't realize was the priest could see me and knew who I was. I also didn't know, because it hadn't as yet raised it's ugly head – I was the village bastard – in the priest's eyes I shouldn't even be breathing let along be wishing someone in hell.

"You are the one who will be going to hell, talking like that"

He sounded almost as if my place was already booked.

"For your penance say three Hail Marys, three Our Fathers and three Glory Be's"

I left the confessional box totally confused, there was not a single gentle word; in my small mind priests were almost saints and I couldn't imagine a priest being unkind. But I knew I had been put in my place and I was very sad. I knelt down to do my penance really upset on a day I should have felt at peace with the world. I saw that all my class mates were smiling and looking pleased with themselves. I wondered what they had confessed, perhaps that they had poked out their tongues or pulled someone's hair

So at seven years old, even before I took my first Holy Communion, I had a hint that things weren't as they should be, I felt a distance from my class mates, but the incident didn't spoil my day, Grandma had done me proud. I had the nicest white dress, white shoes and socks and a lovely veil. It hurts me even now to think how ashamed my beloved Grandma must have been, but she wouldn't give way. How they must have talked in that little village, but she brazened it out.

Grandma was busy early, it was a special day, my eight birthday, and she had been out to the hen house, picked the newest laid egg, tied brightly coloured rags around it and boiled it. The rags stained the shell so that I had a special Googie, my name for eggs, for breakfast.

My favourite Uncle Tom was home on leave, with his usual surprise for me. This time he brought a slice of white bread something I had never seen, spread with fresh churned butter and home made jam. Amazingly that was sixty five years ago now, yet I remember it's delicious taste today, even though I haven't the slightest recollection of any other presents. I was as happy as ever, having no idea that the days of my contented and sheltered childhood were numbered. Still very young, I failed to realize the tower of strength that was my Grandma. While she stood proudly sheltering and protecting me no one would touch me.

A few weeks after my birthday Grandma decided one Saturday that she wanted to go to church and say a prayer. She seemed tired so leaving Maureen with Granddad she and I walked the three miles to church. Inside the church she walked straight to the front row, knelt down and quickly put her head in her hands. I knelt down beside her to say my prayers. I felt her nudge me

"Leila" she said "Light a candle for me"

"Can't it wait, Grandma? I don't want to now, I'm in the middle of a prayer" I whispered.

"If you are going to be naughty and play me up," said Grandma "I shall die and I'll leave you."

At her gentle push I went forward, putting the money in the box. Slowly lighting a candle I placed it in front of the statue of the Virgin Mary. I had never before known Grandma to be cross with me and made my way back to snuggle up close to her for forgiveness.

Soon after we arrived home Uncle Christy came to take Maureen and me to stay with him and Auntie Nancy and their two children. We loved being there although until now we had never stayed over. The front room had bare floorboards and no furniture, just toys everywhere and a playpen in the middle for any babies, The four of us could play and scream to our hearts content.

It was a two story house which made it even more exciting. Half way up the stairs was an alcove, a wonderful place to sit and dream. I was sitting up there one morning playing with my cousins dolls and looking out the window, saw the sun was shining on the garden full of daisies and decided to go outside and made everyone a daisy chain, As I knelt on the grass I realized some one was standing in front of me. Looking up I saw a strange woman, staring at me with a blank expression. Without a word nor even the slightest hint of a smile, she held out a long gold chain with a purse at the end, it was plastic and decorated with pale and dark tiny roses. I knelt up and reached for the purse, with a big smile I thanked her. Without any sign of recognition, she turned and walked away. All I remember of her was her thick black hair spreading down her back, right to her waist. I rushed inside to find Auntie Nancy.

"Look Auntie, at my present. A lady gave it to me. I don't know who she was. Can I keep it?"

"That was your Auntie Sheila" was all my Auntie said "Yes, keep it." I sensed there was something odd about the lady; she seemed cold and I hadn't liked her.

Uncle Christy had joined the Army very young but he didn't like it at all.

Right through the war he supervised fifty men in the bogs at Coolronan, County Meath. He was very involved in sport, especially handball and at lunch times he would allow the men to let off steam. Someone always had a ball for a kick about, and when Brendan was there he would provide a few pairs of boxing gloves, set up a makeshift boxing ring and Christy would be timekeeper if there were any takers for a knock about. When Christy died of cancer soon after the war ended, Brendan dug his grave as a mark of his love for the man.

Uncle Christy and Auntie Nancy were always kind to me. After a few days he took Maureen and me home. A home without Grandma. While we were away she had gone to heaven, as she'd threatened me.

"If you're naughty, I'll die and leave you"

I kept hearing those dreadful words, but I couldn't believe I had been that naughty. In fact I wasn't sure how I had been naughty at all. I asked God over and over what I had done that was so bad that my wonderful Grandma had left me. For a long time the episode in the church was the last recollection I had of my Grandma, but I knew that a light had gone out in my life that would never be rekindled.

Granddad now had two little girls to look after, he set about the task willingly. In the evenings he would sit on the bench by the fire with us standing, one either side of him while he told us the most amazing stories. While he talked we would spit on his bald head and with thumb and first finger we would put the spit on his wispy little bits of hair, rolling it around in our fingers we tried to make ringlets. He stood for all our tricks If truth be told, we probably saved him from despair, he'd worshipped the ground Lizzie walked on.

Back in England Una was seriously ill in hospital. She had a goiter operation and it was six weeks before she was well enough to be told her Mother had died. As soon as she was well enough to travel she came home to Moortown. No more ammunition factory work for her, she would sit the war out with her father and daughter – and me of course.

When I met her after Grandmas death she was a young woman, about twenty five. She wasn't in the strongest of health and I wasn't her responsibility but she was good to me. I loved Auntie Una and Uncle Pat till the day they died.

It was a full house again, Granddad, Michael, Brendan, Una, Maureen and me.

Auntie Una had arrived just before the September term, when Maureen was to start school.

"Now, Leila, I expect you to look out for Maureen, make sure she is safe getting there and back"

Auntie Una said "Make sure you play with her at playtime and you can read to her when you get home this evening." Plenty of instructions, but no problem for me. I loved Maureen to bits, Una absolutely adored Maureen as all Mothers are supposed to do with their children. I did wonder who was looking out for me,

So it was I delivered Maureen safely home. We had been at school for a few days. I might have dragged her through a hedge, ran her through some puddles but she was safe.

Auntie Una had spent the day making her a dress. It had a flared skirt with different coloured buttons, sewn all around the hem; red, blue, pink, white, yellow, green, buttons of every colour Auntie Una could get her hands on. I had never seen such a lovely dress and I was quite envious, longing for someone to make a dress like it for me. I was still sitting there with my mouth open, dribbling when Granddad shouted,

"Leila, time for you to fetch the cows"

We had three cows in a neighbours field and that was my job every night, I knew which three I had to fetch, and was always careful to shut the big gate after me. I had just enough time every night to plait the cow's tails as I walked them home along the quiet country lane. Every night Granddad said,

"Don't do that, Leila" and every night I did. That night, when I picked up the first cows tail I said to it, (I don't know what I would have done if it had answered me)

"You know Maureen has a Mummy and Daddy and now I think about it, all my cousins and all my school friends have Mummy and Daddy's. I wonder why I don't."

The penny had dropped, for the first time in my young life I was aware I was different. It had to come, sooner or later, that dress with the buttons had made it come all too soon. I decided to listen at school to my classmates conversations and try and find out what a Mummy was, what she did. It seemed to be an advantage to have a Mum, so I set about getting one. That evening Auntie Una and Maureen were out and Granddad was telling me a story, I always knew they were not true but they were still magical and as I listened I had a great idea.

"That's it" I said to myself, "I'll make up a story about my Mum and Dad"

I don't think it helped that I made them Misssionaries in China trying to bring Christianity to the country.

When I got the chance I relayed my story in school. What happened is very hard for me to explain or understand, it was as if the whole class was waiting. They all knew I didn't have a Mother or Father and in one they turned on me and said,

"You're a liar, we don't speak to liars," and they sent me to Coventry. All I wanted was to be like them, I didn't want a new bike or fancy gifts, I just wanted to be the same as they were.

After three days of silence and the girls getting great delight out of my distress I was at a loss at what to do. It showed me the way people were talking about kids being born out of wedlock, because whose children didn't think it up on there own, it had come from their parents at home.

When I got home that evening I saw Una's red bead necklace in a saucer on the dressing table. I convinced myself that if I take that necklace to school and give it to someone, they might speak to me. I suppose it was stealing but I told myself I was just borrowing it.

I don't know what I expected Una to do when she missed it, I hadn't thought that far. What she did do was write to all her brothers and sisters, telling them I was nothing more than a liar and a thief. Then she went to see the wonderful headmistress,.

Miss Fitzsimmons was a pillar in the community, a good, holy, compassionate human being, with all the makings of a Saint. She had known me from the day I first went into church in my Grandmothers arms, she had seen me grow up in that small village. I had been in her school from the age of five, and had not for one moment been in any trouble.

Auntie Una hardly knew me, she had no right to call me names.

Did this holy teacher take me aside, and have a quiet word with me, knowing how much I was grieving the loss of my Grandmother? Without one ounce of understanding, this bigoted catholic lady made me stand in front of the whole school every morning for as long as I can remember and say,

"I promise I will try not to tell any lies or steal anything to-day" as if I were a habitual liar and a thief.

I will never know what made Una react like that, I could well have done without it. I would have wished the headmistress in hell, only I knew that kind of wish would lead me straight to hell. What about the priest? There was no way I could talk to him, he would send me away with a flea in my ear. I would have to go to confession and lie. I couldn't say I wished her in hell. I didn't know then that the Catholic Church had a place for a girl like me, one of those notorious homes where decent priests like mine thought I should be. He couldn't tolerate having to deal with me; no-body should have to deal with "Scum"

Weeks passed and I was still suffering the daily humiliation of saying my piece in front of the whole school. I felt completely degraded. On one particular cold morning after a three mile walk without gloves my hands were frozen. As I returned to my place in class having said my piece, I made a remark to another girl. On my word of honour, I know there was no nasty intent in my mind.

"What did you just say" bellowed Miss Fitzsimmons.

The suddenness of her outburst frightened me to death.

"I c-can't remember" I stuttered.

If my life depended on it, I honestly couldn't remember. She had frightened me so much my brain had gone dead.

"Very well" she said, "step up here, put your hand out" and she stroked the cane.

Even to-day, I can remember looking into her eyes and pleading.

"Please, Miss, I honestly can't remember"

I held out my red hand, my fingers so cold I couldn't get them dead straight. The cane came swishing down.

"Get back to your place" I was ordered coldly.

Even at that tender age I wouldn't cry and I held my head high, I couldn't wait until it was the turn of my class to sit down so that I could put my fingers between my knees for a bit of warmth and pray they would stop stinging. I felt so humiliated and suddenly wanted my Grandma more than ever. That witch of a teacher wouldn't have done that had she still been alive. Grandma would have had her guts for garters, she wouldn't hold with a child being abused.

The witch, alias Miss Fitzsimmons then turned her attention on the school bully. Of course she had no idea it was the school bully. This lovely – question mark – child had parents and they were practically neighbours of the teacher. Dealing with her was not handling filthy little bastards. What teacher didn't know this sweet little girl would seek out a couple of younger girls, give them a whole two pence, telling them to spend only one, then send them into the little shop in the High Street, where the owner was a good friend of her parents. They had instructions to mess about and play the shopkeeper up while bully girl nipped around the back and stole lemonade, sweets and biscuits. Sometimes she, one of my cousins and others played truant.

"Why weren't you at school yesterday" asked Miss Fitzsimmons.

"Please Miss I was sick," butter wouldn't melt in her mouth.

"Where is your note" was the next question.

"Please Miss, Mum didn't have time to write one, she was busy"

"Very well" said teacher, "try to remember next time."

"Yes, Miss, thank you Miss" and she would smile, laughing with her friends at the stupidity of the woman.

So you could be a bully, a real thief, a liar, play truant and get a pat on the back but then it was acceptable, as long as you weren't a bastard. It's a funny thing but I didn't tell lies nor steal and I never told tales. I would take my punishment even if it was unjust and watch others getting away with murder. As long as you had parents you could get away with most things. Since Grandma's death I was aware I was on a different planet from every one else., That awful feeling of not belonging, being inferior, not as good as your class mates was getting worse, until I was almost on the point of becoming a very disturbed child.

Life is often very cruel, someone hurts you and you take it out on the nearest person and I went off Maureen. On our way to school, when we got to the hole in the hedge where we cut across the fields to save walking up to the junction and along the Castlepollard Road, I took off. I ran as fast as I could and left her. I had done that route every day, mostly on my own and I knew she couldn't come to any harm. All I could hear was.

"Diddly, I can't keep up. Wait for me, Diddly"

She couldn't say "Leila" and called me "Diddly"

Bless her little heart, she was a sweetie. She was used to having her Diddly look out for her.

Flying across the field on my way to school one morning I stumbled over something. I picked myself up and walked back to kick whatever it was I'd stumbled on. It was a bird's nest with five babies squawking their heads off for food. There was no sign of the parents, I was too young to realize they wouldn't come back while I was around. I waited as long as I could but had to get to school I was never late. I knew I had to save them from starvation and placed the nest carefully in my satchel. At morning break and lunch time I would feed them and save their lives. Once everyone had settled at their desks to work there was quiet, suddenly interrupted by this awful noise. Miss Fitzsimmons ears were flapping.

"Who is making that noise" she asked,

She stood up and started to walk round the desks, stopping at mine.

"Open your satchel. Lets see what is making that noise, Leila"

I stood up, placed the satchel on my desk and opened it as requested. There was the nest with the five baby birds. I thought Miss Fitzsimmons was going to burst. The type to go bright red, the colour started at chest level, travelled up over her chin and continued right up to her hairline.

"Get back over those fields as fast as your legs can carry you and place the nest exactly where you found it. The cane will be waiting when you get back"

It seemed to me everything I did in school these days was followed by, "Leila Merriman, what are you up to now" and the cane was always waiting for me. It can have had nothing to do with me as a person, there wasn't a child in that school as well behaved and good at my work as I was.

The truth was that she thought she, a good Catholic, shouldn't have to tolerate low life. There were institutes for kids like me, kids she thought of as filth. Miss Fitzsimmons was going to make sure I paid for the disgrace I had inflicted on everyone by bring born and continuing to breath. She must have cursed her bad luck and resented having to put up with me.

Auntie Una and her friend who lived less than a mile away had bicycles with large baskets. They would put their daughters in the baskets and cycle off for the whole day. Never missing a hurling match or a football match. They went everywhere, picnics, parties, visiting friends and had the time of their lives, I know it wasn't down to Auntie Una to care for me, I was left and played around the cottage something I had done since I was a small child.

A boy called John arrived home one day with Auntie Una. I didn't know who he was but she seemed to know him well. John was English and bigger than me but I think he was younger. He came to school with us although he wasn't a Catholic. John absolutely hated everything about country life, having to share a bed, having no privacy when washing and was disgusted by the toilet arrangements. The worst thing of all for him was the three mile walk to school and he demanded a bicycle. When the tots were walking, the kids would really have taken the mickey if he had peddled by on a bike. It was lucky he had brought his own boots, because he was the only kid with something on his feet. He left as quickly as he arrived and he was soon forgotten.

Things weren't so prosperous now Grandma was dead and years later people tried to tell me I was hungry but I don't remember that. I think when I stole food, I did it for nothing more than devilment, nothing else. I adored Granddad but he was getting old and although he did his best he didn't understand a little girl. I was sitting on the front step snivelling one day when he came by and asked me what the matter was.

"I've got a stone bruise on my foot" I cried.

"Wait a minute" Granddad said, "I'll get a pin and burst it and get the water out"

With all the drama I could muster I announced

"There isn't any water there."

"Well bloody well sit there till there is"

No cuddles now, I had to grow up and he was getting past it.

At the school the big open fire was lit as soon as the weather turned cold, It had to keep going all day with wood and turf, otherwise we would freeze in the snow and frost. The whole downstairs must be kept warm. Sods of turf had to be obtained every day and we children, as was the case with many other requests had to bring them. Any child who brought in a sod every day was allowed once each day to go up to the fire for a warm. Like every other kid I got cold and needed to warm myself but I couldn't ask Granddad for turf every day. He had enough to do cutting the turf in the summer to last us through the winter at home, but I wanted to be like the other kids warm and fed.

I was used to looking after myself by now. As I was labelled a thief might as well be one, so between leaving home and arriving at school, I acquired what was needed to survive. I would duck into a neighbours hen house or barn and grab a couple of new laid eggs, crack them open on a piece of slate and swallow them in one gulp. I wasn't above taking the odd turf or two.

All too soon it was time for me to be confirmed. My confession was a pack of lies, I can't remember what I said to the priest but I have a feeling it was something he wanted to hear, nothing too controversial. Granddad tried his best, I had a white dress and veil, which someone in our vast family probably gave him but I was really upset by my black boots.

"It's hard enough having to buy something for your feet at this time of the year" he told me

"But"

"No buts, Leila, I'm not buying you white shoes, these will last you through the winter"

That lovely man, his back was as straight as a rod, walked proudly along Delvins High Street to the church with me in toe. A passing neighbour said

"Good Morning. They're lovely white socks, Leila."

I looked down and saw how dirty my legs were. Its no consolation for me to think that, I wouldn't be the only one. In Ireland even the tinkers would be scrubbed for such an important occasion, the boys would have their hair flattened with lard. I realize now Auntie Una never even came to the Mass. If only she had cared enough to see that I had washed myself. Granddad no longer had the patience.

In the two years since Grandma died my life had changed dramatically. Grandma would have brought the pigs extra babies indoors and hand-reared them. Granddad couldn't be bothered and drowned them in a bucket, I hated seeing that.

Out of the blue I received my very own letter from Uncle Pat, Auntie Una suggested I write back, so I sat up at the big table and told him all my news. When I had finished I signed the letter, "Love from Maureen"

"Why ever did you do that" asked Una.

"I didn't think anyone would want to get a letter from me"

My confidence was lower than a worm, my self-esteem vanished. I seemed to become more miserable by the day, No family apart from Granddad, and even my wonderful Catholic faith was letting me down. Ballinvalley School was slowly squeezing and caning out of me the life I had when my Grandma was alive. The funny thing was that no matter how rough times were, when I sat down with my books I seemed to put it all behind me, because nothing stopped me getting top marks all the time, the work was so easy.

The Priest and Miss Fitzsimmons were very involved in a special event at the church. Our class had been invited to sing with the church choir one school morning and we rehearsed for weeks. The morning arrived and Miss Fitzsimmons made a special point of calling out the names of all the girls in my class. Except mine. I ran up and reminded her she had forgotten me.

"Sit down" she said.

"Please Miss, I know the words"

Perhaps, for some reason she thought I didn't. What else could it be?

"Leila, sit down" she said again,

There was no explanation.

The only girl in the class not to go to Church and sing in the choir that morning. I thought about my mop of curls, whether my hair had been combed; I wondered if my face and hands were clean and wished I had scrubbed harder when I washed that morning. If course it had nothing to do with that. What hurt so terribly was that those two christians (I can't think of a word for them) denied me singing in Gods house for no other reason than I was a bastard. God in his infinite wisdom put me on this earth. He chose to place me there without a Mother or Father and I knew I would never forgive them.

I always knew when the war ended Maureen and Auntie Una would go home to London. It never bothered me. I would be staying here with Granddad. I dearly loved my Granddad, and knew and loved every inch of Moortown. Somehow with Granddad and home, however humble there was enough love and security to keep me going.

I was eleven when peace was declared and had become one tough little nut, years of watching out for myself had taught me a few lessons. At school months would pass without an incident. I had even come to terms with Miss Fitzsimmons, but I would never say it was a good relationship. The truth was, I didn't set out to be naughty or cheeky, I only wished to be good and well thought of. However hard on me Miss Fitzsimmons was my work never faltered and at eleven I was one very clever little girl. Miss Fitzsimmons would be taking a Maths lesson, finishing her talk, she would say,

"Leila, would you step up to the board, start the sum off, take the class through it and show them how they work the answer out"

It never entered her head that I wouldn't understand it. Once I was walking back to my place when one girl said, "One day, Leila, your brains will burst"

One afternoon, I came home from school to Granddads devastating announcement,

"You are going to England to live, Leila. I'll come and stay with you for a month, give you time to settle down"

The grown ups had made the decision without asking me and there seemed no point in questioning it.

My farewell to Ballinvalley School was very subdued. Miss Fitzsimmons wished me nothing, no "Good Luck, safe journey, God Bless" not one word of comfort to keep in my heart to see me through whatever lay ahead.

I held my faithful penguin very close as I stood in the High Street opposite the pub where Granddad did his drinking, waiting for the bus to take Granddad, Una, Maureen and me up to Dublin.

There wasn't a soul in the street to say "Goodbye" to me as I left. I wondered if I would ever be back to this place which held my heart and soul, where I had known peace and happiness in those tender eight years of my life with my beloved Grandma. Totally lost, and I couldn't understand why my Granddad was sending me away.

We spent half a day in Dublin, in and out of large offices, probably Government buildings. Maureen and I would be left sitting on benches in corridors or small rooms. I heard Una say to one very official looking gentleman,

"This child doesn't have anyone here to care for her, and she can't be left with an old man. She has no one to sign forms for her either, in fact she has nobody. If we can get permission to get her to England, there will be someone there to look after her."

I was very tired, and worried, I hugged my penguin tighter.

"Who was this someone, I didn't want to be taken away from my Granddad. I wanted to say to them all, "We'll be alright together. I can look after myself now. I'll soon be big enough to take care of Granddad too."

Eventually, they must have got the necessary papers to take me out of Ireland and we boarded the train for the docks. Granddad sat very close to me, bending down so he was close to my ear he said, almost in a whisper,

"When we get to England, you are to call your Auntie Sheila, Mother"

I protested,

"I don't like Auntie Sheila, isn't there anyone else I can call Mummy"

Granddad made a terrible mistake, he ought to have made it clear that Sheila was my real Mother. I looked at Auntie Una for support, but if she saw the panic in my eyes she ignored it. I wasn't her problem

Chapter 7

Sheila was waiting at the station platform. She hugged her father and sister but hardly acknowledged me. It was time to say "goodbye" to Auntie Una and Maureen, who had been my family for three years – Maureen for longer than that. It was such a wrench to be going to live with strangers, especially as I thought when I met Auntie Sheila I didn't like her.

Granddad, Sheila and I made our way to Upminster, only half a mile from where I was born although I didn't know then. It had been raining cat's and dog's and it was damp and grey as we approached the front gate. The path ran down the side of the house to the dark green front door. The dustbin by the fence almost blocked the path. Something rotten had spilled from it and the path was a carpet of tiny white maggot's, there were thousands of them glowing in the dusk, which disgusted me.

As we approached the door opened suddenly and a familiar voice said, "You're here, at last"

It was John, who had stayed with us at Moortown and I said to myself

"Oh, so that's who you are, your Auntie Sheila's son, spoiled little brat. Well, now I know"

Granddad and I followed him to the lounge at the back. A very large man in a brown and white pin-stripped suit and a white collar and tie got up from a comfortable armchair. I wasn't used to this kind of formal outfit, but that was the way Jack dressed all the time. I stared at his long thin face, small eyes, large roman nose and thin lips and saw that he was much older than Auntie Sheila. He held out his hand to shake mine, saying

"Welcome, you're very welcome, little one"

This was my new "Daddy" and it was as near as possible to love at first sight. Straight away I felt at ease with him, there was some kind of bond. My Dad's name was Jack Jacobs, so my new Mum was Sheila Jacobs. He was Jewish, which I was going to find difficult. I'd thought Sheila a devout Irish Catholic. I was Leila Merriman and would defend my name and my religion to the end. I wondered how

I, with my completely different upbringing, was going to fit into a Jewish household. For now there was hope as Granddad was staying for a month and with luck would take me back with him.

The house they were renting was part of a long row of similar semi-detached houses, with a living room, dining room and kitchen and upstairs three bedrooms and a bathroom. It was amazing to have a bathroom with running water and a joy to switch the lights on and off. It seemed posh to me, but in reality was all very sparse. Sheila didn't own even a plate or a hook to hang her hat on. Having my own room did little to raise my spirits.

Granddad had the time of his life with his family. His son Frank lived close by in Grays, Essex; Uncle Tom in London on Army manoeuvres came to visit and his daughters, Mina, Lily, Una and Sheila spoiled him. There were many days at the races, the dog's in the evening, cards, quite a few whiskeys and as many pints as he could drink. All too soon the month was over and it was time for him to go home. We hugged each other for what seemed like forever. I choked as I tried to say, "Goodbye, Granddad" when I wanted to scream, "Take me with you. Don't leave me"

Years later I was told that he cried for a month when he got back to Moortown. So did I, in England.

Auntie Sheila – now to be called "Mum" – seemed to resent me from day one. To begin with, my hair was infested with fleas. She used to spread a newspaper on the table and I would bend over it while she would roughly comb the fleas out, catching them as they bounced and popping them between her thumb nails. She had lived in Moortown longer than I had and should have understood what living in rural Ireland meant, but instead she would mutter

"You are such a disgusting child"

Amazingly for someone who considered herself a clever woman, it never once occurred to her to have my long hair cut. She seemed to prefer almost tearing my hair out by the roots every morning. It seemed to take forever to get rid of those fleas.

There was still six weeks of the school year left and it was decided I would travel to Brentwood every day where my cousin was at school. The journey into Romford, a big town after Moortown, with a change of bus and on to Brentwood was all very strange to me. School work was different from Ballinvalley, but nothing was causing me concern. Each morning at assembly Reverent Mother would offer prayers for a special intention. It seemed very important and the children prayed with all their hearts. One morning Reverent Mother came in all smiles.

"Our prayers have been answered, thank God. This morning we shall say a thank you prayer to God."

It was later I learned that Odette GC, whose three daughters were at the school had come home.

I had no idea about the education system in England – why should I. If I had stayed with Granddad I would have carried on with Miss Fitzsimmons. There was something called a scholarship which I had missed so arrangements were made for me to take an exam alone. I had to attend this large building on a Saturday morning. I remember being greeted very warmly and being led into a massive room which looked like a head's study. A large oval shaped highly polished table was in the centre. I was asked to sit down and told.

"When you are comfortable and ready to begin, you will be given your papers" I did understand the results would determine my next school. I remember how easy all the questions were and I soon finished. Mum and Dad were told almost immediately that I had passed and until very recently I understood I was at a state school, St. Mary's Convent Grammar School.

I hadn't been back there since the day I left and on the spur of the moment in 2006 I decided to re-visit the past. I was made very welcome by another former pupil and during the morning she said,

"When you think our parents paid nine guineas a term fees and seven and sixpence for our dinner's"

"Say that again?" I said.

I knew my parents wouldn't have paid nine farthings a term. It was another six months before quite my accident, I found out the real story.

Towards the end of the war a prominent catholic Bishop asked, "Why is it that Catholic private schools don't get the high marks that other fee paying schools achieve?"

He realized that wealthy parents didn't necessarily produce clever children and persuaded the Church to agree to fund any poor kid with the brains to achieve top academic results. That meant me – so I was educated at a private school.

Now I faced the long summer holidays. I went to stay with Aunt Lily for a couple of weeks and met my cousin, Sheila, named after Mum for the first time. She was four years older than I was and had such a lovely life as it appeared to me at the time. I was so envious of her. She had pet rabbits and played the piano. Uncle Bill was caretaker of Queen Eyot's island on the Thames, which belonged to Eton College. Staying at their country cottage was almost like being back in Moortown. You had to run over the fields to the river, jump into the boat and row over to the island. Once there it was great fun playing around the club house, skipping and swimming. When we returned from the island one day I found that Aunt Lily had taken down a pair of dark green curtains I'd seen hanging in the dining room and made me a dress It was absolutely appalling, I looked like a tramp. The curtains were so old they had faded in the sun until they looked like green and white stripes. Puffing on one of her perpetual fags and stuttering as she always did she said,

"That'll do for you."

I felt so degraded. Perhaps Lily still had designs on downing me.

When I went back to Upminster – I couldn't think of it as home - I was delighted to hear Michael, Sean and Tommy had followed me over from Ireland. Uncle Tom was still in the Army and had got married quarters for his family in the Army Barracks at Sheerness. I didn't unpack, I went straight over to Auntie Maggie. I was to spend many holidays with them. The boys were to become, as they were at home, my second family. Over the next few years the times I spent with my cousins were the best part of my young life.

Auntie Una agreed to have me for the last two weeks. They lived in an upstairs flat in Brixton and were decorating after the long absence during the war years. Maureen and I were allowed to help and had great fun. Our job was "ragging" all the rage at the time. We had to dip screwed up rags into a bucket of paint and pat them onto the walls on top of the first coat. The family who lived downstairs invited us down for tea. I was only eleven and had never seen a black person but there were two sitting in the room. I hate to think what the expression on my face said to them. I must have imagined them to be savages but would hate to offence anyone – they were very friendly and Maureen and I would sit spell bound by their amazing singing. They would spontaneously break into song we would clap and giggle when their glorious harmonies came to an end. We spent many happy hours with them.

During my six weeks summer holidays I had done the rounds being passed from pillar to post like a sack of spuds, everyone taking a turn a looking after me. It had done nothing to bond me with these two people I now called Mum and Dad. I heard a great deal about the job they both had at the Beehive and I wondered why they had given it all up and taken me on. They obviously had no love or even interest in me, why should they, they were complete strangers. I was even more confused and couldn't understand why I had been taken away from Granddad.

I'd lie in bed remembering the conversation I over heard in Dublin.

"This child doesn't have anyone"

Had " they," and I always referred to them as "they" because I never knew who they were. Had they agreed collectively, for what reason I don't know, decided to have me and Sheila had drawn the short straw. It was four months on and I realized I was different again from the rest. They were "Jacobs" and I was "Merriman," a Catholic in a Jewish house. Still, the important thing was I had for the first time a "Mum and Dad." The school authorities might know they weren't my real patents but that was un important.

It was time to start my new school. My Granddad would have been so proud, I longed for him to be there to share my excitement Mum did as little as she could with the list of requirements, she bought me just two of everything I needed, two blouses, two pairs of knickers, two pairs of socks. I learnt later she had ambitions to go to Grammar School, but Granddad and Grandma couldn't afford it and now I was having the chance she was denied off her back, how she must have resented me. The first morning at assembly I saw that the whole of Ballinvalley School would fit into the hall of my new school. We, first years made our way nervously to our classroom and sat quietly waiting for our teacher. She was very young lady, quite small, neat and pretty and wore a tweed suit and silk stockings. She bobbed up and down a little and I discovered she had one leg a little shorter than the other. We all rose,

"Good Morning," we all chorused.

"It's Miss Glass,"

She was smiling.

"Good morning, Miss Glass,"

It was the start of a very busy day.

For the last lesson of the day, we made our way to he dining room for a lesson on etiquette. We each had a plate with a slice of bread and the jam pot was passed round. We had to take a spoonful of jam and place it on the side of the plate, then use a knife to spread the jam. It wasn't etiquette to plonk the jam straight on the bread. How amazing, to be taught how to eat correctly.

One of the nuns, leant over and smiling sweetly said "We'll make a lady out of you, Leila."

I wondered why she had singled me out, I found out later. For now I was just thrilled to be at the school.

Granddad had sent a card signed "Your fond and loving Granddad. I would treasure that and would write "Home" I still thought of Moortown as home – to tell him how well school was going.

What ever anyone said, Mum, always worked her socks off. She played just as hard, but boy, did she work! She was manageress of a cake shop next to Room Stores in the High Street. This was 1945, wartime austerity and sugar rationing still with us, yet the shop was a glorious sight, with displays of rows and rows of cakes decorated with cream and icing of various colours, plus trays of jellies and trifles, all different shapes and sizes with squiggles of cream.

I would sometimes pop in to see her on my way home from school which was in the next street. Had I hoped for a warm greeting? It was never there. I know Mum believed it was not her place to flatter or praise me. I become quite a tough little nut after eleven years with no Mother – any affection I deserved would come from somewhere else. I wasn't charming and lovable, like John, the little creep. I became more than willing to give her a bit of lip as she called it, which would result in a slap across the face and a torrent of rage.

"I don't know where you get your rotten ways from," was one of her favourite phrases.

The headmistress at Ballinvalley School was the only other person who ever hit me. I hated being hit and I hated the teacher, I think I almost hated Mum.

Dad was addicted to gambling: he hadn't done a days work since they left the Beehive, but tried to earn a living by his wits at the dogs, doing a bit of Tic-tac, having a share in a book if he had the money. He would hang around the dog-track and if anyone had a win he would use his silver tongue to charm a few bob off them.

"Easy as taking candy from a baby," he'd say, "They'll not miss it."

Anything that offered him another bet was fair play. He was without a friend, and neither smoked nor drank, calling such pleasures,

"A waste of good betting money"

Mum seemed to encourage him, probably because she too was a gambler, mostly at cards, The difference between them was she worked to fund her gambling. If Dad did get work for a day, his wages were gone before he did the job.

Every Saturday morning Mum gave me sixpence pocket money and as soon as she had gone to work Dad would ask:

"Can I borrow that?" He would take the sixpence out of my hand, rush out and put a sixpence each way on an accumulator.

Over the years I realized if he did have a winner he wouldn't settle his debts or pay anyone back or treat anyone to anything. He would keep on gambling until every penny was gone. When Dad wasn't at the dogs he would potter about at home doing small jobs. We had no radio so he would buy all the racing papers and read them through from back to front. When I got up in the morning he would be there with the kettle on. For me they were cosy mornings even if he did pinch my pocket money. He was a real friend, we could always talk and I loved him to bits. I didn't know for years he was up and about to make sure he got the post before Mum. Someone would always be after him for money and if Mum found out she would probably kill him. He would come home from the afternoon meeting at the dogs to feed John and me, then he and Mum would meet up at the evening meeting.

John and I were left alone in the evenings, something I wasn't used too. I was terrified of the dark and all the strange noises. John knew how much the night times frightened me and he hit on a plan. He tied a piece of string to my big toe then attached the string to his wrist. I only had to wriggle my toe and he would shout out to comfort me. I couldn't sleep until Mum and Dad were home, usually about midnight. Mum was very involved in a serious card school and sometimes she would be out almost all night, which worried the life out of me and I couldn't sleep till I heard her come home, Dad never seemed to mind.

In the morning I would be tired; I couldn't concentrate during the day and cracks were beginning to appear in my school work. I was also in trouble for my appearance. I only had the two blouses and two pairs of socks and they had to stay clean all week. One morning at assembly a nun beckoned me to one side and asked,

"Did you have your blouse ironed this morning?"

I was mortified. Ironed? my blouse hadn't even been washed, we didn't "do" washing and ironing in our house In fact Mum did nothing indoors, Dad was the one at home and fed John and me.

After about a year the shoes Mum bought for me to start school had worn out and I desperately needed a new pair. Dad arrived home one afternoon from the dog track with the shoes. Where they came from God alone would know. They were as near to bright orange as you could find. Of course next morning I was asked to step aside again after assembly.

"You can't wear those shoes here" I was told.

"But" I protested

"I don't have another pair"

Shoes seem to have been the bane of my life.

Sundays was the day we were all at home. I was distinctly discouraged from going to Mass, which was surprising considering I was at a Convent school. Mass was the last word to be uttered in the house. This was a sin which I would have to confess. My own faith meant much more to me than the Jewish faith. I mean no disrespect to any religion, this was the 1940's when there was less understanding than we have now. I was so against the Jewish faith that one Sunday morning I decided to take my Dad on and argue with him until I was proved right.

"How do you think a Jew is going to get into heaven" I asked.

He was so angry with me he grabbed my prayer book out of my hand and threw it on the fire. It landed on its back and opened out, the pages rising up in the flames, I watched it burn. It was the only thing I had that belonged to my beloved grandmother and vowed never to forgive him. But of course I did.

Sunday afternoon the fish man peddled round the streets on his old bike with a big basket in the front, selling cockles, winkles and whelks. Dad loved winkles and I would sit with a pin picking the winkles out of their shells; horrid wriggly things but he loved them and would pig out.

Like Dad, Mum had no friends, work, gambling and card schools were her life, she was never the type to gossip with the neighbours or have girlie chats. Everyone she mixed with during the week was Jewish, but on Sundays she would catch up with her large family. She was a brilliant cook and when her brothers and sisters came on a Sunday, she would prepare bits and pieces to pass around but she would never offer me anything.

"I'll have one after Leila," said Auntie Una one day.

"She doesn't want one," snapped Mum.

"How do you know, you haven't offered her one?"

There was no answer to that. But I still got nothing.

I would wonder again what was behind me being brought over from Ireland, who had persuaded Sheila to give me a home. Why had she agreed?. She obviously had no interest in me at all. She didn't even know how old I was. One day she asked me my age and I told her I was twelve. With that she shoved a book in my hands and told me to read it. That settled my mind. I had began to wonder exactly who she was. I looked briefly in the mirror and I saw her face in mine, we were as alike as two peas in a pod. But this latest incident settled my mind, she definitely wasn't my mother. If she were she would know when I was born

As for the book, I understood very little of it. All those long medical words. What was it all about and what are periods? When were they supposed to start? When mine eventually did I was too frightened of Mum to tell her. I got some rags and paper to put in my knickers. They had a hole in them, so I grabbed my only other pair and they had a hole too. Luckily, the holes were in different places so the two pairs together did the trick. I had to be very careful how I walked and made my way to the toilet at every opportunity to change the paper. I survived this for a couple more months before Mum handed me a paper bag. She said nothing, but I finally recognized the items I would need – quite a revelation.

Auntie Mina lived the nearest to us, up the road at Harold Hill. Mum liked to go there, you could be sure the cards would be out and a couple of neighbours would pop in to make the numbers up. Auntie Mina had four children. Her daughter and I were born only eight days apart. I definitely never stayed overnight there, I didn't at all enjoy being at that Auntie's. I knew when I got home I'd get a smack. Mum would say,

"I'm fed up hearing from Mina how rude you have been to her."

Then would come the thump. But why would I be rude to Mina

and more important, when had I been rude to her? She seemed nasty and spiteful and although it was laughable, she seemed to be jealous. Why anyone in their right mind should be jealous of me God alone knows. I had nothing. Years later Mina was to cross my path and cause me trouble and heartache. I'd like to think if there is a God she got her comeuppance when she got to the Pearly Gates, though I doubt she even got that far.

It was just over a year and we were on the move. Nobody explained anything, Dad simply announced

"Get your things to-gether, we are leaving"

We left the house with two cases and Dad dragging the rest of our possessions along the pavement in a sack. At the station, as we stood on the platform waiting for a train I asked,

"Why are we going?"

"Hold your tongue"

I never seemed to learn and asked again,

"Where are we going"

This time I got a slap, but I found out soon enough that our new home was to be in Southend. More than sixty years on I still live there. But why did they choose Southend that day? I can only think it was because Dad had a brother, sister and daughter living there. At our new place there was no front garden, the front door opened straight from the pavement, into a kitchen-cum-living room with a toilet to the left and one bedroom to the right. All four of us had to sleep in one room which suited me. I was used to company during the night. A small bed, a large one and then another small one took up almost all the space.

I found out then that John wet the bed. Mum would throw the wet sheet over the wardrobe to dry during the day. There wasn't a back yard to hang anything out so she had no other choice. In the evening the sheet would be turned this way and that. The room smelt permanently of wee and there were other smells. My pillow had no cover and as my nose sank into it for the first time I laid my head on it. Someone must have been sick on it so I threw it on the floor and slept flat.

I missed Moortown more than ever, the lake and being out in the boat, fishing in the Deel and fetching the cows home in the evening. More confused than ever. I wondered again what was this all about?

One good thing every morning for the next two years Mum gave me the train fare to Upminster plus my dinner money. She now worked as housekeeper to a wealthy business couple. The gambling lifestyle hadn't changed. She bet£1 at fifty to one that "Sheila's Cottage" would win the Grand National. When it did she came home with the loot, sat on the bed like a child and spread it all about. I'm pleased she sent Granddad a fiver. He would be thrilled to bits.

It didn't do anyone else any good because we moved the next day. I was home from school when the landlady called for her rent. Dad didn't know I was listening behind the door while he talked to her. He said something like,

"I'm sorry not to have the rent money again. I promise faithfully you will have it next week"

"Don't bother" she said. "You can get out to-day"

So that was why we were moving all the time, each place scruffier than the last. Dad never paid the rent, I couldn't imagine what tale he was telling Mum. Whatever it was surely by now she had worked out that it was a lie. She was supposed to be clever but sometimes I doubted it. If she had used her brain, she'd have paid the rent herself, that way she would have a roof over her head for herself and her precious John. The rows when Mum came home to find we were on the move again were terrifying. One day she chased dad down the road with a carving knife. I think if she had caught him, she might have killed him.

John and I were very lonely children. We knew no one in Southend and at school in Upminster I was the scruffy little kid no one ever asked me to a party. I wouldn't have been able to go anyway because I didn't have a dress, nor would I have been able to afford a present.

It was the end of the school year summer 1948. We got our results and I came top in, of all things, history, not one of my best subjects. I did struggle a little with languages, both Latin and French and I was pathetic at Art, but even though my position had slipped I had nothing to worry about. I was thrilled when one of the bigger girls passed her blazer on to me for the next term and looked forward to going back in September.

We moved again to what was to be our last home together as a foursome. It was a turning point for me because Mum said she wouldn't be paying the fares to Upminster any more and I would have to go to school in Southend. I was deeply unhappy at not being allowed to stay at St. Mary's, which offered the only bit of stability I had. I was never unhappy in class even though my work had declined. There was never any thought of failing or giving up and with the help of the Nuns and teachers there I'd have come through.

I have affectionate memories of the Nuns. They may have been a bit tough at times but they were always fair and I got no more than I deserved.

My relationship with Mum was stormier than ever. With Auntie Una's accusations fresh in her ears, to Mum I was always a liar and a thief. Apparently, I suffered from hallucinations, was to blame for everything that might go wrong and last of all, I was mentally disturbed. Too true, too true, I was disturbed but there was nothing wrong with my mental faculties, I was simply very unhappy. Too unhappy to wonder how John was coping with it all. He had been so spoiled and cosseted he couldn't take Moortown, which was Paradise compared to this place. I suppose it helped him to be with the mum and dad he had always known. For me I didn't know who these two people were, except that Sheila was really my Aunt. Yet people would say,

"Aren't you like your mother!"

And I was, the only difference between us was our colouring. When I laughed I could hear Mum, my actions and mannerisms were like hers. In fact, I was so like Sheila I could almost have been a virgin birth. There was no way she was my mother, Granddad would have told me, Sheila would have revealed something herself. Surely, someone, somewhere would have said something.

The strangest thing of all was that I asked no-one, ever. That is the root of all the trouble that was to come. So why didn't I ask? Was I in total fear of the woman, afraid of the consequences, the rows, the accusations? The wall between the two of us was impregnable? Sheila or Mum, whatever, was always talking about herself, how clever she was.

"If I'd been given a chance I'd be a rich woman "she would say, Or

"I could have scaled the heights"

It never entered her head that perhaps she could give a word of encouragement to a little girl who quite frankly was falling to pieces.

Our new home was over a grocer's shop in Westcliff, with two dingy bedrooms in the attic, one for Mum and Dad and one for me. Narrow stairs covered with scruffy lino led down to the landing, with a large lounge and a double bedroom where the shop keeper and his wife lived. A bathroom and toilet shared by all and along the landing a tiny bedroom for John and a kitchen.

We four lived in this cramped kitchen; there were the basic - a table, four chairs, sink, cooker and a couple of cupboards. Next door was a posh butcher's shop, spotless in the front for the customers but they would have died if they went around the back. The butcher was kosher and while preparing the chickens would chuck their heads and feet out the back door into the yard. Littered with old boxes and all sorts of rubbish, the yard was overrun with rats. I have no idea how the rats were kept from coming into the shops.

September came - time for me to start at my new grammar school St.Bernard's in Westcliff. The head, Madame Mildred, might as easily be called Miss Fitzsimmons. From day one I knew I was beaten. My lovely blazer, that present from St. Mary's, was now no good to me. Foolishly I cut the badge out of the pocket; it looked appalling. I had no tie and grabbed one that had been left hanging in the cloakroom.

My first morning I made my way to the back of the classroom, hoping perhaps no one would notice me. I knew now that I was different. Dirty, for one thing - I could smell myself. I perched on the very edge of my seat as far away as possible from the girl next to me.

Lunchtimes were a nightmare, St. Bernard's was in a very affluent area, with girls talking about their parents' yachts, their posh cars, their holidays abroad. One girl had been to Capri, I mean who goes to Capri - that has to be the best ever thing in the whole world. Then there were the horses, I could ride bareback when I was three but somehow this riding was not the same. They went to ballet lessons had loads of friends and on their way home would rush to the local shop to buy magazines, sweets, etc, I would creep by hoping I was invisible. Now and then I had a halfpenny to buy a stale cake.

It's easy now to criticize, but there was no apparent concern for my welfare or my misery. I walked in to class in the morning, spent the day there then walked out in the afternoon. I can't remember anyone ever speaking to me,

John too was miserable and was the first to break rank. Unable to tolerate that awful existence any longer, he ran away to sea, spending his fifteenth birthday aboard a Merchant Navy ship in port in Egypt. His ship-mates gave him a party to remember all his life. They ordered a crate of rum, a crate of Coke and a crate of ice. His birthday present was a tall, very glamorous, long-legged, long-haired blonde to do as he wished with. After a few drinks the blonde took him to bed. He couldn't believe her beautiful breasts and he was encouraged to dig in and help himself. John was totally inexperienced with women but instinctively his hands wander, down, down, until they clutched a pair of "BALLS." He ran screaming through the mess accompanied by roars of laughter, the men's feet banging on the floor and their hands thumping the table. He collapsed, drunk, on the quayside where he slept the night away

Chapter 8

My fifteenth birthday was slightly different. I had survived one term at school and had started back in the New Year. I would be fifteen in March and, as the date approached, I decided things must change. On the way to school I just stopped walking, stood still on the pavement and I knew for certain I couldn't face another day at school. I would take a leaf out of John's book and get a job. I never went to school again.

Instead, I went to the Job Centre and they offered me work in a factory. It wasn't what I had in mind but it was all they offered me and I was too determined to get a job to say anything. On my fifteenth birthday I walked along the front at Westcliff. The tide was in, the sun was shining. I didn't have a bean in my pocket but I was determined things were going to be OK. I set myself a task. I would achieve one thing in my life, whatever it turned out to be, that I was really proud of.

The school proved they thought I was a waste of space – no-one contracted Mum and Dad to inform them that I was missing and it was three weeks before Mum noticed I had stopped going to school and was working. Her first reaction was,

"What have you done with your wages?"

Not

"Why did you leave school"

There wasn't one other question.

"Don't worry" I said. "There here, all quite safe"

I wouldn't have dared spend them. I can't remember how much Mum wanted for housekeeping from my £2.50 a week pay packet, but it opened up a whole new ball game for Dad. Every Saturday morning without fail he would borrow a pound to go to Hamlet Court Road and get some food. It didn't leave much for me to spend on the normal things a young girl needs. Throughout my teens I never once bought a record or a magazine. I still don't buy those things today, although I can well afford to.

The girls in the factory must have thought me peculiar. I didn't smoke, didn't drink, didn't use make-up, didn't chat the boys up, didn't go out evenings or weekends, never went to the pictures. I was amazingly quiet and wouldn't say boo to a goose.

So what did I do with my time? I joined the local swimming club as swimming was my main interest, mainly long distance. I liked being alone in the water. I was independent, no one was there to criticize me or put me down.

We must have been living in that hole for going on two and a half years. How Mum stood it I'll never know, but then she wasn't there very much. On friday nights she gave the shopkeeper the rent — she had learned her lesson - then she was off out. Their routine hadn't changed in the years since I came over from Ireland. When Mum wasn't working, she was at the dogs or playing in a heavy card school coming home to sleep. There was nothing at home for her, just a kitchen with four chairs, not even an easy chair.

Dad and I had this amazing relationship. I never remember him seeing either his sister or his daughter, but he would be up in the morning with the kettle on for me, albeit to catch the post before Mum did. My job was in the next street, so I came home at lunchtimes for a cup of tea and a sandwich. It would be ready and waiting. I wasn't interested in going for a pub lunch and couldn't afford it anyway. If there was an afternoon meeting at the dog track Dad was there, but without fail he'd come home to cook my dinner. He never once said,

"Get your own food."

Then he would be off to the evening meeting

One day I shouted up to him as I came up the stairs.

"Is that you, Sheila?" he asked.

Bouncing into the kitchen I said, "It's me, Dad."

"Do you know you sound more like your mother every day," he said.

The perfect time to ask the million dollar question and settle my mind once and for all, "Is Sheila really my mother?," but as usual the words remained unspoken.

Sixty years later as I read over what I've written about my relationship with my Dad, it seemed basically that he controlled me by taking all my money. It could be construed as systematic child abuse, certainly it was cruel. Yet he looked out for me. Of course he did, I was his next bet. My pay packet was a guarantee he could feed his addiction and like all abused children I would never say a word to anyone, most of all Mum. Yet I loved him to bits, he was my only family.

Not one member of the Merriman clan visited us while we were moving from place to place, on the road as I call it They may have wondered about our continuing change of address, and would have had a fit if they had dropped in and saw the conditions we lived in. We did however get invited to family parties. Mum was so determined to keep up a front, that on one occasion she got things wrong, rather than miss out we caught a taxi to Sheerness. The £5 fare was a fortune to us. Maybe she had a good win to have been able to afford to do it.

Show and pretence was part of Mum's style. What few clothes she had were the best quality, she shopped mostly at Judith Scotts, an exclusive shop in Hamlet Court Road. Still very young, she went out of our pigsty of a home looking like a woman of substance.

One of her sisters was planning a family trip home to Ireland in a year's time. She invited Mum to join her and I was amazed to hear her say

"Sure, I'll bring Leila"

I'd be seventeen. As I was working I was naturally expected to pay my own fares, that caused me a problem. I saw very little of my pay packet and didn't have the strength to refuse Dad on Saturday mornings. I took a second job in the evenings and kept it from him, hiding my money where it was safe from his thieving hands. I could save all the evening wages towards my holiday. I was fast asleep one night when I was disturbed by two men with Mum in my tiny bedroom. They were searching through my things.

"It's OK," said Mum, "Go back to sleep."

Later I heard her crying and rowing furiously with Dad, calling him all the names under the sun and blamed him for the position she was in. She screamed at him,

"I'll probably go to prison."

It was getting close to the time for our trip to Ireland.

All I want to do is to go home to see my father. You're so useless I have had to do a burglary to get there"

There wasn't much he could say, he knew she was right where money was concerned. It was her day off. She knew the couple she worked for had gone out for the day, so, in the middle of the afternoon, in broad daylight she walked up their path, let herself in and removed enough money to pay for her holiday. Now is that desperation?

Unfortunately, for Mum a neighbour was peeping out from behind net curtains as they do. The culprit was discovered straight away, but they didn't press charges. They thought the world of her and would have given her the money if she had only asked. They told her not to come back to work. What neither they nor I knew was that she had made other plans and wouldn't have gone back to work for them anyway after her holiday.

I had a great time, I was out shopping till I dropped. I bought myself a pale lavender dress in seersucker, which was all the rage. It had a very full skirt with a belt round my waist; then there were matching white shoes, bag and gloves, and a half moon hat that clung to my head, with white feathers. Clothes were still on ration after the war but I could afford to buy some coupons on the black market. A mackintosh was a vital piece of clothing in Ireland and I bought a gold one. (it was plastic, not solid gold) plus some bits and pieces. I wanted to hold my head high when I got home.

The moment arrived when I stepped off the bus in Delvin. It had been six years, the lousiest six years of my life. I had been away too long, and I was fabulous to see my Granddad again. I had missed him so much. I wonder now why I didn't stay home, instead of going back to Southend. At seventeen, almost an adult, able to make my own choices, except that then you still had to be twenty-one

My first stop after Moortown was Ballinvalley School. Scrubbed up well in my new dress and accessories, I was unrecognizable. I wasn't aware that I had grown into quite a pretty girl. I bounced in thrilled to be there, back again in the place where I grew up.

"Good morning"

I simply gushed, for the want of a better word, at that wonderful Miss Fitzsimmons, who looked at me without a flicker of recognition on her face.

"Can I help you?" she asked.

I was thinking

"It's only been six years, I can't have changed that much."

"Can I help you?" she repeated

I can still hear myself saying to her,

"I'm Leila. It's me, Leila"

Her face didn't alter, still the same acid expression, the greeting was cold and I left after about five minutes. Had she given me the time of day I would have admitted I had screwed up and she was right all along, I really was a waste of space. To her it was simply a case of the return of the village bastard. The sooner she got rid of me the better, my kind were not welcome in her school. It wasn't going to spoil my visit home.

I think Mum loved Moortown even more than I did. After all, she had spent more time there and had completed her education at Ballinvalley School. Like me she knew everyone, but now she was a woman of the world, so to speak. There were many gin and tonics at the pub, rounds of drinks for the old crowd. She flitted in and around like a butterfly. Granddad, Mum and I took the boat out on Dysart Lake. Mum caught a large pike and posed on the edge of the lake laughing like a child she held the fish out shouting.

"Look how clever I am."

The women all had to sleep in the one big bed, aunts and nieces, three up and three down so there was a feeling of closeness; I liked that closeness with my mum but of course, I was just kidding myself. Mum had plenty of time to have a word with me if there was anything on her mind. I'd have understood, whatever she had to say. If Sheila was my mother surely there was something there however slight. Did she not feel she owed me something, that she shouldn't treat me like a mat to wipe her feet on and walk all over. Whoever had given birth to me must owe me some tiny spot of affection. I went to sleep; there was no point in puzzling over the unsolvable. One of the Barry's prize greyhounds had just had a litter of pups. Remembering how much I loved animals as a child, Mrs. Barry invited me down to see the litter. I spent a very happy time there. As I left, instead of going home I turned right and walked the short way to the River Deel, smiling as I saw the bridge with the three steps Granddad had chiselled out for me. The bridge seemed so small now, I could rest my elbows on it and look over. The water looked inviting with the sun shining on it as it glistened and flowed along on its merry way. I decided to take a walk along the bank. Memories of Grandma and my cousins ripe in my mind as I recalled the happy times I had playing along the bank and fishing. I had walked quite a way and looking back to the road there was no sign of life, not a movement of any kind, no bicycle or horse and cart were passing. It was hot and the water looked so tempting. Sitting down on the bank, I slipped off my shoes, popped my dress over my head and slipped off my bra and knickers. Time to do a bit of skinny dipping, it was glorious. Dragging myself out onto the bank, I stretched out on the soft grass to dry my front and then turned over to let the sun dry my back.

There was only one small cloud in the blue sky on this holiday, going to confessions and Holy Communion. We had been home for two weeks and I could no longer get out of going. Granddad would think we had completely lost our way and would be so ashamed. I didn't discuss it with Mum. She didn't need any help from me, was quite capable of putting on her own act. As we walked along the three miles to church chatting I fell back and walked alone.

I was back in time with my dearly beloved Grandma. I saw her with all those children, on her hands and knees scrubbing. Giving more than she could afford to the Priest every week was top of her agenda. I had come to think of priests as part of a set-up, employed by the Catholic Church, that fabulously rich organization, to rule people like my grandparents' with fear, threatening hell and eternal damnation. The priests took the last pennies out of the hands of the poor without a second thought, making the Church they worked for even richer.

I was none too happy at the thought of going on my knees and confessing my indiscretions to a man hiding behind a curtain under the umbrella of the Catholic Church. So many priests had proved to be adulterers, fornicators and paedophiles. Not all priests by any means, but enough of them to gave Priests in general a bad name. What was the Catholic Church's attitude to these abusive men? What did the church do about them? It certainly knew what was happening. Ordinary people in the street knew, so how could the Church possibly avoid knowing? Were these men held up to ridicule and shame, treated as they treated a young girl whose only sin was to have a baby without being married. Worse still, the innocent newborn baby who had no say in being born was also seen as the scum of the earth. Everyone made sure the child knew it had brought shame on the family.

What happened to the priests was that they were cosseted, sheltered and protected and if they were paedophiles, they were recycled and put to work in another children's home where no-one knew about them. Silence was their main weapon, none would dare speak out against a man of God at risk of having your tongue cut out, in the next world if there is one.

I went through the charade of confessions, by now I realized about ninety per cent of confessions were like mine an act. My only consolation was it made an old man very happy. I still believed in God totally but didn't have any faith in his representatives on this Earth.

All too soon the holiday was over and it was time to bid a tearful goodbye to my wonderful Granddad. We held each other close, I didn't know it was to be the last time I was going to see him. He was an old man now and the years caught up with him. When he died I was unable to consider coming home for his funeral. Every penny I earned was running on a dog somewhere.

Dad had the kettle on when Mum and I arrived home. The kitchen looked scruffier than ever.

"Good time" he asked.

I was full of it, wanting to tell him everything, but Mum suggested I should get to bed as it was back to work next day. I. had washed out a couple of tops for work before I'd left. I owned two, one I wore for four days of the week and the other for three days and the next week I would do it the other way round, although now I had a couple extra. To dry my clothes, I would put some newspaper on the top of the cooker, fold my clothes and lay them on the paper. They would dry by the warmth of the cooking. God alone knows what they smelt like with the frying. My clothes were still there on the cooker, just as I had left them ready to start work in the morning, nothing had changed.

I had no bad feeling about work so next morning I was up bright and early. Mum wasn't around so I asked Dad:

"Where's Mum?"

"She's gone," he replied

"Gone where?" I asked.

Mum had return to Solly and May at Gants Hill. I demanded to know more.

"When did she make the arrangements?"

"Before we went off to Ireland."

So when she did that burglary she knew she wasn't going back to work for them, so she didn't care. She had left without a word, she didn't even say

"Goodbye, Leila be seeing you"

Nothing, she just went. She knew all through our holiday she was going to do this, abandon me. If she had told me when I was home, I might have stayed there. I was just seventeen and seventeen-year-olds then were just children. I sat there in total shock and disbelief staring into my tea. Dad's words interrupted my thoughts.

"When you find somewhere to live I'm going to join your mother," he said.

I think he hurt me more than Mum had done. All those times he had the kettle boiling for tea, all those comfy chats. Knowing I was going to be alone and would need money for rent and food, he had taken my last penny before we went to Ireland. He didn't have the guts to tell me about their arrangements. Neither of them cared. The bottom seemed to have fallen out of my world.

Still dazed by the news I was wondering whether to skip work and look for somewhere to live when I spotted the window cleaner giving the shop window a desultory wipe. He was a revolting little creep, less than five feet tall with beady little eyes under the thickest of glasses perched on his thin hooked nose, hair a frizz ball, a local character everyone knew. When I was nosing through my mother's things one day I found a photo of him signed. To my darling Sheila - All my love, Ben. My Mother must have been desperate to fancy him. I tore the photo into tiny pieces thinking if Mum missed it, she would think Dad had found it and she'd never dare ask him.

Ben liked an excuse to stop work and chat and began immediately when he saw me come through the door. Searching for something to say, I said

"Mum's gone, Ben, and Dad's going to join her later, I've got nowhere to live"

"That's solved, you can stay with my wife," he said.

When I told dad all he said was

"That's a relief. I can get going"

It didn't take me long to pack and when I got round to Ben's, Lil, his wife said "You will have to sleep with my daughter."

God knows what the teenage daughter thought, but I was a paying guest and money was tight in that family so probably she had no say. At the weekend Lil gave me the bill for bed and board. Fair enough, I expected to pay, but bed and board in a good hotel would have cost less than the bill Lil handed me at the weekend. It was more than I earned in a week. I smiled as I paid up and left myself with nothing. I knew I had to move on quickly and luckily saw a notice in a newsagent's window, "room to let" and moved straight away into a house in the next road.

Home for me was now the upstairs back room in a large house

where twelve other families lived. My landlady, a red-haired larger than life character, well known to the local constabulary, lived downstairs. She would sit in a big padded chair holding court in her back room, weighed down in gold rings, bracelets, chains, a cigarette in a long holder in her hand. It was alleged she had a string of convictions as long as her arm for prostitution and keeping a disorderly house. There were always people coming and going, but I lived there for three years and she was always fair and straight with me.

My little room had a window overlooking the garden, with a table and a couple of old rickety chairs in front of it. A bed stood against one wall, with a sink, a two hop gas stove and a cupboard opposite. A shelf above the fireplace completed the furnishings. When I could afford it, I bought myself a single wardrobe and a rug on the tally.

One of the women tenants was very nice to me. She wore her hair rolled around her head with bits hanging down all around, so she always looked scruffy. She had four equally scruffy children. One day she said

"If you're short of money the landlady could set things up for you"

"How's that"

"What do you think"

I raised my eyebrows, shrugged my shoulders and walked away. It didn't worry me if all the guests were on drugs and into prostitution as long as I was left alone.

I was completely on my own in the world now, with no one to criticize me, no more moving on. I knew where I was from day to day. Life was actually quite good. My job wasn't mind-blowing but I was safe there and my swimming was going very well.

I had a couple of long swims under my belt and the English Channel was my next big swim. I had a coach and a boat man who accompanied me at times. Weekends, if the tide was right, I could get a good training session in. I would just set off from the beach. It never entered my head that I would be in any danger - get cramp, get stung by a jellyfish or worse still get carried out to sea. Silly girl, I knew no fear and I was to learn one of life's hardest lessons. On one of my long swims I was so far out that a fishing boat on its way home after a night at sea stopped and picked me up. The two young men on board were concerned and read the riot act. The wrapped me in a blanket, cooked breakfast and brought me home. As we nearly reached the shore they joked:

"Let's throw her back in,"

I hit the cold water.

"We will look out for you next week," they called as I started out for the shore.

Good as their word, there they were the next week and I was quickly yanked on board. Breakfast was just as good but this time there was an extra ingredient, SEX. That was my virginity gone but at least I knew what sex was all about!

Almost as if life was planned, that was my last long swim. The rage at the time was Esther Williams - Water Ballet - and it had come to Southend. The Water Ballet team was formed and suddenly swimming became fun instead of a cold hard slog. Long distance swimming had left me alone with my thoughts, isolated from conversation. There was no one out there to argue with me, undermine me or hurt me. I was alone and that was how I had liked it. But now I was part of a team mixing with a great bunch of girls, and life felt so much better.

Every Wednesday afternoon throughout the summer we put on a show at the open air pool on Westcliff seafront. The costumes were very glamorous and the routines were fabulous. I never thought I'd have the confidence to put on a grass skirt and wriggle around a pool in front of hundreds of people. Invitations came from all over the place. There was a "Miss Lovelies" during the show and when the entries were low some of us in the ballet team made up the numbers.

One afternoon the American Navy was stationed off the Pier. Sailors from the Warship were guests of the Corporation for the afternoon. They were short of entries for the "Miss Lovelies" and it was my turn with a couple of other girls to step forward and make up the numbers. I wore a one-piece red bathing costume and this particular afternoon my hair fell naturally in dark curly ringlets. Of course I came nowhere but later on a sailor asked if he could speak to me.

"I think you're beautiful, you should have won, can I take you out?"

We met on the Friday evening at Westcliff Station. We went up to London and dined at a superb restaurant, where I tried not to panic when I saw the puzzling assortment of cutlery and glasses. Then he took me to the famous Windmill Theatre. Well, it might be famous but I had never heard of it and I was shocked. Of course, it was all very new and exciting to me. As I left the station later that evening to walk the short journey home a taxi driver called out,

"I didn't think I'd see you home tonight."

"Goodnight," I called back. I was too happy to tell him off for his cheek.

Every Sunday I took the Green line bus to Gants Hill to have tea with Mum and Dad, who were still living with Solly and May. They never had children, had worked their socks off for years and had now retired to enjoy their vast wealth. Solly had a stroke and was a complete invalid. May never stopped telling him she hadn't worked all her life for this.

It was a measure of Mum's desperation that she was living with this old woman. May was so mean that when she boiled an egg she knew how long to let the water boil before turning the gas off and letting the egg stay in the water until it was done. One cup of water was measured when she boiled the kettle for a single cup of tea, but they had made money from this thrift.

The house in Beehive Lane was small – with three bedrooms and a bathroom upstairs, a lounge, dining room and kitchen downstairs. It was exquisitely furnished, with flock wallpaper everywhere and carpets your feet sank into. I didn't know anything about antiques but I knew the ornaments, pictures and glass were pretty valuable.

There was never an invitation to dinner on Sunday, just tea. It would be the smallest of meals - a sandwich and a slither of cake served on priceless china. One Sunday when I was just about to pop my piece of cake into my mouth, May asked "How did your parents die?"

I looked at her in amazement. The idea had never entered my mind: as I never had any parents, why would I ever wonder about them?

Mum scalded May

"Why ask the child such a silly question?"

Child? I was seventeen.

Dad stayed silent and neither of them offered an explanation when they were seeing me out, and I never ever ask for one. It further confirmed to me that Sheila wasn't my Mother and I could bet my life Jack certainly wasn't my father It did show the state of my mind, admitting that I had never wondered about my parents. I was too confused to take that on board.

Chapter 9

From the time Mum and Dad returned to Gants Hill, Jack's daughter, Betty (her name was the same as mine, Elizabeth, but she was called Betty for short) fed me once a week. It was tragic for her that her mother died when she was four but she seemed to have led a charmed life. Sent to a very affluent aunt in Southend, she was sheltered, protected and completely spoiled. Throughout the war, unlike my experience, her schooling was uninterrupted.

After one or two romances she became involved with Bernie, a married man with children and was determined to marry him. Betty told me that the day of his divorce hearing his now ex-wife had turned up in court looking ill and scruffy just to get the judges sympathy and hopefully get more maintenance.

"Made me sick" she said

It may have made Betty sick but it made me angry. Perhaps the woman was ill having been abandoned with young children. Betty like John, was so spoiled she didn't realize what a tough world it was for some people.

It was a very quiet wedding with two other people besides me. We went back to their flat for tea and Betty asked me if I could persuade Bernie to take us to the Kursaal. They had met there and she wanted to make a sentimental journey back.

"You ask him" was my reply.

"He won't do it for me,"

I didn't ask why not, but she was so persuasive I finally found myself whispering into Bernie's ear.

"Please, please can we go to the Kursaal?"

I had never been in the place in my life, dancing at the Kursaal wasn't my cup of tea but fate was playing a part again. Bernie said

"For you, yes"

The Kursaal, the centre of pleasure and entertainment in Southend, was the biggest thing for miles around, bright and noisy with a live band. You couldn't help noticing the fleet was in.

A large ship was anchored off the Pier and dozens of young men in uniform hung around. Towards the end of the evening someone in civvies came up to me.

"Would you like to dance" he asked

I was no dancer and luckily for me the dance floor was so crowded you couldn't put one foot in front of the other. Making conversation, he said

"I'm in the navy but not in uniform tonight,"

I don't know if he felt he needed to impress me but he certainly didn't. My reply was slightly tart.

"If you think all I'm interested in is a uniform, you are very much mistaken."

They were the first words spoken between me and my future husband, a local lad, home on leave. In the early 1950s, no-one had cars, so the Kursaal put on a free bus to get all the young people home. As we ran for our bus he introduced himself.

"My name's Alan. Will you be at the dance next week?"

The short time we had spent together certainly hadn't been earth-shattering. I didn't answer but I might perhaps give it a try. Alone to my small room that night, I made myself a cup of tea and sat at my little table feeling a tinge of pleasure. At least the day had been different I had seen Betty and Bernie wed and I almost had a date. That was unheard of. I wasn't into dating. I may have been nineteen but I still felt very young. I thought about Alan and wondered.

By the time Saturday evening arrived I had decided, much to their surprise, to join my workmates at the Kursaal and there stood the man himself. We seemed to get on really well from the word go. Fairly tall, lean, according to his official statistics Alan had auburn hair and green eyes. He also had a superb set of teeth - a horse would be proud of a set like that. They matched his attractive smile and I thought he was gorgeous, so easy going.

After we'd been going out for about three weeks I invited him home for a coffee. If he was surprised to find home was a little room in a multi-occupied house he didn't say, he wasn't at all inquisitive. I chatted away about my mother and father, Sheila and Jack at Gants Hill and told him I visited them every Sunday and asked if perhaps he would come up with me next week.

A week later I was pottering about in my room planning what to wear for my evening out with Alan, when at around 11 o'clock, I heard a gentle knock on the door. When I opened it I couldn't believe my eyes. There stood Mum. We looked at each other for a few seconds without saying a word, then finally Mum said

"I've come home."

After the way she had walked out on me without saying a word. Sometimes it seemed I was the parent and she was the child. I put the kettle on. We couldn't go back to the life as it was before she ran away but for now I was glad to share the little I had. It wasn't the first time I had gone without for her.

I can't remember a thing we talked about all afternoon and around teatime she stood up.

"I'm going to Romford with Dad, I'll be back after the races"

So it wasn't Jack she had quarreled with but she never again visited my little room.

Events had taken a shocking turn. When Dad had left for the afternoon race meeting Solly and May had seemed quite comfortable. He returned to Beehive Lane for tea and as he put his key in the door he could smell gas. He rushed into the kitchen and found his brother with his head in the oven. May had laid him on the floor then she had gone down beside him with her head next to his.

They were both dead.

Dad'a first thoughts, after the ambulance and the police, were for Mum. He phoned my landlady, asked if he could speak to me and passed on the absolutely appalling new. His news was dreadful,

"Mum has gone to Romford to meet you," I told him.

Mum arrived at the dog track she heard her name being called on the loudspeaker. At the information kiosk she found the police waiting to take her home.

When Alan arrived that evening I was very subdued. I told him what had happened.

"Was she mad?" he asked. An add question? Perhaps, but May was no relation of mine so it wasn't as if madness ran in my family. Ironic, though, that mental instability was already raising it's ugly head. My mood soon changed. It was almost Christmas and Alan had bought me a present. Something in my life that was very rare so I was absolutely thrilled. There would be no decorations in my little room, no stocking pinned to the chimney for Father Christmas to fill. Christmas was a time I specially missed Moortown. I was used to big family parties there. Now I had a prettily wrapped present and I couldn't wait, so I opened it there and then. It was a box of hand-made lace hankies I would treasure them.

Next day was Sunday, I travelled as always to Gants Hill. I
don't know why I changed the route, but I went by the steam train
instead of the bus. Not that it made any difference.

I was startled to see a police car outside the front door with two
policemen on guard, one policeman stretching his legs, strolling up
and down the pavement. The second was leaning against the fence
observing us all.. Mum and Dad had little to say, nothing had changed
except Solly and May weren't there. I stared at the closed door of the
oven as I walked more slowly than usual into the kitchen to put the
kettle on. It was hard to believe that only a few hours ago two people
had died at that spot. I shivered and didn't stay in the room. My visit
was shorted than usual. Dad was half asleep in the armchair, not
wanting to wake him I gently kissed his forehead. Mum was fidgeting
and seemed anxious to see me to the door. As we reached it she
suddenly slipped an envelope into the top of my coat, saying

"Take this to Lew,"

I knew who she meant.

The two policemen watched me as I walked down the path.
Sweetly sick to the stomach I smiled at them and walked slowly across
the road. What if the envelope slides over my boobs and landed with
a thunderous noise? Once out of sight I retrieved the envelope and put
it in my bag. The train compartment was empty. Curiosity got the
better of me and I had to open the envelope. I held in my hands three
of the most beautiful rings I had ever seen, one a solitaire diamond
big enough to choke a donkey. I wondered why I had been given the
rings in such an underhand and risky way. Obviously they were a little
bit of well earned security for Mum and Dad was to be told nothing
about them.

Mum and Dad settled down in Beehive Lane to await their fate
They assumed possession was nine-tenths of the law. There was a
Will, but it wasn't signed. May had promised Mum a fortune to look
after Solly. But she had broken the contract that morning. She could
have lied about it, said I was ill or made up any story to cover her
absence that afternoon.

Mum said

"I'd like to have you live with us Leila but I'm afraid you'd have
rows with the neighbours"

"What do you mean, rows? I've lived with some pretty rough

types over the past few years. There've never been rows"

What was Mum talking about? I had been prepared to share my home without question, but she seemed never to want to make me part of her life. I had been in the factory over five years and was now a member of the Water Ballet team, a crowd of lovely ladies. I got on with nearly everyone.

"Don't worry yourself" I said, "It suits me being alone"

Subsequently I heard stories going around about Solly and May's deaths. They were all bare-faced lies I was shocked, but whatever my mother said or did I was always quick to defend her. Jack's daughter, Betty, put the story about that my Mum had helped May with the events of the afternoon and then stole May's best ring off her finger. It was in fact Betty's Father who had last seen them and who found them later. Mum was in Southend with me. A particular ring had certainly disappeared, but in my book Mum had earned something for spending two years of her life with that nut case of a woman.

I tackled Betty about the lies. Bursting into tears, she said "Don't accuse me, I didn't say a word."
I wasn't going to let it drop
"Then who did"
She went on sobbing, saying I was upsetting her
"I'm not used to life's little nasties. I can't cope with all this"
As if I was always mopping up suicides. A married woman of about twenty-four I thought it was time she grew up. I didn't know until years later that Betty saw Mum as a young interloper who had married her father. If I had known about Betty's hatred, I would have had nothing to do with her. It would have saved me a traumatic experience later on.

Things moved along very quickly with Alan. He took me home to meet his parents and I prized out of them all the information I could. Perhaps women are naturally more inquisitive than men, or perhaps I needed to know about his parents. His mum died when he was young so I met his stepmother.

Originally he'd wanted to go to sea for a couple of years to get away from home, but there was a waiting list unless he signed on the dotted line for twenty two years, then they would take him straight away. He was then about two years into the twenty two.

The day finally arrived when we were going to meet my

parents. We chatted away intently as the bus wound its way through the country roads to Gants Hill. If I was nervous it was because I hoped they would liked him. I was hiding nothing, in my eyes there was nothing to hide. It didn't seem to matter that I was about to introduce these two people to Alan as my Mum and Dad when in fact they weren't. They were the two people who were my only family in England.

As an intelligent man away at sea seeing something of the world, not a mollycoddled mummy's boy, Alan was nobody's fool - or so one would assume. Imagine the scene as we went into the house and I introduced him to my parents. Mum wasn't much older than me. There were times when I looked older than she and people would ask

"Is Leila your daughter?"

She would reply,

"Actually she's my mother."

Mum was a Christian, a very Irish Catholic married to a much older man. You couldn't miss the fact he was Jewish, even a blind man could see that his nose covered his face. The afternoon went extremely well. With hindsight I do wonder what was in Alan's mind. Maybe he had no idea that at that time Catholic's and Jew had little in common. He must have been brain dead to be so uninterested. He certainly wasn't inquisitive like me.

Once back on board ship he wrote to my parents thanking them for the meal and also to me. One envelope was addressed to Mr. and Mrs. J. Jacobs, the other to Miss Leila Merriman. Still no questions.

Alan embraced the large Merriman clan. He went to Maidenhead to meet Auntie Lily, Uncle Bill and cousin Sheila, rowing over to the island to pick apples and he spent lots of time with Auntie Una, Uncle Pat and cousin Maureen. There were few members of that large family he didn't know, no huge conspiracy of silence. I had been around the family for a long time and was accepted for myself with all my human faults. They had long stopped talking about me.

Alan seemed to see nothing strange in the different surnames and never once asked a question. Had he asked about it and I had lied to him, it would have been different. He could have asked just out of curiosity

"Were you adopted? Did your real father die?"

Divorce wasn't an option, women didn't get divorced as there was no support for them and nowhere for them to go, but he could have asked

"Has your mother married twice? Or

"How comes a young Catholic girl married a Jewish man so much older than her"

There were so many questions he could have asked but he didn't and I accepted that. I, just me was the most important thing to him. I had suddenly blossomed, found such confidence through this man I was so in love with. The uncertainties of the past disappeared. I thought how lucky I was to have landed a chap like Alan. He never asked a question. The important thing to him was me.

My swimming was beginning to suffer. On the weekends when Alan was home I skipped training and soon got dropped to the reserve team which hurt, so I retired from the sport that had kept me sane in earlier years. It was a small price to pay for the happiness I had found, any sacrifice was worth it. Two years passed, with regular trips to Beehive Lane. On one of these, out of the blue Alan asked me to marry him. Sitting on a bench at the top of Pier Hill he slipped a diamond ring on my finger. We sat there for ages looking out to sea, at peace, totally in love and committed to each other for life. As soon as Mum heard of the engagement she demanded I come and live with her and Dad, so she could plan the wedding and organize everything.

The move to Beehive Lane wasn't a problem for me, although my boss was upset when I told him I was leaving. Having been with him since I was fifteen I was now the charge hand in the factory. I'd progressed well and was designing pieces of jewellery which was being sold all over the country. Quite an achievement considering art and design was my weak subject at school.

Now at twenty-one, my brand new engagement ring on my finger it was time to start a new life and new job. Mum was unusually excited about it. It was a large firm; I worked in the showroom demonstrating the range to buyers from major stores. It didn't keep me busy all the time and I became dogsbody – that's a good word – to the youngest of the bosses three son. Only a little older than myself, he took an instant shine to me which I found embarrassing. All the other girls must have noticed, and the last thing I wanted was to be the boss's pet. He invited me to accompany him in the directors box to the Arsenal Football match the coming Saturday. No way.

I wasn't ever going to let my husband-to-be down, I was so in love and with him away at sea I was going to be one million per cent loyal. My boss was a millionaire - don't people do some foolish things when they are young. I could be at home now polishing my diamonds!

It was a very glamorous job and I loved it. There were delightful lunches out and at Christmas the party was at a swank Soho restaurant. For that first Christmas party I bought myself a black sleeveless dress with a wide red cummerbund. As I was getting ready, Mum came into my room with a brown paper parcel. It was rare for her to do anything like it. On opening the parcel I found a white fun fur jacket. It was beautiful. With that over my dress I looked like the cat's whiskers; someone would want to sweep me off my feet. I had a funny feeling Mum would be delighted to see me split with Alan, she was certainly pulling out all the stops.

I told myself she was just concerned at the length of time he was away at sea and that I had chosen a lonely life for myself, nothing more sinister than that. I certainly wouldn't let her come between us because I was too determined to marry Alan. I wonder sometimes if she sensed something in him that I was too besotted to think about?

I absolutely loved my job and the people who worked with me. More importantly I had a fiancé and the house in Beehive Lane was sheer luxury. What more could a girl want? I seemed to have it all. Life seemed a long way from Moortown, from the poverty and that little girl of eight who lost her grandmother and later lost her way along the road. The months passed happily. There was only one fly in the ointment - Dad started meeting me off the tube and borrowing the fares to the dogs plus enough for a bet. Mum was back to her card-playing ways and her own gambling. They didn't work, there may not have been rent to pay but gas, electricity, phone and other bills arrived. Where did the money come from for food and clothes. Still young and beautiful, Mum often stayed out all night. I always wondered what she was doing, but Dad never said anything, and never seemed to mind. As long as he had his daily bet nothing else mattered.

I was now earning very high wages, so I didn't mind giving Dad the few quid every day. I was saving very hard for the wedding, keeping my money at home as I didn't have a bank account. It didn't enter my head to hide it from Dad. My only concern was to keep it safe from burglars. In my bedroom was a large old fashioned chest of drawers. My woollies were in the third drawer down. It wasn't very original but it seemed safe to hide my money between the folds of my jumpers. The day came for me to achieve the ambition of a lifetime and go to buy my trousseau. As it was giving Dad his daily cash meant I'd gone without little extras young girls need. I opened the drawer, plunged my hand in amongst the woollies. Nothing. Just a note which read

'Sorry, I had to have it.'

" What the hell am I going to do?"

I spoke aloud – but there was no-one to hear. It had taken me nearly a year and it was all gone. The theft was never ever mentioned by either of us.

We were still in the 50s when it was rare for an Irish Catholic woman to be married to a Jewish man. It was never mentioned between Alan and myself. Nor did he question our different surnames, or make any remark that would lead me into saying something about my parents. I could imagine replying to the slightest comment

"Well, I don't know if Sheila is my mother. Jack certainly isn't my father. How could he be?"

Then one day he said

"I'm going to become a Catholic"

"Whatever for?" I asked.

He had spent a lot of time with my cousins and his answer was.

"Our wedding day is going to be perfect. You have a right to a nuptial Mass and I'll not deny you. A mixed marriage would mean loosing your nuptial blessing. We are going to have the full rights of the Catholic Church."

I wasn't particularly impressed; a mixed marriage, Catholic and Church of England didn't worry me at all. I had long since been disenchanted with the Catholic Church although I definitely believed in God.

The day came when Alan became a Catholic. Did he now believed we were all God's children created in his image? I mean this is a man who had deliberately become a Catholic for practical reasons.

It was time now for meetings with the Priest to discuss the wedding.

"What are your plans?" he asked.

We both said

"We want to have a home first, then a car and later a family."

The Priest almost exploded.

"You're not thinking of using those filthy contraceptives."

He could have said delicately something like –

"You know the Catholic Church forbids birth control."

But instead he sent us home with a flea in our ear. Mum phoned to complain to him and he told her,

"It had to be said."

Fair enough but it was the way it was said. The strange thing about all this was that Alan, a man of the world about to embrace a faith willingly, was already practicing birth control, something forbidden by that the faith. He was quite happy to be two faced about it, accept Catholicism and carry on with his birth control. On our next visit to the Priest we assured him, straight-faced, that we would not use anything. Hypocritical, two-faced that's the Catholic faith, making liars out of people. At the end of the day believing in God is the only important thing, leading decent live and trying to be a good person.

As for me I had broken all the rules since I was seven by lying to the Priest. I booked my place by the fire years ago, but I was born a Catholic and didn't choose the faith. I believed in God and would take my vows seriously in his house

Alan had just started a two-year posting ashore at Portsmouth. We had a couple of rooms in a large house occupied mostly by service families.

The wedding plans were well under way. There wasn't going to be time for a honeymoon. Someone from my firm drove down all my possessions. I'd had a great time working there and partly because they were sorry to lose me they couldn't do enough to help. They acted as though they were losing a member of their family.

Working in London I had all the big shops to browse through. My wedding dress was very fancy - satin, lace, frills and bows. I had always wanted a tiara, so a tiara it was. Because of Jack's duplicity I had to watch the pennies. The silly bits of underwear I had planned to buy were left on the shelf. If I had wanted to take my workmates out for a meal that was no longer possible.

It was going to be an Easter Monday wedding. Mum had pulled out all the stops and most importantly taken care of everything. If she hadn't been so protective and had left my birth certificate lying around for people to see things might have turned out differently. She had baked a three-tier cake and prepared a wonderful spread. The family started arriving on the Good Friday. Uncle Tom was there to give me away. He had always been there for me. As a little girl I remembered when I met him on the road, there was always a half 'penny for sweets at Tierney. Dad wasn't coming to the wedding. He couldn't miss the afternoon's dog racing for anything especially something as unimportant as my wedding. That wasn't a problem. Michael, Tom's oldest boy, was best man. Beautiful Maureen was to be bridesmaid. She would look lovely in her dress and all the boys would swoon over her afterwards. I loved my cousin to bits but I was always envious of her. Una and Pat arrived. Lily was there with a fag in her mouth stuttering and swearing like a trooper. The cards were being played day and night and there would be a fight over the kitty if it reached a few shillings. The whiskey and gin flowed. The frying pan sizzled the whole weekend. Family crashed out for a nap where they could. The younger members of the family sat up all night singing songs of home. One or two played an instrument. It was a great weekend.

As the wedding morning arrived I felt sick, a mixture of excitement and nerves. Almost ready, I glanced out of the window. There to my amazement was Alan, pacing up and down on the opposite side of the road. He looked wonderful but I did wonder for a moment why he was there. "Silly" I told myself, "Of course he's here" He wouldn't let me down. I didn't have on doubt: my husband to be would never let me down, like people had in the past. To-day was for real We had been to-gether three whole years, must have written a million words to each other, discussed almost every subject except my past that you could imagine and knew each other through and through,

I still wasn't sure if Sheila was my mum or not and accepted Dad as her husband. After today I'd be away from them and they would fade into the background. I wondered if my darling grandmother and lovely granddad would be sharing my happiness. It would have been fantastic if they had lived to see this day.

In the mirror, as I put a final dab of powder on my face, I saw a young girl about to start the most wonderful journey of her life.

Mum knew how to put on a show. The wedding car, a black Humber Snipe arrived. On the way to the church we had to negotiate a roundabout. Sitting there in my gorgeous dress, clinging to my bouquet, I was conscious of the shoppers stopping to have a peep at the bride as they do. I wanted to enjoy every moment and with Uncle

Tom at my side I wished the car would go round the roundabout again and again. The family had done me proud. There was a small competition among the cousins jealous of the one who got the most members of the immediate family at their wedding. No one missed my day. They were all very proud.

The service was beautiful and very nerve racking and I was glad when it was all over. What's in a name? I had my own now, Mrs. Leila B. We had just exchanged our wedding vows

"In sickness and in health, for richer or poorer, for BETTER or WORSE...," and the nuptial mass and nuptial blessing Alan had insisted on, done with the full might of the Catholic Church. No second best for him, hadn't he just embraced the Catholic Church where all children are God's children? The marriage certificate was signed and now we faced the walk down the aisle. There were smiles of approval all round, the photographers were busy, non-stop photos, handshakes and kisses all round and finally home for the reception. All smiles cutting the cake, plenty of food and drink for everyone. The Priest popped in for a brandy.

All too soon it was time to gather up our things and head for the station.

Loads of hugs and kisses from uncles, aunts, cousins and friends. Some guests insisted on coming to the station to see us off, though others were too well-oiled to stand up straight. The rest were anxious to get back to their game of cards. The train pulled into the station.

"Take care of yourselves"

"Good luck."

More hugs and kisses and we were off.

Chapter 10

We had a compartment to ourselves. I sank back into my seat: happy doesn't seem a strong enough word to describe that feeling of knowing you belong, the magic of being two instead of a lonely one. It was a wonderful feeling, alone with that lovely man I had just married. Surprisingly he took the seat opposite and as the train started to pull away sat bolt upright, ashen, glaring as if he might explode. He started to undo the buttons on his jacket and held the left side open. Reaching into the inside pocket with his other hand he took out a piece of paper and handed it to me.

"Explain this?"

Trying to keep my composure, I took it from him. Opened it and read it quickly. It was our marriage certificate.

"Explain what," I asked.

"Read it again" he said through clenched teeth, so I read it again.

"Elizabeth Winifred Merriman – Father unknown"

Well that's not surprising. So what, I thought and asked again, "Explain what"

Sitting opposite me was the man I had married that very day. A man who had made a vow, for better or worse, till death us do part. I thought he was going to burst.

"I've just married a fucking bastard! Who the fucking hell are you?"

Hitting me over the head with a sledgehammer would have been less painful.

"I'm me, Leila, I'm me,"

Useless words, he'd just told me I was no longer Leila, or not the Leila he had wooed so sweetly. But we were strangers to each other, the Alan I married disappeared in those few minutes.

"Who the fucking hell are you?" he shouted

"Whose fucking blood have you got in your veins? You're a liar, a cheat, a conniving bitch. You've tricked me into this marriage. I'd NEVER have married you if I'd have known."

He leaned towards me threatening, terrifying me.

"Do you know what we do with bastards in the navy?"

I sat there absolutely stunned. Had I at that moment been capable of reasoning I would have stood up and with quiet dignity, pulled the communication cord, stepped off the train and walked away. Unfortunately dignity was a word I was less familiar with than naïve. I thought this was a small blip brought on by the combination of shock to a fairly conventional system and the alcohol we'd consumed at the wedding feast. Our marriage would begin properly when he sobered up.

The rows began from then and became physical. Yet no matter how violent, Alan still demanded his rights as a husband. I would convince myself he still loved me, really needed me, that a man doesn't sleep with his wife just for sex. Given time he would trust me, would realize that we were the same couple who had gazed dreamily out to sea, had exchanged rings, had vowed

"I'll love you forever"

I'd sit in front of my mirror saying to myself

"When we are old and grey sitting by the fire, surrounded by children and grandchildren we would laugh about this. We'll remember how stupid we were on our wedding day."

But as the days, weeks, even months passed I realized he was never going to forgive.

Fortunately, or looking back perhaps unfortunately, before I had time to unpack fully the Suez Crisis happened and Alan was posted overseas for eighteen months. We wrote to each other, but our letters being censored did nothing to help the relationship. It was a strain writing at all, but knowing a stranger was reading and perhaps laughing at your words made matters worse. In one letter Alan wrote:

."........ am keeping my head down. I'd rather be a live coward than a dead hero"

That figures, I thought, a live coward. Any man who beats up a woman is a coward. The seeds of doubt were well sown in my mind from day one of the marriage, and his long absence gave me time to build up a resistance.

So within six weeks of the wedding with Alan posted, I was back with Mum and Dad and back in my old job. Nothing seemed to have changed, except that now I was married and already knew what a terrible mistake I had made.

There were times when we got on when he was home, but the

closeness of our first years to-gether, before we married, never returned. If anything despite my best efforts to find a breakthrough – his bitterness deepened.

I would keep my secret very close to my heart. No one would know I was a battered wife.

It was tough, Mum, Dad and I were like three strangers living under the same roof. We had never talked about the important things and there was no way I could approach Mum. If I ever hinted anything, she would fly into a rage and scream,

"Go away, haven't I got enough on my plate without having to cope with a mad woman" Alan desperate to find the answers couldn't accept that I knew nothing. No matter what I said, he believed I had always known and that I tricked him into the wedding.

One thing Mum and Alan had in common, they both agreed I was totally mad. Alan honestly believed he could have me certified, put away in a madhouse. That because I was born out of wedlock I was rotten to the core. Certainly, years ago some women who had babies out of wedlock were put in asylums, but their children? Alan said that being illegitimate, mad and conniving to deceive meant that I would one day just die. That would have suited him fine. I used to wonder how he thought I would die, I wasn't ill so It wasn't going to be that easy to get rid of me. Perhaps he planned to kill me.

The eighteen months flew and Alan was due home. On the way to the docks to meet him I wondered what things were going to be like after such a long time. My feelings were mixed; apprehensive but also thrilled, standing on the crowded docks with the band playing and the tremendous sight of the warship coming home and all of us straining to get that first sight of our loved ones.

Naturally, loyal and faithful being second nature to me

I had played it straight while Alan was away, so I was puzzled by his request one day when he had been home some time,

"Lets have a look at your private parts?"

"You won't be able to go to work for a while – you've got crabs"

"What the hell are crabs" I asked,

I soon found out.

So that was how he behaved when he was away from home. It was another nail in the coffin. He said I was the one who was no good, yet you don't behave much lower than he had.

Cousin Sheila was next to get married and she asked me to be her matron-of-honor. It was the first time I had been asked to be bridesmaid. I was thrilled. When the invitation arrived, Mum said I had been asked because I was ugly. All the cousins were beautiful and Sheila didn't want anyone to outshine her on her day.

I travelled to Maidenhead alone the day before the wedding and stayed at a nice hotel. After a leisurely breakfast I made my way to Auntie Lily's to prepare for the big moment, no way was I going to be late. Alan arrived with Mum and I was surprised to see Dad too. He couldn't be bothered to cross the road for my wedding yet he had traveled all the way to Maiderhead for Sheila's.

How I envied Sheila on her wedding day. Her husband's parents owned a garage and it was obvious they were financially well off. The reception was at a very smart hotel and was a lovely affair - not like my home-made do. His mother wore the most gorgeous mink coat and was dripping in diamonds.

Sheila was four years older than me which put her in her late twenties. She had done well by waiting, what a good catch. A year before her death we had lunch in a very smart restaurant. We were both financially secure then so we ordered the best. I had long been trying to talk her into putting her life story down on paper. Like me she thought the children would be upset. I knew by now quite a lot of her story and if I thought mine was traumatic it doesn't touch hers. Chatting over lunch that day she told me about her violent upbringing. Something I find very hard to believe. Even in her twenties if she came home late, her father would order her upstairs and as she walked up the stairs, he would thrash her legs with a cane. In the end the violence was so bad she vowed that the next man to ask her to marry him she would accept even if he were a tramp.

The man she did marry, Gordon, was in his thirties. He first asked her out because he needed a lady companion to accompany him to a presentation dinner. It progressed from there. Now Sheila was one sexy lady, always up for a laugh and with a terrific sense of humour. She thought it a bit odd that he never touched her and put it down to a combination of respect and shyness. The first bombshell came before they were married. Sheila had noticed that her husband-to-be had a lot of illnesses and he asked her to accompany him to the doctor. He had some sexually transmitted virus and the doctor wanted to check that she hadn't given it to him. Sheila was appalled. This was the 1950s, so gay man and the illnesses they carried weren't in the vocabulary of ordinary people. She told me that day over lunch with all the signs she never twigged. But when she was in hospital having her baby he was cautioned for offences against boys. The news shattered her life and she vowed when her youngest was eighteen (there were two children) she would walk away. He continued with his men lovers and she kept her word. She walked away. When she first approached a solicitor for a divorce, she was told her husband having an affair with a man wasn't grounds. She did get her divorce in the end. The whole experience put her off marriage ever again and she lived alone for the rest of her life. Gordon had dozens of lovers through the years. His favourite haunt was Bournemouth. He would stay away weeks at a time, scouring the gay bars there. Sheila kept her finger on the finances mainly for the children's sake.

Almost on his death bed Gordon fell passionately in love with a twenty-six-year-old man. He gave this lad a great time - swanky hotels, smart restaurants, designer clothes. Gordon mentioned to Sheila one day that he was going to give this lad control of a sixty thousand pound insurance policy so he could learn about finance and responsibility etc. It took Sheila five minutes to get to the solicitors and block it. On hearing he wasn't going to get his hands on the sixty grand the young man did a runner. Gordon was distraught. He cried on Sheila's shoulder.

"I love him. Please get him back for me."

He couldn't understand that a diseased-ridden skeleton of a man as he was then was only wanted for his money.

Sheila had started to put it all down on paper and from then on we spent hours on the phone. Sadly, she died prematurely.

Sheila never let me down, she was always there for me and it was a privledge to have spent the time with her before her death. Sitting in that smart restaurant, two ladies in our late sixties, we were very much at ease in each other's company. She was shocked at the story that she had asked me to be matron-of-honor because I was ugly."

"On the contrary, all the cousins were jealous of your beautiful dark looks."

We had both had a bad life but now at the end of the day we were at peace with ourselves. We laughed about the film moguls turning our life story into a blockbuster.

"Who would play you?" Sheila asked.

I said I fancied Julia Roberts.

"No, no," said Sheila

"She wouldn't be nearly pretty enough."

How we giggled, doing each other's confidence the power of good. We had come a long way since Sheila's mother Lily, had asked why I hadn't been drowned at birth.

Sheila was surprised at the ignorance of our aunts and uncles, most of them seemed so uneducated, never developing any social graces. I told her she was being hard on them. She hadn't grown up in Ireland as I had and I saw things differently. Our aunts and uncles were born at the turn of the century into poor families and never had a chance to make anything of themselves. They were all Catholics indoctrinated with the bigoted religion. Mind you Christians all, they wouldn't sit next to a black man or woman in church.

It was so good to see her. Someone up above had told me to get in touch. A year later when I sadly learned of her death, I was very grateful for the lovely memories.

Alan's next posting was at Chatham, just across the water so I joined him. We had two rooms with a very pleasant landlady. She was so spotlessly clean that when the coalman dumped his load down the shoot into the cellar she went into overdrive. I was asked to go down into the cellar, sweep the coal to the side, sweep up all the dust, then wash and polish the parts of the floor not covered in coal. For once I agreed with Alan on that one, I must have been mad to do it.

While we were there, Mum and Dad moved back to Westcliff. With their pay out from Beehive Lane I thought they were set up for life, However difficult things were they were my only family, so I was keen to see the new house and have a nose around. Life with Alan was like treading on eggshells, never knowing when the next smack would come or what I had said or done to start him off.

At the first opportunity when he was at sea again I made for home. Funny how a place I had never seen was home. As soon as the ship pulled out of the docks I was gone.

The front door looked impressive. Mum and Dad had rented a downstairs flat in a very old house so the rooms were huge with great high ceilings. Standing at the front door you looked down a straight hallway to the back bedroom. The huge lounge in the front had a wide bay window. It should have been called the red house. Everything in the room was red - red carpet, red curtains, big red suite with red cushions. The dining room was next - red carpet, red curtains, dining room chairs with red seats. Unbelievably, the kitchen and bathroom were painted red and white. It was a large flat, but I vowed never to have red in my home. The important thing was at last Mum and Dad had a home where they could settle down and hopefully grow old together.

I slept over for a couple of nights in the big back bedroom. Little did I know that later it would be home for Alan, myself and a baby. On the first morning Jack came quietly into my room and handed me a box of chocolates.

"What a lovely surprise." I said

It wasn't Dad's scene to give presents.

"Could you just lend me fifty pounds?" he asked.

That was a lot of money to me at the time, but what worried me more was that he had just received a pay out from Beehive Lane and here he was broke and borrowing already. The future looked bleak for Dad.

Chapter 11

Next stop for Alan and me was Rosyth in Scotland. We had a very pleasant flat over a shop next door to the swimming pool in Dunfirmlin, Most of the other naval wives were housed at Rosyth, but Alan always seemed to make sure I was away from them, stuck on my own. It was pretty lonely especially at night after the shops closed. The ship was out at sea for weeks on end and time dragged particularly at weekends.

There must have been hundreds and hundreds of other wives but I never came in contact with any of them. I began to wonder what secrets my husband was hiding, if he needed to go to such great lengths to keep me from finding out.

On Sundays I would go for a long walk in the park in Dunfirmline, but I always made sure I was home while it was still day light, I was scared of going indoors in the dark.

To pass the time and partly to keep myself sane I went job hunting. First I got a job selling Christmas cards in Woolworths, then I got a job at Paten and Baldwins the wool factory in Alloa, although this was a problem. Not the job, the firm was very good to me, but I was pregnant. There were huge tubs all around the factory floor, where the sheep coats were soaked to clean them and remove the oil. Whatever cleaned was used in the water, the smell made me vomit. I put up with it - the alternative was to stay at home without a soul to talk to. Maybe my dying of loneliness was part of Alan's plan to get rid of me.

The huge looms were awesome, I thought I would never master them. All those strands of wool spinning around, needing to be kept under control, whizzing into balls of wool on the pegs. My other problem was the language. Everyone was speaking English – well, Scottish – but with accents so broad I couldn't understand a word anyone said to me. It hardly mattered as my whole day was spent trying to conquer the looms. January and February in Scotland were freezing and we made a very early start. Every evening I'd go home to a cold empty flat, bolt the door and not move until it was time to begin the routine again the next morning.

There was a dance hall across the road from the flat and on Saturday nights I'd perch on the arm of the chair and watch the youngsters coming and going, laughing and hugging each other as they went on there way. They all seemed to be having such fun,.

Two members of the Salvation Army called on Thursday evenings. The first time they knocked I said

"I'm a Catholic I don't have a lot of time for you"

"That really doesn't matter – we're happy to talk to you" and insisted on calling regularly anyway. They would sit together on one side of the fire and chat. I realize now that the fire didn't heat the flat very well and they probably sat together to keep warm. I found them a little odd; what did they get out of their visits? Looking back I think they read my misery and loneliness and decided to keep me company.

As if I'd had a premonition, from the very start of my pregnancy I traveled home to Westcliff for my antenatal appointments with my own doctor.

I have one lasting memory of Scotland. I have no idea who the people were I'd never heard of them before and never saw them again, but Alan and I were invited to spend the New Year with them. It was a huge place standing in it's own grounds and the Hogmanay celebrations were amazing. Dozens of guests, a huge turkey with all the trimmings carved at midnight, the first footing, many drams of the local bevy – except for me of course. We played games after dinner, the Hula Hoop had just reached Britain and there were all the adults, some more than merry trying to swivel their hips and everyone falling about laughing. By three o'clock in the morning I was feeling rather groggy and I asked quietly if there was somewhere I could lie down.

My sympathetic hostess showed me to a beautiful room where everything was in Chintz and lace. I slept like a log. Alan hadn't missed me, he probably wouldn't have noticed if I had gone home.

I had found an admirer who knew I had gone to bed not feeling too good. He apparently checked on me now and then and must have had at some point an urge to wake me up, couldn't think of a reason, then had a brain wave. In the early hours he took a jug outside and with the snow up to his ankles milked a cow. He came into the bedroom with the jug of warm milk, made enough noise to wake me and offered me the milk. He couldn't have known about the morning

Tom & Me.

Ballinvalley Girls School - 1920
Bottom row - Far left Sheila, far right Una.

Granddad & Me rowing on Lake Dysart 1951.

*Me at my Conformation
with my black shoes.*

Colin my Husband.

Granddad & Me on Grandma's pig.

Mum and Me.

That's me greasing up for a long swim.

That's my election address photo.

My beloved Grandmother.

My beautiful Mum.

sickness and I threw up all over the beautiful bedclothes. I must have been the only one that night who wasn't drinking, yet I was the one to show myself up. That was the only time I have celebrated a Scottish New Year, I will always remember the kindness and generosity of the Scottish people. It was five days before Alan and I returned to our flat, it was one party after another.

Alan was soon back at sea, it must have been about March/April I had a letter to say he was in hospital. The ship had put into port somewhere up around John O'Groats. The lads had gone ashore for a football match and he had broken his leg, the Navy had flown him to Portsmouth. That was the end of our time in Scotland, the flat had to be vacated. I had nowhere to go only home to Mum and Dad. I wasn't too thrilled at the thought of us all together plus a baby when it arrived. Alan hated Mum like poison he'd say things like

"She's the wickedest woman on this earth.

All she had done as a naïve young girl was have a baby, but the problem for me was less her having had the baby than the continuing secrecy about who that baby was.

As Alan was recovering from his broken leg he slipped in the bathroom and broke an arm I said a little prayer – not that a truly wished him any harm but....

"Please, God, make it his bleeding neck, next time"

Mum and Dad were renting a corner premises and were in business. Dad was in his glory with his betting shop at the front he could gamble all day. Round the corner Mum had her cafe/restaurant she had always wanted. The two of them were in heaven. With Lily and Bill moving to Westcliff to help, it was going to be a great success.

It was a baking hot summer and my bump was getting bigger. To pass the time I got a job on the broken biscuit counter in Woolworths. I suffered miserably with lumbago but ploughed on. How hard I had worked since my wedding day. In Portsmouth, it was a grocer's, in Chatham, the Phillips factory, Woolworths and Paten and Baldwins in Rosyth. Never a big spender, I didn't smoke or drink and never visited a hairdresser but Dad was still up to his old tricks and made sure most of my spare cash was running on a horse or a dog – as far as I was concerned the animals were still running.

I had to give up work when I was seven months pregnant and once more spent my time pretty much alone all day. After their two shops closed Mum and Dad were always at a race meeting, a card school or the casino. There was always something going on somewhere. On most nights Mum would give John the petrol money to take her and dad to the dogs, then give John five pounds while they were there to have a bet as well as treating him to eats and drinks. Even after all that Dad would come home broke and on the borrow again, usually from me. John too was broke. Like his Dad, John could tell a story with the best and hadn't worked out you don't make a living from gambling. Mum and Dad had lent him the cash to set himself up in a carpet business out of the Beehive Lane money, but he went bankrupt owing Mum and Dad two grand.

Nobody but me was interested in housework – but then they were never at home. I was so angry about the life they were leading that I took it out on the furniture. The best thing would have been to leave everything as it was and live in a mess but that wouldn't suit me so the place shone. Feeling fed up with it all one day, I walked round to see the other half of the comedy act, Dad's daughter, Betty. It was a surprise to see Bernie open the door.

Betty's out" he said

No problem, I'd known Bernie very well for nine years and I went inside happily. I plonked my seven month's pregnant body on the settee which was fortunately right by the door. Without any warning Bernie leapt on me, I managed to push him off and get to the door. Then I ran. I could hear him shouting,

"Come back Leila, come back."

It wasn't far to the end of the road and I stopped to check if I was safe and see how far behind me he was. He was leaning casually over his gate. I never spoke to him again as long as he lived. I didn't go round any more and when my baby was born I didn't phone. I stopped sending Christmas cards and when Bernie died in his fifties, I didn't get in touch. Apparently he went outside one day to clear the snow away and dropped dead. I still see Betty who lives less than a quarter of a mile from me. Conversation is very stilted and polite, it would be pointless for me to say anything to her. She wouldn't understand what I was talking about and would probably say

"I've no idea what you mean, growing up I was protected from all life's nasties, Leila"

Then there'd be the bursting into tears and

"You're upsetting me. I think you should go"

Alan was home when the baby was born - well, up the road in

a pub, which was where he spent most of his time whenever he was in Mum's house. He was a father now, but it didn't stop his criticism. His conversation stopper when he got angry, which was on a regular basis, was

"Whose fucking blood has that baby got in his veins"

All mums think their babies are beautiful but Stephen definitely was a cracker with dark eyes and my dark hair.

"Why can't you accept it's our good blood?" I would ask Alan, "Because I fucking well can't," he would shout, fists flying, doors banging as he went off to the pub. One day I was so pissed off I marched into the pub to confront Alex, my husband's drinking buddy and reminded him that Alan was a married man with a young baby.

"We can't afford for him to spend all his money on beer" The chap looked me in the face, sneering "Darling, if he doesn't want to be at home with you, there's nothing I can do about it."

Humiliated yet again.

Mind you, this great friendship between Alan and Alex came to a sudden end. When we were first married Alan had bought himself a smart car. Public transport was good enough for me but not for him. On Alan's next overseas posting he asked Alex to sell the car for him, which Alex was happy to do. Then he asked for his commission, no messing around.

"Come on Alan, cough up the money"

Alan's reply was short

"F off."

Alex wasn't having that

"If you don't bloody pay up I'll see you in court,"

Alex meant it and of course was awarded the money he was entitled to. What Alan had to say is unprintable. Why did he think he could get away with it? I honestly think Alan considers where is one rule for him only and another for the rest of us.

The following summer Alan was posted overseas again for six months. Dad was getting even more deeply in debt. At the bookies he had taken some very large bets and hadn't paid out the winners. He sold Insurance policies and raided all the piggy banks. As always, he came begging and borrowing to me, but I just didn't have the amount of money he would need to bail him out. I did have some money, but what there was would have made very little difference, so I told Dad the kitty was empty. Now that I had my son, who was already over one year old, I decided it was time to look after myself.

"Even if I had given Dad my last penny, he would still be broke, so I have no regrets.

It was a lovely warm Sunday and I thought I would take Stephen out for the day to picnic on the cliffs, walk along the seafront, perhaps sit down in a deckchair and watch the world go by. My first stop was the restaurant for a cup of tea with Mum. When Dad walked in I was sitting alone with Stephen at a small table next to the counter. I can't believe I didn't speak to him. I was probably so deep in thought that I looked right past him as if he were a total stranger. He didn't see me. Mum was busy preparing dinner and I hadn't spoken to her either. Dad called

"Sheila"

She left the kitchen and came out. If she saw me she didn't acknowledge me.

"What"

Dad said

"Please don't make me do it, please Sheila don't "

"Go home and do it," was all Mum said and went back into the kitchen.

Dad still hadn't seen me; head bent he walked out without another word. It hadn't seemed to me a particularly significant conversation. It could be anything and nothing. But I noticed that he walked away like an old man. I let him go without calling out. I don't know why I didn't rush after him and walk along the road with him. I couldn't help him out of his financial troubles but I could have offered some kind of comfort. Instead I did something quite unlike me. I cleared off for the day and left him totally alone.

It was comparatively late when I got home, well late when you have a young baby to get to bed. Dad was in their bedroom asleep and there was no sign of Mum. God alone knew where she was.

I saw to Stephen, then pottered about all evening. Dad never stirred. I looked in on him once or twice but my instinct was not to disturb him. At least he is getting some rest after all the sleepless nights he has had lately. Normally I would have whispered something like

"Are you awake, Dad, fancy a cup of tea?" But that evening – I did nothing

It was finally time to get to bed myself. During the night the baby stirred and woke me. My bedroom door was ajar and I saw that the light was on in the long hallway and Mum was sitting by the little table where the phone was kept. She had the telephone directory in her hand but I gave it no further thought, simply got back into bed and went to sleep again.

By 6 a.m. the baby was as usual letting the world know he was around. As I switched on the bedroom lights I heard Mum on the phone

"I've just woken up and I can't wake my husband, send an ambulance"

I quickly picked Stephen up and went out in the hallway. I suspected she might have spent the night sitting by the phone, but self-preservation told me to keep quiet. If she kicked me out I had nowhere to go with Stephen. In their bedroom I saw. Dad still lying the way he had been the evening before. Not asleep but unconscious and that's how he was taken into hospital. Later in the morning I phoned to ask how he was.

"Are you a relative?" I was asked.

"I am his daughter." I said

Well, he was the only dad I'd ever known.

The doctor was very hostile.

"Do you know your father has taken sixteen sleeping tablets?" He made it sound as if it were my fault.

"No I certainly didn't know. Why the hell would he do that?"

I had enough sense not to say a word to Mum. The outburst of abuse I would get would be unbearable. She would present it as something else I had imagined in my mad mind, another of those hallucinations I was suppose to suffer from. I couldn't confide in my husband either. Better keep this to myself. Thinking things through, I asked myself if I was seriously suggesting that Mum had first demanded Dad went home to kill himself and then sat up all night without having a change of heart. Had she really waited as long a she possible could (which would be when I woke) hoping it would be too late. I told myself it didn't happen like that. No, she couldn't, ever. But I knew she had.

When I got to the hospital, Dad was in a deep coma. While he could never be described as good looking, his big very serious face so long and thin, rarely if ever smiling, the small eyes, large hooked nose and thin lips, it was now like cardboard, absolutely lifeless.

I leaned close to him and whispered,

"It's me, Dad."

He responded immediately, frightening the life out of me. Amazed that there was any life there I ran to call a nurse, then leaned over him again and pleaded

"Please, Dad, please, don't die like this, not like this. Please, I beg you."

From that moment he slowly came out of the coma and three weeks' later he was home.

He lived for another five years but the episode had affected his health.

His weight had caused him to have horrendous varicose veins and both legs were covered with open ulcers and he was usually in excruciating pain. I would watch him binding his poor legs with miles of bandages. My heart went out to him but I couldn't help, it turned my stomach over.

One very cold night I decided to go to bed early. As I passed their bedroom door I slipped a hot water bottle in Dad's side of the bed. Next morning he said

"I could hardly walk to bed last night I was in so much pain. Then I was overcome by the luxury of that warm bottle. It saved my life"

Mum wouldn't have been happy to hear I was saving his life. She was so desperate to be free. Every time the doctor wrote out a prescription she would say,

"Another ten years of my life"

In a way I understood her predicament. Every penny she earned Dad gambled and lost. She was still only a young woman and had worked her heart out all her life. She'd survived a couple of years of misery looking after Dad's brother and his wife, was given a chance with a few bob from Beehive Lane. And what happened to that? It had gone like the rest, on horses or dogs. She was desperate and apart from murdering Dad herself, what else could she do? Those years were desperate times for Catholic, Irish, unhappy marriages where people had made a mistake and wanted out. The church has a lot to answer for.

But why not just walk away again? Respectability, that was what. Mum came from a large close-knit family and wouldn't admit to failing in her marriage. Being divorced wasn't very respectable, she'd not have much sympathy. In the 1950's even non-Catholics thought twice about taking such a huge step. They were horrendous years when I came over from Ireland. She had neither love for me nor the finances to look after me, but had obviously been pressurized by her large family into on the responsibility she'd never wanted and had run away from once.

I knew all about respectability through my own marriage. As a good Catholic I was still wrestling with the vows I had made. Something very extreme would have to happen before I broke those vows. I suppose respectability was what kept Alan with me too. With all his airs and graces, as a Chief Petty Officer. P-e-t-t-y, that word couldn't be more fitting —Alan wouldn't want a divorce either. It would be far more respectable to have a wife in a mad house, even better if he were to be widowed. He really went on telling me I was so evil that I would die naturally

"Or perhaps I'll have you committed" he would sneer.

More than once he said

"Seeing you makes me feel ill, even the hairs on my arms stand up"

Yet there were reasonable times, when he was at least civil and I had married him because I loved him. Until the end I kept hoping there would be a breakthrough. I understand now that most battered wives hang on, hoping, but I know better now.

He reckoned that the reason I stayed around was that I needed his allowance book to live on. I'd be rich if I had a penny for every time he screamed at me

"All you're interested in is my allowance book."

He forgot I'd been fighting my own battles since I was eight. I was no weak little woman who needed a man to support me. I didn't need his blasted book.

Most of my time now was spent looking after Dad and Stephen. I tried to spend as much time as I could talking to Dad but we never mentioned the hospital incident. One day Dad said, "Teach me how to say your prayers, Leila."

"Don't be silly, Dad," I said. "Prayers are all the same. There's only one God."

"I want to make sure I'm going to the same place as you," he said.

So Dad became a Catholic, in my opinion it was ridiculous, I wasn't impressed. I knew that if he had the opportunity to stake my life on a dog with a fifty-fifty chance, he would take the risk, but I honestly loved him. It was funny how close we had always been, even with his unstoppable gambling.

Mum had now taken over both businesses. She was out all day and usual most evenings as well, so it was great to hear out of the blue that Tom my favourite uncle was coming to visit.

"I'll make a special effort for lunch" I offered.

Mum was not keen

" It would be easier for him to eat with me" she said

I stood my ground.

"I want to spend some time with him, we've got a lot to catch up on"

Uncle Tom had long left the army and was now working in Lyons Corner House. I was anxious to catch up on all the family gossip.

When he arrived he sat himself down in an easy chair and the first words he spoke were:

"How about you and me going into business together, Leila?"

Once again I was the last to know, but Mum was selling the café to pay off their debts and keeping the betting shop, hoping to make a living from gambling. Lily and Bill had long returned home to Maidenhead. So that was that, Tom and I would invest in the café.

It seemed a wonderful idea – Uncle Tom and me in business together. There was nothing to discuss. I totally trusted him and we could work it out as we went along. One thing was for certain, Tom had never, and would never, let me down. I would trust him with my baby's life.

Tom gave his notice in at Lyons and to make things even more cosy he rented a flat a couple of doors away from us. Maggie was settled in Sheerness and didn't want to uproot, she was happy with her life there.

For the record and for the benefit of a certain section of my family, let's get this straight. When Tom and I discussed buying a business, we were simply talking about buying the goodwill of a poxy cafe stuck on the corner of a side road. We actually each put in three hundred and seventy-five pounds for the goodwill only.

From day one Tom worked harder than me. He would open at seven o'clock to get breakfast for workmen I came along at nine with

Stephen in the pram, he would be sleeping outside or sitting inside in his high chair while he was awake. I worked as hard as I could in the circumstances, going home at teatime while Tom would stay open until eleven at night. Not an ideal situation but Tom was happy about it, he knew that was how it had to be. He was in his element, for him the most important thing was to be his own boss.

At the bottom of the road a couple of hundred yards away, was a very large hotel which accommodated the overflow of army wives from Shoebury barracks. Most of them, like me, had husbands overseas. They would come in for their cigarettes or a cup of tea and a chat. After all his years in the army, Uncle Tom was on their wavelengths and they got on like a house on fire. When I arrived there would be a couple in the kitchen helping Tom with the breakfasts and another couple of ladies waiting on tables. I knew there would be a crowd there to help in the evenings after I left – some of the women must have thought I just came in for the company. I was quite happy with everything. I never even asked Tom how much we were paying them. There was no need to ask questions, Tom seemed so contented. He was working hard, we were very busy and that was exactly as he wanted it.

As the months passed Stephen grew into a very lively little boy and he became more and more restless. Which I began to find difficult to cope with. It seemed the time to have a chat – things seemed to be going really well and Tom was in top form.

"Look, Tom," I said, "You seem to have it made. Would it be OK for me to stay at home?"

I had never taken a penny in wages, you don't expect pay when you are building up a business and I made it quite clear to Tom that the money didn't matter, I didn't want anything back. Tom honestly didn't mind me leaving and I retired from the restaurant. If I did think of money I would tell myself that one day I might get a surprise. Boy did I get that surprise – and sooner than I thought.

The time had flown and Alan would be home in about three weeks for Christmas. Could Alan coming home and maybe asking questions have been the trigger?

Dad and I were having a cuppa; he missed me when I was on cafe duty and enjoyed having me around again since I had given up work. Mum had left for the betting shop, where she seemed to be making a success. As soon as she opened up it was in to Tom at the café for a cup of tea and a chat. She would pop back several times a day, for more tea for her dinner at lunchtime and then more tea in the afternoon. If there was anything wrong, however slight, if the café was dirty, or there were no customers, or Tom was down, she would have known. Mum was no fool and I know for certain that Mum and her brother Tom were very close they thought the world of each other.

Suddenly the peace was shattered for Dad and me by the sound of the phone.

"Hello, who is it?"

"You won't know me" a total stranger informed me, "The cafe isn't open. Do you have a spare set of keys?"

"No! I didn't have any keys"

"No, I know nothing about Tom but I'll check his flat"

Then Mum phoned.

"No, I've no news and no suggestions"

At about 11 a.m. someone went around to the back of the café and looked through the kitchen window. There was a body on the floor, all that could be seen were the legs. Distraught, Sheila phoned her sisters with the terrible news that their wonderful brother was dead, then immediately came home. Soon Mina arrived. If there wasn't trouble already Mina was sure to make some. I was right. She laid into Mum with her fists yelling

"Whore. Going to bed with two men at the same time"

What did all this have to do with Tom killing himself?

It didn't matter to me what Mum had ever said or done, nobody was going to hit or speak to my Mother like that. I threw myself at Mina and dragged her away.

"What the bleeding hell has it to do with you? Mind your own business"

I pushed her towards the front door and manhandled her out of it.

"Get out." Dad shouldn't have to witness such a disgraceful scene, poor old sod. Not in his state of health, you spiteful cow."

Then the threats began. Where did this lying, foul-mouthed woman come from? Surely she couldn't be a Merriman.

"It'll be my mission in life to see Tom's boys get their share"

Tom left only one note, to me in which he wrote,

This will be a nine day wonder. You will soon find something else to talk about. Make sure you give the boys their share.

One of my few regrets in life is on that day I didn't pick the phone up and phone Auntie Maggie or any one of Tom's three boys but Mina had left me totally shell-shocked. I had a baby to care for and I suppose the responsibility of a café. One of them would surely phone me. The days passed without a word from Sheerness, not even news about the funeral. Mina had done a good job. I was so traumatized by it all that I couldn't think of phoning and facing any more rows or rejections. For no-one to contact me, especially as they were part owner of a café, there must have been some very bad feelings.

Alan arrived home for Christmas to a re-run of when we first met - just before Christmas when Solly and May died, now it was Tom. I hadn't been able to go near the cafe and, credit where it's due, Alan took on the task of opening the place up again. Who knows what happened on the day Tom died. We did find one thing though. The fishmonger had delivered a box of wet fish and it had stayed on the kitchen table. No- one had put it away in the fridge. The smell turned your stomach. Alan set about scrubbing the whole place out. It took the whole of his two weeks' holiday to get it fit to re-open, but it offered him a whole new arsenal of ammunition. He was married to a family of nutcases and I was the nuttiest of them all.

"If it's the last thing I do, I'll have you locked away"

It never entered his head to go out and find a flat for Stephen and me, he preferred to accept the hospitality of these nutter's yet abuse everyone. Nothing was right, he complained about his meals, my Mothers cooking, whatever came into his head.

Mum was to get rid of the betting shop and help me out of the mess I found myself in, making it clear she wanted paying for every second she worked. That was fair enough she had an invalid husband to support and a home to keep up.

The first letter I received was from the landlord of Tom's flat, saying he had never paid the rent and enclosed the bill. It never crossed my mind to challenge it - as if he would have let Tom stay there for six months without paying any rent at all. Next Tom owed the tobacco company over a thousand pounds. In 1960 a thousand pounds was a tidy sum. There were bills from every quarter.

All I could think about was my desire to continue living in the place I loved, to be able to walk down the street with my head held high owing not a penny to a soul. But for now it was serious business.

I had inherited a mountain of debt, none of it mine, but I had to work to pay it back. Mum and I rolled our sleeves up and set to.

All the book-keeping had been left to Tom, there were no books. Something else, we, Tom and I weren't paying any rent, insurance or taxes of any sort. The whole building was owned by Lew, the gentleman I had taken the Beehive Lane rings too. He and Mum were lovers, I found that out the morning Tom died. It was one of the many accusations Mina threw at Mum, so even she knew. It was obvious the ground floor was free to Mum for as long as she needed it. What we had bought into was a chance to trade illegally, a one hundred percent fiddle. I pretended I was stupid, never said a word to Mum and as I intended staying only to pay off Uncle Tom's debts, I carried on.

Stephen would have to be put in a nursery which was awful. At that time ordinary kids didn't go to nursery but waited until they were five to go to school. It broke my heart. I had never been parted from him. As I walked away the tears fell freely. It was like putting him in care. When I got back that tea time he was standing in a corner. He had wet himself. He didn't do it again, he was too frightened.

Still more weeks passed without a word from Sheerness. If they had been in touch to offer some words of comfort the café might have had a different ending. A great sadness remained with me, as I thought constantly about missing the funeral and couldn't come to terms with that fact. I would ask myself if Mum was to blame for involving us in the café, then if I was to blame for staying at home. I didn't know then that anyone involved in a suicide had similar feelings of guilt. Those thoughts soon passed because it was a really good business and one by one the debts were settled. Funny enough not one of the crowd of army wives came near the place. They seemed to disappear off the face of the earth, not that it would have been fair to ask them if they could throw some light on Tom's suicide.

One thing I knew for certain I didn't want to work and live with my mother for longer than necessary. There were two other certainties – I didn't want to be in the café business and I didn't want to benefit by one penny from Tom's death. So when the last bill was paid I said

"I'm out of here"

Lew said

"You're timing is perfect. I have been waiting to put the building on the market"

His solicitor wrote and asked me if there was anything I needed - I said £375, which was my Goodwill investment. Guess what - I heard from those three lovely lads in Sheerness. So they did have tongues in their heads after all.

I grew up in Ireland with those three boys who were the backbone of my life. We knew, loved and trusted each other. When they said "jump" I knew I wouldn't land and hurt myself, we ran barefoot, wild and free. There was very little but we shared whatever we had. Now they thought there was a few bob to spare they forgot the rules. They had left me with a baby, sweating my guts out to settle their father's debts as a matter of honour, debts which had nothing to do with me. Now they wanted their share. You meet a few bastards in life, yet I've always been told I was the bastard. I didn't reply to the letter for one reason. I was hoping everything would eventually blow over and however friendly we became secretly they would always think,

"She still had our money" when in fact there wasn't any. So I asked the solicitor to deal with it. That way they got the truth.

If people had pulled together when the tragedy happened, if one ounce of support had been offered, if that wicked bitch Mina, hadn't set out to destroy things might have been different. It was a very sad chapter in my life and today, fifty years on the rift remains. Mina is long dead and I never forgave her. All I hope is that when she got to those Pearly Gates she got her comeuppance.

One job that fell to me was to clear out Tom's flat. I wondered why the boys hadn't been along to pick up their dad's possessions and put it down to them not being bothered. Painstakingly, I went through his mail trying to find one clue, however small, as to why he had killed himself. There was a letter from Auntie Lily, a reply to one Tom had written. He had obviously wanted to buy me out and had tried to borrow my share from Lily. Was he planning the deed and wanted to spare me the responsibility of his debts? Lily wrote back saying

"Sorry, I can't help and anyway if the little cow wants her money (which I didn't, there was no question of it) let her wait."

It was a particularly bad time for Mum, the spoils from Gants Hill had gone. It had taken eight years for May and Solly's will to be settled from the day Mum walked out on me without a word when I was seventeen. Now everything had disappeared and she was back where she had started, only in a worse position. It had taken Dad less than two years to get through every penny and now he was an invalid. Mum was that much older and she was forced to work harder than ever to support them both.

She got a job housekeeping. It didn't pay that well but she was in a very serious card school and always had the money to play cards. Dad, frail and almost blind, would wander to the phone and ring the bookies to place a bet, but they wouldn't accept it. They knew from long experience there was no money to settle his debts, so Dad would wander back to his chair and sit down very dejected. He never went out and had become a very lonely old man.

Alan was back and forth. Without his drinking pal Alex he was even more frustrated and bitter. If anything Mum hated him more than he hated us. I used to ask myself what it was with those two. We had been married about five years now; I spent my days as a lodger in someone else's flat with a crying baby and a sad old man for company. Mum was out day and night and Alan when he did come in, found it easier to start a fight, have a punch up, then disappear down to the pub. I was at crisis point.

The crunch came for me one Sunday afternoon. I had reached the ripe old age of twenty-seven; the years had not mellowed Alan at all, in fact they had made him even more bitter. I had hoped with this baby we would have found something to break the deadlock, but he grew more angry with every day that passed. Totally fed up with the non-stop verbal and physical abuse, I was lost, despairing. I hadn't been sleeping well for ages and craving some sleep I took Mum's sleeping pills. They had no effect, I might as well have take a handful of Smarties, so I took a few more. It was like a curtain coming down, Boom.

Next I woke up in Southend General, with a doctor leaning over asking,,

"Why did you want to kill yourself?"

That was the last thing on my mind, but it was just the shock I needed. It was the beginning of the end. I had received my wake up call. It was almost the last straw for Alan, who shouted,

"How much more do you think I can stand?"

It was less how much more he could stand than how much more I could stand. My brush with death, as the doctor at Southend General called it had shaken me to the core. I thought I would never get over the incident, Grandma and granddad would be so ashamed of me. The strength and courage they had shown when they took Brendan and me on wasn't for this. But in a strange way it put an extra bone in my back, you don't go through an experience like that without changing and some good coming out of it. Never again would I shrink from a fight, I would always have the courage to go for what I thought was right. At that moment nothing was going to help me with my unhappy marriage. Domestic violence didn't exist, nobody spoke about a thing like that. It was as dark a secret as being born a bastard.

I seemed trapped whichever way I turned; having married in the Holy Roman Catholic Church was going to be hard nut to crack. No one seemed to be willing to help me so I was going to help myself. It was desperate measures.

Anything that involved leaving Dad would be desperate. I was going to buy a house for Stephen and myself. I looked around for a little place and finally found my ideal home - a small two-bedroom bungalow. Most important it was not far from Dad, so I would able to visit every day. Alan, away at sea, got his father to check what was going on. Old Mr B, bless him hurried around and was quite impressed, he reported back to his son that he saw no problem at all. I got on with all the arrangements, visits to the estate agents, solicitor and all the others involved. As was the case in those days, it was all in the man's name, so that having run myself into the ground, Alan arrived home to sign the deeds. The married woman's property act wasn't law.

I moved with my son, sure I was doing something his father had never done, provide him with a home. Leaving poor Dad was a very sad day for me but it was a question of my own survival. I knew how lonely he was and now he would be even lonelier, but I had to think about my son and most important, myself. In my heart it was the end of the marriage. If Alan got a long posting overseas which he was due, he'd be going without us. I'd taken enough physical and verbal abuse, but there was to be another child and another five years before the final break came.

114

Chapter 13

The housekeeping I had managed to save while I was doing my two stints at the café covered the deposit, now there was some serious shopping to be done. After five years of marriage we didn't own so much as a saucepan, the consequences was partly my fault for not keeping my eye on what we were spending. Now we needed everything to set up home and it was all on the never-never. We bought a lovely three piece suite, table and chairs for the kitchen, a top of the range gas cooker and a large ornate mirror which I hated.

Our bedroom was full of old junk, two dark wardrobes and a dressing table, no love nest then, which should have told me something. I made sure Stephen's room was newly furnished. Alan already had his car on the tally and with the mortgage repayments, plus normal bills our outgoings were exactly twice my income. I soon realized I would have to do something pretty desperate if I was going to keep the roof over my head.

You wouldn't win a prize for guessing who my first visitor was, even before I had settled in, Dad was on the phone to say,

"Mina is here, she wants to know, where are you"

Poor old Dad couldn't remember where I lived. Nothing had been heard of Mina since the fight but my concern at that moment was for dad in his frail health. My move was no secret; I said,

"I'm so sorry Dad that you have been disturbed. Tell the rat bag, to get lost"

I had no idea she had snatched the phone out of his hand and was listening. I watched out of the window as she waited to cross the road and I said to myself,

"Why not just jump on your broom stick and fly across"

Her journey was a wasted on, I soon showed her the door. I wondered why she was so spiteful to me, she seemed to have hated me like poison ever since I was a child. I remember the hidings I got because she told my Mother tales, always untrue, about me. Perhaps my very existence was the problem. Like Mum, Mina too, as a young girl, had a baby out of wedlock, but she was a bit luckier as she was able to keep it a secret from most of the family. Her little girl, Carmel,

115

died and was buried in Ireland. I suppose the trauma may have been ever greater for her than for Mum and maybe in her warped mind she thought I too should have died.

It was heaven having a home of my own and a garden for Stephen to play in. One morning, as I was racking my brains for a way out of the financial mess, there was a loud rat-a-tat on the front door. Standing on the doorstep was a tall dark haired man who looked about my age, a double for Cliff Richards.

"Good morning" he said "My names Paul. I've been talking to a friend of yours. She suggested I should call on you"

I'd no idea who this "friend" could be, hardly anyone knew where I was living, but he looked harmless enough so he was invited into the kitchen and the kettle was soon singing.

"Now then" I said while I made the tea, "What's this all about"

"I've just had my pay-off from the Merchant Navy and I've bought a café on the seafront at Westcliff. I heard that if I could get Leila to work for me I'd be on a winner"

No need to guess what my answer was.

Poor Stephen, he had enjoyed being with me in his new home, now it was back to Miss Cheeseman every weekday as I agreed to work Monday to Friday from nine to five.

Paul opened just after Christmas, a desolate time of the year down on the seafront. I don't remember having a customer during the first week, we were so quiet I said

"Forget my wages this week. You've a family to support"

I considered him a real friend and as the days got lighter and warmer we got really busy. We had to take on more staff; Paul was on his way.

My evenings after Stephen was in bed would be spent quietly watching TV, my knitting needles going nineteen to the dozen. When Alan was around it was amazing how easily rows started. Take a normal Saturday morning, everything peaceful, nobody looking for trouble, Alan had to go out and on his returned he asked:

"Who have you had in?"

His tone suggested he wasn't talking about old Mrs. Jones next door dropping in.

"Nobody's been in," I replied.

"You're just a liar, I can smell him."

"Smell?"

Now what was going on in his mind? Was it all part of the wearing-down process, actually trying to drive me mad. After the questioning I would get a slap for playing him up. By evening things would be quite violent. He really believed there was no harm in him trying to hasten the process of my state of madness so that I would die naturally.

One of my lovely cousins phoned.

"I'm a bit depressed Leila, could I come for a break" I need a change.

I was delighted.

"It'll be great to see you. Stay as long as you like"

The very first morning of her visit Alan was home and I left him the money to get some shopping, decent chops and everything for dinner. I didn't expect him to have the spare cash to feed my family. Neither did I expect them to buy a bottle of whisky and a bottle of gin and spend the day in bed together. There was no dinner when I got home from slogging my guts out.

There was no point in saying a word I would be told it was all in my imagination. It was a pretty bad weekend but thank goodness I was still alive when he returned to his ship.

I am about to give the impression that Alan was right, I was truly mad, but it is impossible to explain.

It was midday and I was busy getting Stephen's lunch. Nothing happened, I saw nothing, heard nothing, felt nothing but I knew someone was there and had something to say to me. No, that's not true, nobody said anything. All I knew was that someone called Dorothy was looking after me and that everything was going to be alright. A couple of days later Mum called in. I was still looking around expecting to hear or see something. Mum said.

"That's three or four times you've done that, what's the matter?"

"I don't know," I said and told her about the happening. "The funny thing is," I said, "I don't know any Dorothy."

"Yes you do," said Mum. You remember Alan's mother died when he was young. She was a Dorothy."

It certainly was a weird experience and never happened again, but I did wonder if Dorothy was doing her bit when a year later Alan got a year long posting overseas.

That long a break without a fight - heaven. What Alan and I

wrote to each other about I can't imagine it must have been very shallow stuff. One thing we definitely never discussed was having another baby. Alan swore he didn't know whose blood was in the veins of the one we did have, so goodness knows how I would have responded if he mentioned anything about a baby.

Phone's were used far less than they are now, so the only contact was through letters. I never bothered if they weren't very regular, I was too busy working to pay off the never-never.

It was hard work in the cafe but I always enjoyed it. The customers were great and many became friends. Some would come in every morning on the way to work for breakfast or a coffee. Wednesday was half day closing in Southend so I knew I would see the same people for lunch or afternoon tea and sometimes they would have a laze in the sun. Which didn't please me because they would occupy the best seats and I wasn't getting any tips. Fridays was fish and chip days and the same crowd came, they were a great bunch. There was always the odd one who fancied his chances, when I cleared away his cup there would be a fiver under it. Next time I'd remember to be a little cold.

One of the female customers, Pearl had a profound effect on me. Looking back I can't believe she liked me, we came from such different worlds - she was so rich and I so poor, but I liked her – and envied her – right from the start. I'd hate to think she was using me, pretending friendship to get at her husband. Pearl and I were about the same age but that was where the similarities ended. She was a tall, slim redhead, with polished fingernails and toenails. Her jewellery was extremely expensive, her clothes exquisite and she smelt divine, her perfume wafted over the smell of the cooking. We did have one thing in common, a lovely smile. Having been brought up by a Jewish man and a very pro-Jewish Mother I did have a rapport with the Jewish faith and Pearl was very Jewish.

We had something else in common which wasn't apparent to me at the time. With all the material things she had Pearl was totally lost and desperately unhappy, perhaps what drew her to me was she sensed my despair.

Our friendship spanned only a few months. Pearl kept inviting me to call on her and eventually I visited her in their flat on the seafront at Westcliff. The last time I had sat in such luxury was at Solly's and May's house at Gants Hill. Immediately I arrived she picked up the phone and ordered steaks. The butcher, the same butcher I had lived next to as a seventeen-year-old, jumped into his car and delivered them straight away. I wondered if the rats were still around but reckoned the cooking would kill the germs. Pearl had one daughter who she lived for, adored and thoroughly spoiled.

Her husband owned a gown shop off Southend High Street. Pearl had grown up in the North of England and I gather she came to London as a teenager to better herself having had little as a child. It was obvious she had married well; she said very little about her husband, but I gather his status had grown and her Northern roots of poor education and background were letting her down in her husband's social circle. She would say things like,

"I waited until he was in the bath to speak to him, a bloke can't be pompous when he is in his birthday suit."

She never expanded on her conversation with him, but I think she suspected he was having an affair.

Perhaps if I were in a different frame of mind I would have responded differently, maybe I would have been shocked. As a battered wife, anything she had to say on the subject of her husband was so tame to me. One Saturday night there was a knock on my door and Pearl was standing there

"Can I stay with you?" she asked.

Of course the door was open and she was very welcome. They'd obviously had had a major row; Not wanting to pry and make her feel awkward, we chatted away all evening about anything and nothing. I never even got around to sorting out where she was going to sleep. About eleven o'clock the phone rang, it was her husband, he was on his way to take her home. He didn't step inside my home, he behaved like a perfect gentleman and was very polite. As for Pearl I had the feeling she felt she had scored a victory, he had come after her. After all she would have to have left him my phone number. I went to bed thinking the row couldn't have been all that serious.

I had started working on Sundays as money at home was still tight, most weeks it didn't stretch to meet all the bills. This particular Sunday morning I didn't see Pearl sit down at the table, when I did the greeting on both sides was warm.

"Just a coffee, please," she said.

We chatted away between customers, but Sunday mornings were always busy. As always I gave her every second of my time I could spare. She looked calm and relaxed, as beautiful as ever wearing her valuable jewellery.

"My daughter's spending the day with a friend, so I've got a lazy day to myself"

She paid and left with her usual lovely smile,

"Goodbye"

I watched her for a few seconds as she walked away.

A few days later I was walking along the road and a stranger stopped me.

"Aren't you Pearl's friend?" she asked

"Yes, that's right".

"Did you know she is dead?"

Pearl had walked home from the cafe that morning, closed the kitchen door and gassed herself. That was the fourth time I'd lost someone that way. In those days people kept their troubles to themselves, I certainly never talked about mine. Still I ask myself, why didn't she say something that Sunday morning? I phoned her husband, I felt he was holding his own. I had the impression he would have liked to say

"Piss off and mind your own business" but he was far too well bred to do such a thing.

I've often wondered about the little girl, I'm sure she has had a good life materially. I'm sure there was a stepmother waiting in the wings but she would never take Pearl's place. That little girl will be about fifty now, I wonder if there was anyone to tell her about her beautiful mother, I doubt it.

The year, an unusually uneventful one for me, flew and Alan was due home. On Saturdays I'd take Stephen to the park, perhaps to the zoo, do whatever families do at Saturdays, You couldn't help notice families together, talking, laughing, Dads doing their bit. I longed to be like them, a family unit. Not with Alan, though, I knew if he was home it would be nag, nag, nag, slap, slap, slap. I wanted no more of that, but I longed to be happy and less lonely. Stephen and I plodded on by ourselves, I'm sure he was missing out not having a dad to guide him, but there was nothing I could do about that anyway.

The job at the cafe had gone well, it was tiring and hot in the summer but I was grateful to be able to work and keep the house going. Paul now opened until midnight or later. He did the evening shift and had a manageress/cook for the daytime. Patricia. She was middle aged, with one of her legs half the length of the other, rather like my Uncle Michael in Ireland. It was fascinating seeing her bobbing up and down in the very small space, but her disability was a handicap and there was no way she could cope with the work. I needed the job so I worked my butt off to keep things going. I guess Patricia had been let down in life; she wasn't a pretty lady and she seemed bitter which gave her a hard look.

One day she sent out four salads without washing the lettuce - they were covered with creepy-crawlies. I was so rushed of my feet I didn't notice and anyway I wasn't in the habit of checking her, I accepted they would be perfect. There was no reason for anything to be said, mistakes happen all the time and they are soon put right. But Patricia close to blame me and let out such a torrent of abuse that I walked out. It was probably quite good timing, Alan would be home in a few days. For what it was worth he would have my full attention. The relationship between us was still very strained. One day without any previous discussion he declared in his unusually gruff voice.

"I want a daughter."

Why he should want another baby amazed me, there was no way to work that one out. What would be different, would he still question who's blood was in it's veins. It certainly did nothing to bring us closer, weeks later Alan had to ask,

"Have you got any news for me?"

"If you are asking am I pregnant, then yes I am," I replied, thinking poor me.

There were no hugs and kisses or rejoicing just the bare fact that I was having a baby. I needed this baby like I needed a hole in my head.

Almost from day one I was ill, sick morning and night. It was a good job I had taken that heavy dose of sleeping pills earlier, it had put me right off tablets and wouldn't take one to save my life. The sickness was unbearable, but I still refused tablets. Someone up there was looking after me - if I had taken the prescription I might have had a thalidomide baby as so many other women did that year.

More pressing was the state of the finances;

The only work I knew was the cafes but I couldn't go back to Paul as he still had his disabled lady in charge. So I walked along the row of cafes; I knew most of the people who ran them, so it wasn't too difficult asking if there were any jobs going. I'd do anything. I did feel a bit like a worn-out tramp, pregnant and begging for work, but things were very tight and I couldn't afford to be proud.

I came to the very last café, my last chance with no idea what I could do next if I was unsuccessful. Peggy, the cafe owned, took me on. I would work nine to four, Mondays to Fridays for five pounds a week. I didn't tell her I was pregnant but I was already suffering from awful sickness. When she handed me the first plate of cooked breakfast to take to a customer, the smell turned my stomach over. I felt so awful, tears came into my eyes, I had no idea how I prevented myself from being sick all over the place. Peggy must have thought me a very surly young woman. Sick and miserable, I had to shoulder on.

Peggy was a very bright bubbly character, Tall, blonde, and very athletic she played tennis, drove around in a sports car and had lots of friends, a bit like my mum in that as she worked hard and played just as hard. Every day she fed me sausage and mash for lunch. I was very grateful for those months of sausage and mash. I don't know if my diet was deficient but I craved chocolate and would pig out on peppermint Aero. I had the luxury of a washer-upper; at Paul's I did all my own washing up.

Tilly, the little old lady at the sink, was what we now call "Special needs" Her family dropped her off every morning; she spent her whole life standing at that sink. You could say her family was getting rid of her, but she was as happy as a lark and always had a big smile on her face, although in some ways Tilly was such a poor old lady. She always had the same flowered dress with a wrap around apron and even on the hottest of days she wore thick woollen socks. He only make-up was sweat, she was bent over and would shuffle along but there was a twinkle in her eyes. She knew no other life and to her it was good. Tired as I was, if it meant a rest for me, I would rather give her a hand and a hug. She would smile exposing the only tooth she had in her head. She was such a lovely person and she stood at that sink almost to her dying day.

Eventually it became obvious I was pregnant - very - I had worked through the heat of the summer, every week I expected Peggy to give me the sack, she never did and I never gave in. I would leave home every morning at 8,30. Push Stephen in the pram uphill about a mile to London Road, struggle to get across the main road, down Crowstone Road, about another mile to the railway line. I would physically pick the pram up and carry it over the bridge then down to Miss Cheeseman's, drop Stephen off and walk down to the cafe.

It would probably spend a full day on my feet without a break, except to eat my sausage and mash. Even that would often be interrupted by someone wanting something, more bread and butter more tea, etc. Then at four o'clock the process of getting home would be repeated.

I kept my appointments with Dr Pearson.

"Now then," he would say, "you are taking things easy aren't you?"

"Of course, doctor"

"You are leading a lady's life, breakfast in bed?"

"Yes," I assured him.

"Well I don't understand this. I'm warning you as things are you are not going to make this pregnancy"

Without working I wouldn't be able to afford the baby. I pressed on thinking doctors don't know everything.

Time was passing, the days were getting colder and the nights were closing in. It was 1962 and it was one of the coldest winters on record. When I picked Stephen up from the nursery and started to push the pram up to the railway line it was already dark. He would run over while I struggled with the pram, then it was the uphill climb to London Road. My bump was big now and I had difficulty holding my water. No I didn't have difficulty, it was impossible, I couldn't hold my wee. It would run out as I pushed the pram up the hill, all down my tights. By the time I got to London Road I was soaked. It was so cold that winter the wee had practically frozen on my legs before I got home. Finally, just a week before Christmas, Peggy and I called it a day.

There was still plenty to do before Christmas, I was desperately worried that I might not be well enough to cope with the cooking. Alan would be home in hours and I was dreading it. The home had to be run as efficiently as Her Majesty's Ships, he certainly wouldn't tolerate dust under the bed. There were still presents to buy.

It was a bitterly cold day and I had nothing to put on my legs, so I pushed the pram to the shops with them bare. Alan wanted some photo frames for his Dad I searched for the right ones. I still had nothing for Alan and I was utterly exhausted. Maybe that accounts for my next action. There in a window were some lovely covers, exactly what we needed for our three piece suite. I'd get him the covers for his Christmas present, sure he would understand. After all it's the thought that counts I persuaded myself plus money was extremely tight..

On Christmas morning he presented me a gold charm for my bracelet; it was a whistle.

"I thought you would like this," he said. "Next time I beat you up you can referee and blow your whistle for time"

I wasn't quite sure about either the gift or his sense of humour, but I didn't have to wait long. He unwrapped the covers I'd bought and went stark raving mad

"Call this a present!"

But it wouldn't have made any difference; if it wasn't the covers it would have been something else, the only certainty was that there would be a row. Thank God when the day came and he could sod off back to the ship and leave me in peace to try and hold on to this baby.

January 14th, the date of my antenatal appointment came. It was bitterly cold and the snow was inches thick as I struggled with the pram against the wind to keep my balance. "You are doing well," the midwife informed me.

As I struggled home with the pram I felt so awful the tears streamed down my face. I took things quietly at home that evening, I knew I wasn't doing well at all. I waited until the morning and I gave my midwife a ring.

"I only saw you yesterday afternoon and you are fine, I'll be in all morning if you need me though"

"Silly cow" I thought, " I rang because I need you now"

I was suddenly quite panicky – not unnecessarily, after saying she would be in all morning the midwife left the house to take her daughter to school. Luckily for me I was on her mind. Later she told me

"I was thinking you are quite sensible, if you rang it would be for a reason, I made a quick detour to check. Just as well I did"

As I opened my front door I got that feeling - if someone stops this world going round, I'll jump off. Then I was gone, unconscious, it was her turn to panic. She called the doctor out of morning surgery and he arrived in record breaking time I think he had always expected that phone call.

To add to the confusion Mum arrived at the same time, Of course Mum would never do anything quietly, she could always be trusted to be dramatic and put on a show. Throwing herself on her knees on the floor she screamed

"Please God don't take her. Give her a life, take me, please."

I heard the doctor say,

"This patient could die of the cold, if nothing else"

With that the midwife opened my wardrobe to get something to keep me warm. I remember thinking how neatly I had stacked my bits and pieces. Later the doctor told me at that time he thought I had died. The flying squad arrived, with orders to crawl as slowly as can be and not to give me any bumps on the way. The doctor told Mum as long as I remained pregnant it was fifty-fifty whether I would survive. He also told her they wouldn't do anything at the hospital to save me at the baby's expense and he said the baby was in the worst position now because it had been starved of oxygen during the time I was unconscious.

Matron met the ambulance, I heard her say,

"We haven't lost a mother here for five years, make sure you don't lose this one."

All was quiet until midday; a lovely nurse was fussing about and I said to her,

"Can I breathe out now, because I'm holding my breath to stop the baby coming."

"Don't be ridiculous," she said. "If that baby wants to come you holding your breath wont stop it."

"Okay,I'll breathe out now."

With that the baby popped out - that made her move,

I heard someone shout,

"Get the mother. not much point delivering a baby one end and letting the Mother slip away at the other end."

The little baby was perfect and a real joy. I just fell in love with her before she was taken away, then I was sedated and placed in a private room.

A day later, barely with it, I realized my lovely doctor was sitting by my bed. I was aware that my mouth was open and I was dribbling. He sat there for ages looking at me, Finally he said,

"I'll remember you on my death bed, you are engraved on my heart in gold. You gave me an awful fright, I thought you had died on me"

I stayed in the private room for five days. The night before I left the staff asked, "Did I have any requests?"

"Could I spend my last night with the other Mums"

I wanted to feel I had been in the maternity hospital, my bed was pushed into the ward. It was visiting time, Mum rushed in with some pink carnations explaining

"Stephen is outside in the taxi crying"

I told her "Don't leave him, I was OK."

I knew my baby was crying and one of the mums came over to tell me.

"I knew but I didn't have the strength to hold her"

I was unaware on the afternoon Alan learned he had become a father again; he was asleep and was woken up to be given the news.

"Another bastard, that baby's not mine, find someone else," he told the messenger.

"I've been at sea for a year, I've not been home long enough for her to have a baby. Well not one of mine"

But having this baby had been his idea in the first place. At Christmas he hadn't noticed how ill I had looked or how tired I had been, He wasn't interested. From day one the doctor had said I wouldn't make it and he was almost right, I nearly didn't. I had struggled as hard as I could to get the hire purchase paid off and in doing so I had risked both our lives.

The first night I was home from hospital Alan phoned and was surprised when I answered. He wanted the baby called Ruth. Where that came from I have no idea, there was no discussion so "Ruth" it was with "Elizabeth" after my wonderful grandmother. When Alan did eventually come home Stephen rushed to the door and excitedly told him where the baby was, he wanted so much to show his dad his little sister.

"I'll have my tea first," was his cold reply.

When he did finally see the baby he said

"It makes me feel sick to look at her"

Funny thing that it made me feel sick to look at him.

It was 1963 one of the coldest winters on record. The snow was too deep for me to consider going out I stayed indoors happily with my little boy, nursing my baby. they were relaxed carefree days. The baby had to be kept warm and I needed to build my strength up. Finally after six weeks the great day arrived when I put Ruth in the pram and sat Stephen at the other end. Exited about the new addition to my family, I met a neighbour.

"You are so brave," she said,

"I think it is wonderful of you to have adopted a baby and pretend she is yours"

"But, she is mine" I protested.

With all the drama the morning Ruth was born and Mum would have added to it, I think the people around me all thought there had been a death.

Mum and Dad were delighted but poor Dad said he had one regret. He knew he wouldn't live to see the children grow up. He died ten months later in his sleep.

It had been a quiet time for Mum and Dad, Mum was working very hard to keep the home going. Dad was now in his seventies, very frail and he spent a lot of time alone, which made me sad. Mum would never alter her habits, no way would she give up her card school or her nights out at the dogs. She turned up one day with two tickets to see the game show, Take Your Pick with Michael Miles It was being recorded in London.

"Did you want to go," she asked.

"I'd like that"

I got a babysitter and off we went.

I had an idea Mum fancied her chances of getting on the show and winning a big prize. At forty-eight she was in her prime; she'd been to the hairdressers and had an air about her that people warmed to. If she had met the quizmaster in person I'm sure she would have twisted him around her little finger but things don't always go your way. I sensed she was keyed up as we were shown to our seats about five rows from the front.

In Take Your Pick, there were twelve contestants and twelve boxes, plus box number thirteen. Answering three questions correctly won a key –the boxes contained either a fabulous prize or a booby and one key also opened box number thirteen. The quizmaster would try to buy the key off the contestant, who had to decide whether to take the money or take a chance. We weren't sure how the contestants got picked, but finally Michael Miles came on stage and got the show started.

"I've got a coach party here from Milton Keynes," he said.

Cheers, clapping, foot stamping from Milton Keynes party

when they had a mention. "Anyone from Milton Keynes want to come on the show?" he asked.

More cheers, shouts of,

"Yes."

"Right," said Michael, "I want one of you to stand up and give a commentary on an imaginary horse race."

Someone did stand up and they were brilliant.

"WE have our first contestant," said Michael.

Mum looked a bit flat.

"If that's how it's done," she said, "We don't have a chance, sitting here on our own." Next someone from a party of office workers had to be a market trader selling tights with three legs. So it went on, it was a riot, it's exciting to see how talented people are. By the time eleven contestants had been picked the audience ached with laughter. Looking directly at me and pointing a finger Michael said, "That lady with the dark hair in the red dress"

I put my hand on my heart and mouthed to him, "ME?"

"Yes, you, please would you stand up,"

I was in such a panic, no way was he going to get me to make a fool of myself, it would only take me a second to sit down again.

"What's your name?" he asked. "Are you married? followed by, "What does your husband do?"

"My husband is serving in the Royal Navy, he's at sea at the moment" Michael had been in the Navy and was very pro the services.

"Please join us and be our last contestant," he said.

It was so exciting, I couldn't believe it. The make-up lady was fussing around all the other contestants, each more nervous than the one next to them. Me, I was petrified, shaking when my turn came I was sorry I was up there. What if I couldn't answer the questions? They were easy and I picked the key to open box seven, my lucky number. Bells were ringing everywhere, it was the key to open box thirteen as well. First Michael would try to buy the keys from me. No way was I going to open the box. I came from a gambling family and tonight it was my turn to throw caution to the wind and gamble; if it was a booby so be it. Michael was offering more and more money, the audience were geeing me on,

"Open the box, open the box," they chanted. Quite determined I was going to open the box, I kept shaking my head and saying, "No, thank you"

The money had gone up to what seemed to me a fortune and as with determination I said, "No," again, I saw Mum she was screaming,

"Have you gone mad!"

Michael made an even higher offer and so I quickly said,

"I'll take it."

Everyone went very quiet as he counted out the money in my hand, then I had to open both boxes. Would you believe there was a booby in each? Mum would have gambled to the end but she just didn't want me to take any chances. The show went out in three weeks and I'd be counting the days to watch it.

I rushed round to tell Dad all about it, although Mum had already told him everything. He was so pleased for me and said how much he was looking forward to hearing me. His old eyes couldn't see but he could listen. He didn't live to hear me, he died the week of the show.

The night Dad died was weird. It could just be a coincidence. I woke at three in the morning feeling dreadful. I was freezing cold yet the sweat was oozing out of my pores. It didn't surprise me to hear the doorknocker going at seven in the morning. I knew someone would be standing there to tell me Dad had died at 3 a.m.

Sure enough John was standing there.

"Dad's gone, Leila. He went at 3 o'clock"

It was almost as if Dad's spirit had tried to say,

"Goodbye."

A daft thought, it was as if he had left something unsaid and he was trying to tell me; too late now, he was gone. I went to see him in the chapel of rest. He looked at peace, holding his hand I said to him,

"You know I've lost my best friend."

I reminded him of the TV show in a few days' time and I told him off because he was going to miss it. But I said,

"I know you will be there with me."

The night the show went out Mum bought a bottle of wine and sat with me to watch. The show was great and next morning out shopping I bumped into a neighbour.

"Saw you on the telly last night" she said "You looked beautiful"

It was a rare moment of happiness, a bit of excitement tinged with regret that Dad had missed it. When I finally spoke to Alan he said he had watched it in the mess with his mates.

"You looked deaf, dumb and stupid "he said

I couldn't believe Dad was lying in the morgue up the road. It was still a couple of days to the funeral and having been Jewish all his life he had become a Catholic, I can't say Mum was distraught with grief, she was just a little quiet. To me she was a very capable lady and I never gave any thought to her future. Still young and beautiful she had everything going for her, a lovely flat, a wide circle of friends, I assumed life would go on as it was, I certainly gave no thought to her coming to live with me. For one thing, Alan would have a fit, but if I had to chose between my mother or Alan there would have been no contest. For now she seemed in control. I had no idea then that as the car came to take Dad away she would immediately move in with John. They had always been close and she could continue her gambling and nights out at the dogs with John.

Not many weeks had passed when Mum called

" John is moving and there isn't a place for me, I had nowhere to go."

"Well, you had better come here," I said. "In fact, you should have come here when Dad died."

She could always put on an act and still doing the old sob stuff she said,

"You never asked me"

I hardly had the chance, she was gone in a flash. I never bothered to ask what she had done with a flat full of possessions. Shortly afterwards she arrived with everything she had in the world in a suitcase.

"You know he's had everything."

I didn't need to ask her to expand. I knew about the two thousand pounds John owed her. In 1964 I suppose that was a lot of money and I'm sure when she had nothing she would have liked it repaid. It never happened. She sat deep in thought and from her attitude I guess she thought her life was over. I made the tea.

"You know," she said again wearily, "I spent all my young life working to support two kids that weren't mine."

Mum appeared tired out, confused – sad.

So much for the two wealthy Aunts who'd taken on Jack's son and daughter when his wife died.

While I was running around without a pair of shoes on my feet

John and Betty were being mollycoddled and spoilt on my mum's back.

Mum settled in straight away, not that I saw much of her working all day, she came home for a good home-cooked meal, then it was off to the Casino or a card school. She was no bother. The worst task was writing to Alan and telling him we had a lodger. Well, she'd provided a home for him for long enough, now the boot was on the other foot.

A year passed. Over breakfast one morning Mum reminded me it was Auntie Una's birthday and she was forty-something or other.

"Gosh." I said, "isn't she young."

When I was young - eight, nine or ten - and she looked after me in Ireland Auntie Una seemed so old. Now I was a mother of two and Una in her forties, she was suddenly so young.

Mum could always put on an act and with a tear just ready to roll down her cheek she said,

"I'm only a year older."

"Well here you are, still only a baby, you have a whole life to live yet!"

With that Mum decided the world was her oyster, rushed out to get a paper and go job-hunting. Fairly soon she got a job as cook/housekeeper to a very wealthy millionaire bachelor in London. I never saw his flat or knew who he was but was told it was full of priceless paintings. Soon I learned she was spending her day off with someone living in Basildon. Jewish like Dad. He was a bachelor in his fifties and they married three years after Dad's death. Mum was fifty-one, he was fifty six. The old Mum hadn't changed her spots; when she was down I was always there, without question, but as soon as she got going I was out in the cold again.

She told me her husband-to-be didn't like children and that her grandchildren weren't welcome at the wedding. Harold, her new husband, might be a thorough gentleman, well educated and financially secure but someone who didn't want my children could get stuffed. On the morning of the wedding, I sent them a telegram wishing them all the happiness in the world. It might have been different if it was a huge, posh wedding but apparently they made the journey on their own to Brentwood, stopped two people in the street and asked them to be witnesses, then travelled back to Southend for a small reception with about half a dozen people.

I couldn't work out here children would have upset things. After that whenever the children and I saw Harold we couldn't get away quick enough.

He was a very quiet gentle person, for whom manners were paramount. Confrontation was not in his nature. One evening he was so fed up he picked up the phone and told me exactly what he thought of my rudeness to him and my children's rudeness.

"What do you expect?" I asked him.

He was amazed at my reply. He hadn't understood why I hadn't come to the wedding. He'd puzzled over it and thought perhaps I considered it disloyal to Dad that Mum had re-married. No way had he said he didn't want the children there. Of course Mum had her defence ready, she wasn't going to let herself down. Back came the usual abuse, she'd had to put up with my lies all her life. I suffer from hallucinations and quarrel with everyone I meet. It wasn't long before Harold got the measure of Mum and we became great friends. He grew to love the children and couldn't see enough of them.. I find it odd that I got on so well with both of my step-fathers – me being a Catholic and both of them being Jewish. One day he said I was all he had. He and Mum were married for more than twenty years and Mum was widowed for the second time at seventy three.

Chapter 13

Ruth was now several months old and like all babies was getting bigger. Stephen, very dark, looked just like me, no-one would argue who he belonged to. Ruth, on the other hand, was pale and looked like neither of us. She could have been fathered by a total stranger which didn't help matters. It seemed that Alan was treating his daughter as he treated all the other women in my family. He considered his Mother-in-law the wickedest woman in the world and of course was so allergic to me, accused me of being a health hazard. Ruth, like the two of us another female might only have been a baby but she knew. One day Alan took her out in the car, throwing her at me on his return as he shouted

"Take her, the little cow's wet all over the seat!"

Ruth often shit herself when Alan was around. Another time I left the children at home while I popped out to the shops; when I came back Stephen was playing but there was no sign of Ruth.

"Where's Ruth?" I asked.

Alan had locked her in the dark oak wardrobe in our bedroom. How naughty could that little tot possibly have been? I opened the door in a panic to find Ruth sitting on the floor keeping as quiet as a mouse. She just looked up at me with her big eyes – already she knew better than to cry.

There was the time Alan threw a small cuddly teddy bear with such force it took a whole glass window out. When he came back with the new window pane he fell and it smashed. It was worth the hiding he gave me because I was doubled up with laughter. But joking aside things were getting scary. There is absolutely no suggestion that Alan would deliberately hurt the kids but all it would take for an accident to happen would be one unlucky blow, or something thrown in a fury that hit the mark

I worried constantly about what I would say to the police if anything did happen, or what the neighbours would say. They would whisper amongst themselves that I must have known he was violent and had allowed it to happen, it would all be my fault.

From day one of the marriage, I think I knew the day would

133

come when I had to get out. In the 50s and 60s Domestic Violence was as much a taboo subject as illegitimacy. That word "taboo" sounds so stupid when no one knew it existed. No one talked about it, the police didn't get involved, they turned a blind eye, claimed they couldn't interfere in relations between husband and wife. If people were told about the violence they hardly ever believed it. There was nowhere for the battered and abused wife to go so women just put up with there violent lives, kept their mouth and their front door shut

What puzzled me was that all this was because I was born out of wedlock, as they say. I had no say in the matter. Yet Alan, who considered himself intelligent was perpetrating an even worse crime freely, was committing it off his own choosing. One thing he forgot in between his ranting like a madman, I was abandoned the day I was born. You grow tough in those circumstances and I considered myself a far stronger character than he, even if he was a Petty Officer in Her Majesty's Navy.

I knew I had the strength to support my two children on my own. What life would be like I had no idea but I knew I would be failing my children if I allowed them to grow up in such violence. Worry as much as I did, I found it hard to make the break and renege on my wedding vows. It was like having a sick animal around. I had to be sure, needed time to say my goodbyes and make peace with myself over what I was thinking of doing. When I put that sick animal down (i.e. sue for divorce) I had to be sure there would be no regrets. Another year or so passed and unbelievably we had been married for nine years. Alan was home on a week's leave. One evening we were both slumped in our armchairs, one each side of the fireplace. Alan sleeping - to an outsider a scene of domestic bliss. Half waking, he must have completely forgotten where he was. Sitting up and stretching he said,

"I'd love of cup of coffee, Margaret."

"Who the hell is Margaret?

While Alan was trying to get his act together I said

"It's a pity she isn't here to make it. I've had enough."

He was immediately back to his old self.

"Oh! Here we go again, you're crazy, imagining things. She works at the base. Her old man's a friend of mine.

Where have we all heard that one before?

"Oh yes?" I said

"I like her kids – I'll invite them all here – that will prove how paranoid you are, madwoman"

"You're not bringing your bit of spare into this house," I told him.

Now we were back to the usual routine.

"I'll bring who I fucking well liked to my own home. It's my house – remember? I'll get you committed if it's the last thing I do, then everyone, especially me, can get on with our lives."

An anonymous phone call a couple of weeks later told me Alan and Margaret were laughing their heads off behind my back.

"No, they're not," I told the caller, "Everything's under control"

She was welcome to the bastard but I still had to be sure. If Alan had had one streak of decency or honesty in his bones I would have found it acceptable if he had said,

"Look, I've met someone else. You have a divorce, I'll leave the roof over the kids heads."

He possibly still had this crackpot dream idea that somehow I was going to die. What of, for God's sake, I was as tough as an old boot, every bit a match for him. He had nothing to lose now and the rows became even more violent.

One evening I was so scared I grabbed the children and ran to the police station for protection. I told them I was afraid for my children's lives and my own. What those two babies sitting on that long bench in the station thought God alone knows. Talking and laughing among themselves the police kept us waiting for an hour, which unnerved me even further. They then decided to be kind offering us a lift home. To protest any further would have made things worse for the kids, so we quickly got into the police car. The policeman escorted us to the front door and knocked. I stood there silently, the children beside me. I wanted to scream, fall on my knees, beg not to be returned to the home, but that would have been too traumatic for the kids. Alan, cool and calm, answered the door.

"Have you hit your wife?" asked the stupid policeman.

"By accident, I assure you," replied Alan very pleasantly.

"Promise there won't be another accident,"

The policeman was still being pretty stupid.

"Of course not," Alan's promise oozed charm and sincerity. He was good at charm.

Placing one hand on the front door and pushing it wide open, the policeman placed his other hand on my back and firmly pushed me indoors. I wanted desperately to make a last protest, but those two children following me in would be even more confused and I knew as far as the police were concerned it would fall on deaf ears. I put Stephen and Ruth to bed as calmly as I could, kissing them goodnight. Calmly and slowly I left. Absolutely mortified I stood outside their closed bedroom door for a while. There was no alternative but to join Alan and face the music. I went into the front room closing the door behind me, terrified.. It was as if a button had been pressed, up until then he had stayed in control but now.......?

"How dare you go to the police and show ME up like that." You take the hiding hoping and praying you are going to survive the night.

It is appalling that a human being should find themselves in such a position.

Things were deteriorating more quickly than ever; when I laid the table for meals I always set a carving knife beside my plate. I knew what was going on at Portsmouth and I knew Alan wasn't going until he had every penny. He underestimated me; I would fight for my kid's as long as I had breath in my body. Mind you I thought often about that carving knife. I'd rest my hand on it for comfort, resisting the temptation to plunge it into his heart. I was quite determined there would be a life for me after Alan and killing him might have made that life a little more difficult. Besides, how would I face Stephen and Ruth and say

"You did have a Father but unfortunately I killed him."

As autumn approached it seemed as if Alan came home to start a fight deliberately, hoping to wear me down. This particular evening I decided to have an early night and get out of his way. I didn't want a fight so I went to bed to get some peace and quiet. When he finally came to bed I felt two feet flat in the middle of my back and I was kicked out of bed on to the floor.

"I'm not sleeping with a bastard," he shouted.

I didn't reply that was alright with me, if that was how he felt I wasn't looking for a fight. On the contrary I was looking for nothing but peace. I went into the lounge and made myself comfortable on the settee. In a rage Alan stormed in and pulled me off the settee by the hair on my head. I wasn't to sleep in a chair either. He dragged me across the hall into the bedroom and dropped me on the floor. I was wearing a thin nightdress and there was no central heating and I was to lie on the floor uncovered like a dog. Except that even a dog normally has a blanket or a basket. Emphasizing each word with his boot he told me to stay there and make sure I didn't move. Every time he got up in the night to relieve himself from his drinking, he would put on his leather slippers and kick me as hard as he could as he passed.

Next morning, exhausted, freezing and very stiff I went into the bathroom to wash. As I tried to lift the flannel to my face the pain was unbearable. It was far too tender to bathe around my hairline where the hair had almost been pulled out by it's roots. With gentle dabbing the warm water brought a little comfort. I asked my reflection in the bathroom mirror how it would all end. Yet I cooked breakfast as if nothing had happened, although I knew the violence was becoming really dangerous.

A few weeks later, like any normal couple we went out for a meal, just the two of us, so there was no room to accuse me of flirting as he might if another couple had been with us. On the way home as he was driving downhill Alan suddenly leant over, opened the car door and tried to push me out. Was he really trying to kill me? What would have happened if I had fallen out and been run over by a following car? Would he have told the police I jumped or would he have wept crocodile tears, saying

"My wife can't have closed the door properly. I was always telling her to be careful"

Once again I wondered why he didn't just walk away – but I knew the answer. He wasn't going empty handed. He was going to make sure he got what there was to get. Even more amazing to me now, however bad the fights were, he never went without what he called his "rights."

When we were first married I would get a good hiding over nothing and then he would want to make love. I told myself then that he really did love me, that he needed me and wanted me. One day he would suddenly change back to the man I'd thought I was marrying. It was one of the reasons I hung in there waiting for the breakthrough.

I know now that most women in this kind of relationship hope all the time it will change, until the day they either realize it won't or they are killed. One day when we are both old and grey, the children grown up and we are grandparents, Alan would say,

137

"Sorry."

But the going was getting too rough and I could see there was no fairy tale ending. I would rather have two bloody good hidings one after the other than be beaten once and then have to succumb to forced sex.

The end came very quickly, if you can class as quick ten years of marriage with nothing but hassle from day one. As Alan approached the back door, home for another weekend, he was still my husband so I opened the door to greet him. I felt his fist in my face — bang. What was that all about?

"I didn't like the expression on your face," he told me I didn't know at that moment it was going to be the last together. It was the whistle of the kettle that ended a ten-year nightmare. Remember the old fashioned kettles with a whistle on the spout? When the kettle boiled the whistle screeched and you knew the water was hot. Saturday was as usual, criticism about this and that, looking under the bed and finding a speck of dust. I was working full-time with two kids, but deserved a punch for dust under the bed. When I got up Sunday morning once again an attempt had been made to rearrange my face. As the children came in for breakfast, Stephen was old enough to see the bruises, you couldn't hide them, but all was calm. The carving knife was in place. I stroked it once or twice. Sunday dinner was happy families played to the full. In the afternoon the children went to their rooms Stephen to play and Ruth for a sleep in her cot. I had washed up after dinner and was in my bedroom, tidying up. Only another couple of hours he would be away; I would have survived another weekend. When the neighbours saw my face in the morning they would know he had been home. They were used to it by now and would ask,

"Been walking into doors again Mrs B?"

Domestic violence had no place in any vocabulary,

Alan suddenly appeared in the bedroom, pushed me roughly on the bed and without one word helped himself. Suddenly there was this loud screech, he had put the kettle on and in the short time it took to boil he was going to rape me, because that was what it was. There isn't another word for it. He finished what he was doing and without another word got up and left the bedroom. I rolled off the bed and fell on my knees and resting my head in my hands on the bed I tried not to cry. I had to be brave for the children but I vowed it would never,

ever happen again. I was no longer willing to be made to feel so dirty, be so degrades and used. This isn't living I told myself, I have reached the time when that sick animal has to be put out of his misery.

The next morning I went to see a Solicitor. I was prepared to go through detail after detail of the rows and the violence. All the bruises had been measured and recorded during my many visits to the doctor's over the years.

"Start with the first day of the marriage," the solicitor said.

It was painful to tell a complete stranger the details of that first day when Alan had asked me to explain the marriage certificate. I had to repeat his words

"I've married a bastard. Had I have known, I'd never have married you."

"You've got your divorce," the Solicitor informed me. Alan had a good laugh when he was informed I was divorcing him.

"Your head's buried in the sand if you think you'll get away with it." He had just been given a medal for fifteen years' good conduct in the navy, so a nutter like me trying to sue him wouldn't get very far. From day one of our marriage he had been a pig, he'd given me crabs, had been up in court for not paying his dues, and now he was accusing me of trying to get away with something, one of us was definitely mad.

To boast about his good conduct medal from the Navy – well, shame on the Navy. He thought I was weak because I didn't fight back when I was being punched and kicked, if I had I would be dead. I was going to let him see what fighting was from now on. He was about to be given a lesson on the rules in Civvy Street, not Royal Navy rules,

A horrendous three months later I got my divorce on the grounds of cruelty. During this time Alan made a point of coming home, where he would alternate between laughing at me or shouting. He would go through the place tipping everything on to the floor, all the stuff in the wardrobes, emptying out the chest of drawers and any cupboards. When he left the place had been ransacked.

"You do as you please but not in my house." he would say.

Chapter 14

The day of the divorce hearing arrived. I was nervous as I approached the Court House. I wasn't looking forward to seeing Alan nor listening to his ranting, but my solicitor as he greeted me added that Alan wouldn't be attending and wasn't going to contest the divorce. That was a surprise although it made sense; behaviour like his was the mark of a coward so he wouldn't have the guts to face me in court, where he might be shown up for the BASTARD he was.

As I took the oath I looked at the Judge and was warmed by his kind expression, but when his questions started I began to get worried. All I could do was tell the truth. Was he biased in favour of men, especially service men, maybe he had even served in the navy. At one point, I thought he would grant Alan the divorce, but it wasn't a contest. Whoever won we were both losers. I didn't much care who got the divorce as long as the marriage was over. The Judge said

"Perhaps your husband has strong views about bastards, has he?"

That seemed to me both a statement and a question, but I answered honestly. "Yes, he has very strong views."

I said also that I felt sorry for Alan, that everyone is entitled to their opinions and that I completely understood his views, but I had no idea he felt that way. In the three years we were courting the issue never came up. I explained the two different religions, Catholic married to a Jew and the two different names. Nobody, I said, had set out to lie to him or trap him, I only wish I had known how he felt. He never asked a question and I'd often wonder what was in his mind all those years. The Judge sat quietly reading some papers, then he looked up at me.

"This is the worst case of cruelty I've ever come across."

Granting me a divorce on the grounds of cruelty he gave me care and custody of my two children. He said he understood an eviction order was coming up in another court, to get us out of the house and that I was entitled to have something. I was awarded five pounds a week for life or until I remarry and two pounds fifty for each child. A measly ten pounds to keep his two children was peanuts, an absolute pittance, but I didn't want a penny. I wanted him to leave the kids in their home, not order them to be thrown onto the streets so he could provide a home for this other woman. Mum sat through the court hearing and afterwards she said she was taking me out to lunch.

"I saw you into this marriage and I'll see you out," was her comment.

She ordered a large steak each and double cherry brandies followed by a couple more cherry brandies. Chatting away, not once did she mention the morning's events or say a thing about the past. Even though Mum was in a calm, relaxed mood I knew not to test it. One thing Mum had in common with Alan was a large mouth. Neither of them knew when to stop, when on the attack they always went for the jugular.

A few days later with the eviction notice in my hand I went to the Council. It was still possible to put married women and their children out in the street, homeless and penniless, if that was the husband's wish. Not that it happened very often because few couple's got divorced, women had to put up with worthless lives to keep a roof over their heads. We had been in the bungalow only three years but had put down quite a large deposit. If I couldn't have the house I wanted half of every penny he got and I was going to fight for it. I owed it to my kids. Let him and this woman of his marry with sixteen pounds in their pockets as we had done and work for what they wanted, not take the roof from over the kids' heads. That was the second thing I was never going to forgive.

The Council offered me a house in Tennyson Avenue, for which I was very grateful. The only thing it was lacking was fleas. It had everything else. The toilet was outside and the wind blew through as you sat there. The back door had a frame so you could lock it but the door itself was just a few slats of board. There was an antique butler sink in the kitchen. Double glazing or central heating was definitely out. The bath had no enamel on it and the first time I tried to bath Ruth, she wouldn't sit down. I was so tense I smacked her legs from under her.

The last occupants had dumped a double mattress in the overgrown garden and there were needles everywhere in the long grass. I don't know whether stray dogs got into the garden and tore at the mattress, large holes appeared in it. One day there was a gale and I arrived home from work to see thousands of feathers all over the neighbours' gardens. Yes, life was going to be hard.

Years later, our happy humble home was refurbished and we loved it. We lived there for twenty-five years. My life had been spent constantly moving around, being settled was everything to me.

The bungalow had been sold and Alan was waiting for his cheque. It was in his name and he wanted it all. I was going to get nothing. I was still fighting. His problem was that he had temporarily forgotten I was mad and should be certified. He should have remembered, he had spent years trying to drive me bleeding mad. In my madness, I reckoned I might as well keep fighting in court spend the proceeds from the sale of the bungalow. Weeks passed, I wasn't in any hurry. He was screwed up trying to beat me and finally he stormed home and shrieked at me:

"If you keep going the way you're going there'll be nothing left."

He wouldn't dare hit me now, we were divorced. It was time for me to be in control so I calmly told him

"I'm going to keep fighting, I'll make damned sure I get half of your nothing. Isn't that how mad people think?"

It worked - he gave in and that was the last I heard of it. I was amazed that the Judge awarded me half, it was only the second time in the country that had happened. Now the married women's property act is law so women don't have to go through what I had had to go through. In a final settlement the court gave Alan the car while I had the furniture, I was pleased about that - at least I had a start.

My heart was full of hope, although my worst nightmare had come true - I was not only a bastard, now I was divorced. Life was going to be bitter sweet, bitter because I was on my own with two kids. Sweet because I was free, no longer would that bastard come through the door and completely humiliate and degrade me. Life would be hard but it would be a good life.

One day I sat the two children down for a chat, not that they understood one word of what I said. They were too young. I think I wanted to hear myself say those things aloud. I told them that there couldn't be anything else bad ahead.

"We are at rock bottom, we can't get any lower which means there is only one way to go and that is up!"

I promised them I would do everything in my power to make

142

things a success. I would work as hard as I could and in return, I wanted them to work just as hard.

"I only have one ambition in life, there is one thing I want to be able to say on my deathbed, I gave my kids a chance"

No-one had ever given me a chance, not since I left Ireland.

I was quite determined that I would not take one penny from Social Services. When the children started school they each had the ten pence for their dinner money in their little hands. There were no free bus passes, I got them around under my own steam. I had felt different all my life and knew how it screwed a soul up. It would be over my dead body if my children were made to feel different at school. I had the ten pounds a week the court had given me and I would earn the rest. I would scrub floors, peel potatoes, wash up, whatever it took.

Six weeks passed after the divorce and I hadn't received a penny from Alan. He was probably enraged that he didn't get all the proceeds from the bungalow, but if he thought he would get out of paying he had a nasty lesson coming. I would have preferred to have told him to get stuffed but I needed that bit of support the courts gave me. I did phone him and got his woman, she already had her feet under the table. If anyone had told her I was a mouse who could be walked all over she was going to find out otherwise. I reminded her when she lay on her back for my husband (which at that time he still was) she knew he had two children, one a baby still being nursed. I was so furious I could have ripped the two of them to pieces. I made it quite clear that before she put a cigarette in her mouth my kids would eat.

"You're welcome to each other but not at my kids' expense" were my final words

All through the worst times I had been working with Paul. He would sometimes give me a look and ask,

"Are you alright?"

"Yes," I would say, all bright and breezy.

We three had settled down in our little home. Stephen was doing well at school and Ruth was with Miss Cheeseman. Every morning Miss Cheeseman brought her little charges for a walk along the sea front. Ruth's big eyes would stare at me as she passed the cafe, but although I smiled and waved there was never a return smile from her. She held on to the side of the pram and walked along looking

143

back until I was out of sight. I have never forgotten the look on her little face, almost as if she was never going to forgive me. I'm nor sure she ever has. I could easily beat myself up and go down a guilt road. I was such a hard mum and I made so many mistakes but I believed at the time I was doing the right thing. We didn't have to be so poor, there was help available from Social Services but my pride stopped me.

Time was passing, funnily enough it always does; Stephen was seven and Ruth four. Mr. Grimes, Stephen's headmaster asked me to call in at St. Helen's school. A charming man, I liked him very much He said he was concerned about the children and wanted to know how I was coping. He understood the major problem for me, getting the two of them to different places every morning and picking them up in the evening. "Look, why not leave Ruth here with Stephen, she won't be on the register for another year but we will look after her."

That brilliant offer made my world suddenly very bright.

I didn't want to waste my life. I wanted to do something with it, achieve something. After my experiences, I would be good at marriage counselling. I would certainly understand people's problems so that was what I would do. I applied to join the Marriage Guidance Council – now called Relate. Everything was doing fine, the meetings were good, it was achieving my ambition to have an outside interest and there were loads of text books to read. The next task for me was to talk to a panel for ten minutes on Oral Sex. Now I know I'm wrong - I'm sure there was a reason for it. The experts will say we have to sweep out the tough from the shy etc. but I couldn't see what that had to do with people's problems. Whatever the explanation was I didn't hang around to find out. Remember this was 1960 and although I had been married ten years I had never heard of oral sex let alone experienced it. I couldn't talk on the subject for ten seconds let alone ten minutes. I felt they had lost a good candidate.

Next I joined the Labour Party, meeting there didn't suit me so I joined the Conservative Party. That was the start of a twenty-five year roller-coaster ride.

Early one Saturday evening shortly after the divorce the phone rang. Alan and his woman were on their way round to take the children out.

"They're swimming in the Gala tonight," I told him.

"We'll be there,"

And he put the phone down.

We, I thought, suddenly very nervous. Feeling very odd as I sat in the back row at the swimming pool. My children's father here with another woman. She's got some nerve, hasn't she got any shame, I wondered. All the other mums and dads had been my friends for some time and it felt very embarrassing. As fate would have it there was an empty seat next to me. I turned round to see if they had arrived I saw the blushing bride-to-be standing at the back looking as if she owned the place. I lifted a finger and beckoned to her to come over which she did. It was the first meeting between the first and the soon-to-be-second Mrs B.

"As you've insisted on coming tonight, would you please sit here" I patted the seat beside me. "You're making my bleeding nerves bad standing behind me."

This woman duly sat down and looking at me she said,

"The trouble with you is you don't understand Alan."

I looked at her in utter amazement,

"You're quite right, I'm afraid I don't understand BASTARDS."

I almost laughed out loud. I didn't understand Alan! Bleeding cheek. who the hell did she think she was! When I had calmed down I couldn't resist a sideways glance. She looked a lot older than me, her skin was dull and colourless, there was nothing pretty about her, even her clothes were matronly. It certainly wasn't her looks that had won him over. It wasn't a lack of the other either because he never went without; I didn't have a choice. She must have felt she had died and gone to heaven. After all Alan was still a very handsome man, if you liked that sort of thing. Outside, after the Gala, she stuck something like a cigar in her mouth - smoking, UGH! Alan's pet hate.

Some time later Alan phoned again

"We are going to take the kid's for a week, show them our new home."

It wasn't a case of "would it be convenient?" or "would I mind?" He still acted as though he had the upper hand and he hardly knew the kids.

It would be over my dead body was my first private reaction but I knew it was one argument I wouldn't win. Alan would go back to the courts and he would get visiting rights. Then he could always use it as a weapon against me and I didn't intend giving him any ammunition.

I was distraught at the thought of parting with my children. I thought perhaps the answer was for one to go and one to stay with me, but which one could I bear to part with. In the end, mustering up all my strength, I packed their favourite little bits and pieces and when Alan arrived I gently pushed them out the door with a big smile

"Have a lovely time, be good for Mummy"

Then I sat on the stairs and cried for hours. I hadn't expected Alan to tell the kids to give me a ring. I knew better than to expect kindness from him, but was it too much to hope that woman, who had kids of her own, would say to my children,

"Give mum a ring."

She must have known I would be worried. Would I find out they had changed their names and disappeared? When you're in that state all kinds of weird thoughts go through your head. Finally on the Friday evening with the week almost up, I thought I was entitled to phone. Alan couldn't accuse me of interfering after all these days so, heart in my mouth, I dialled. It was such a relief, yes, they would be home tomorrow. I spoke to both kids all bright and breezy but I could hear the tension in their voices.

Suddenly they were home, to their favourite tea in front of the TV. I asked them no questions. I was simply so pleased to have us back together. I wasn't one bit interested in those other two people.

It was weeks later Stephen had gone to play football. Ruth and I were walking down the High Street.

"Mummy," she said.

"Yes, darling,"

"If you knew how naughty Daddy was you would never let us see him again"

My ears pricked up. Whatever happened that week when they stayed over? Ruth told me when she and Stephen got up on the Tuesday morning Alan and Margaret were quarreling. Alan punched Margaret in the eye. She threw a teapot and broke it. I was always too mean to throw anything. Besides when it was smashed I couldn't afford to replace it, so better not to throw it in the first place.

Alan then punched her again. Ruth said they were terrified. Suddenly he grabbed them and ushering them out of the door, took them right around the streets until they came to a park.

"Stay here until I come back for you," he told them.

But he didn't come back, cold, hungry, thirsty and frightened they decided to try and remember their way back to the bungalow, scared of what they would find. I was appalled, Anything could have happened, I never let them out of my sight. I couldn't get it out of my mind. I would have his guts for garters. But as things were the children never mentioned their dad. So while things were quiet leave well alone.

Months passed without a word from him. Birthdays were ignored, Christmas came and went without even a card. Time stretched into years and there still this complete silence. Even the old grandad down the road, Alan's father, never got in touch with us.

The children never mentioned Alan, he seemed completely out of their lives.

I still kept a large photo of Alan in the lounge. I had always, even in my darkest hours, kept the picture in pride of place in the house. It was my way of reminding the children of their father. It is very important to know you have parents and who they are. I was never sure about Mum and I found it difficult to believe she was my mother and my father was unknown. So I insisted the children would know they had a father and not suffer as l had done. I hoped they would grow up without any hang-ups. Not that the children ever mentioned him, nor did they hear me slag him off. Why this picture is being mentioned is because when we were married, every time he came home he would bin the picture. It started a row every time. He accused me of taking the piss and putting it up to wind him up when I knew he was coming home. He never admitted that most of the time I didn't know when that would be, it was just another excuse but the photo stayed in the lounge, at least while they were young.

Shortly after marrying Mum, Harold achieved a lifetimes ambition. They bought a newsagent's and tobacconist's shop in Thundersley, about half an hour's drive from Southend. Secretly I don't think Mum was too thrilled, she hadn't married at her time of life to work one hundred hours a week. Gone were her card-playing days, she really missed the gang of ladies she had being doing battle with for so long. Their card schools seemed like a battle to me, winning was the name of the game. Gone too were her visits to the casino, her dog-racing nights, and her gin-swigging days. In return she had stability, after her life with Dad that had to count for a lot.

147

Out of the blue they got a fantastic offer for the shop, as long as they could move out in twenty-four hours. It wasn't a problem for me, they were welcome to my bedroom for however long it took, so they moved in with their baby - that was a whippet called Nobby. To be honest I was glad to see a few extra pound notes around.

Considering Harold had been a bachelor until he had married Mum - he had lived all his life with his old mum and could be described as being a bit stuffy – he was really laid back with the children. Stephen and Ruth had their own dog - a Chihuahua called Tommy Tucker. The two dogs enjoyed each others company, they played for hours and had us in fits.

Harold would take Nobby for a walk every morning, stop and get the paper, then just relax and have a read. He soon learned the shop around the corner was for sale, so they bought it and as quickly as they had arrived they were gone. There was mixed feelings on my part having Mum live on my doorstep. But I threw my lot in with them and went to work for them.

We were still struggling to fit in with the neighbours, some of them were a rough lot. One family of drunks would shuffle up the road, one or other of them shouting abuse at anyone who tried to pass. They were a disgusting lot, swearing and spitting. Just across the road the lady earned her living in the bars on the seafront; she would prop the bar up one end of the pub and her fourteen-year-old daughter would be in competition propping up the other end. Next door was a young family with seven kids. Neither of them worked; I mean no disrespect to anyone being genuinely unemployed but they were bone-lazy, sat on their fat backsides all day smoking. I had worked my socks off getting my garden straight for myself and the kids. Flowers were in bloom, I had some lovely dahlias; their garden was a wilderness. They had a brainwave one day, only they could have thought of it. They got a goat in to eat its way through the weeds. Naturally it wouldn't enter their heads to tie it up, it cleared my fence and ate all the tops of my beautiful flowers. I yelled at the scruffy bitch next door,

"Get this bleeding goat out of my garden, it's eaten all my flowers."

Her reply is unprintable, but it boiled down to the fact that I was making an awful fuss over a few weeds.

I had another barney with them, when a new family move in

across the road and the two men struck up a friendship. Gossips had it our new neighbour had just come out of jail. Apparently he had a list as long as your arm for robbery, burglary, you name it, he had done it

Disturbed by a noise one night I looked out my bedroom window and saw the two men push something through the back door into next door's kitchen. At that moment I was pleased to see it was only them, God alone knows what they were doing in the middle of the night, it didn't interest me, I would get back to sleep. Just before dawn, I sat bolt upright in bed, in shock. There had been a bang loud enough to waken the dead. It was none of my business, I wasn't going to get involved.. My task was to get us all up, get the kids to school and get myself to work.

I hadn't been at work five minutes when the police came in.

"We're making enquiries about a robbery last night across the road. Anyone see or hear anything"

My big mouth was in overdrive before I could think,

"I could tell you a story," I said.

I hadn't seen a safe but it didn't take too much working out and the police went round to their house. The safe was still in the kitchen, they hadn't managed to blow the door off. When I walked home for my lunch break the police were still there. The two wives were standing on the driveway, With a few choice adjectives added they said in front of the police.

"If we thought it was you who bubbled us, we would tear your guts out and stuff them down your throat,"

I looked at them.

"So you reckon I'm scared of you, I can tell," I was smiling and very cocky,

"I'm scared to death,"

Believe me I was, I was shaking like a jelly, so frightened I sat on the stairs and cried.

Hard as I tried to mind my own business, and keep out of trouble with the neighbours, there was always something. Our house was at a crossroads, on one corner were the Riley's, a tough lot, another large family, eight in all, parents ex-jailbirds. Ivy, a single parent with three kids lived on the opposite corner.

Ivy was quite a character, tall and imposing, her dyed blonde hair was always well combed and she was neatly dressed even if all her clothes did come from jumble sales. However hard she tried she never looked clean. It was probably the cigarette in her mouth non-stop that did the damage. If she asked me in, the white cupboards in her kitchen were dark brown stained by the smoking. Ivy spent her whole day gossiping, she knew everyone's business; what she didn't know, that was her task for the day, to find out. She could swear for England. Her eldest was the same age as my Stephen and as thick as two planks. None of her children went to school, on the rare occasion when they did she gave them instructions on how to play up the teachers. Simple things, telling her kids to walk in a zig zag line when they lined up in the playground to go back to class, anything that would annoy those in charge.

It was difficult really for us, as Stephen and Ruth had both passed their eleven-plus and were both at grammar school; they were away from the estate all day and in the evening they had homework or school activities. We didn't mix, we were not being stuck up, that was the way things were. I was a nobody, trying to get on with my life and do my best for my kids. Ivy was into all sorts of mischief, I liked her but you couldn't trust her. She enjoyed stirring things up and obviously hadn't learned not to mess with my family.

On this particular day Stephen had his best friend from primary school to play. They went out for a ride, it hadn't been many minutes when I saw the two of them running for their lives across the road pushing their bikes. A gang led by the Riley brat, their mouthpiece, had pushed them off their bikes and had started hitting them. There were quite a few kids and the size of the gang had frightened Stephen and his friend.

I phoned Mum to say I wouldn't be at work that afternoon and told her why. She was as cold as ice,

"Are you working here or not, only I can soon get someone else."

I was frightened to leave the children but I couldn't afford to feed   them without working so I told her I would be along, to which she replied, "and don't bring your troubles with you into the shop."

Mum worked in strange ways; days later the Riley brat, a real tearaway from the tip of his head to the tip of is toes, came in for some sweets, His hair looked as though he had stuck his finger in an electric light socket, it stood straight up. Shirt adrift, tear in his trousers and holy socks hanging around his hobnailed boots, he stood with his halfpenny, pondering how to get the most sweets for his money. Mum had been waiting patiently for him and approached him nicely.

"Why did you terrorize my grandson last week?" she asked.

Frightened of no one he wasn't a bit put out by the question, an old biddy like my mum wouldn't phase him. In his Cockney accent he replied,

"Weren't me, Missus, Ivy asked me to do it."

Ivy's son was standing outside the butcher's. Mum pointed to him.

"I'll give you fifty pence" (a fortune to a kid like him in those days) "if you go out there and kick him in the shins."

Out went the Riley brat and landed an almighty kick on his friend's shin. It's OK for their kids to go around in gangs, aided and abetted by the parents, but return the favour and they squeal police.

Two big burly police walked into the shop but Mum was a real hard nut.

"Is it true you gave the Riley kid fifty pence to kick a boy?" they asked.

"What nonsense. Do you honestly think that a lady in my position would do such a thing?"

"We wouldn't have thought so,"

Apologies all around and that was the end of it. I could imagine Ivy - she would be plotting all sorts of revenge, but perhaps she realized she had met her match. It was a message to the urberts on the estate not to mess with us, we would fight fire with fire.

John was around but not that often as Harold had no time for him as long as he made no effort to repay his debts. John was selling second-hand cars for a living and offered to look out for one for me. Years earlier I had learned to drive and acquired an old banger and it had passed its sell-by date. True to his word he found me a "Beauty," and I parted with my hard-earned cash.

I arrived home from work one day to find this superb Austin Cambridge Estate on my drive.

"Wow!"

John had done me proud. I couldn't wait to get the keys off the mat and get going. There wasn't a squeak out of the engine, so I hurried around to the local garage, asked if they would be good enough to drop by and have a look. The mechanic who came laughed.

"You're having a joke with me, aren't you? The Starter Motor is missing"

I wasn't quite sure what that implied but I was furious. I went to tell Mum what had happened and asked if she had an address. She was as angry as could be with me, how dare I criticize her wonderful boy and she bellowed

"John doesn't understand cars, he only sells them."

Then I had a dose of the old chestnut. I was having hallucinations again and she had to put up with it all. In the end all I could do was pay the garage for the repairs. The children were all over the place in the evenings and weekends and a car was essential for taking and collecting them. We would just have to tighten the reins a little for a while, they didn't have a lot of "give" anyway.

Shortly after that incident the phone rang one evening. It was someone from Southend Police Station.

We would like to send a couple of detectives round to speak to you on a very delicate matter.

"What delicate matter?" I wanted to know but they would say no more other than it was delicate.

"They'll be round in a few minutes"

I wasn't too happy to have strangers calling after dark and immediately they got off the phone I dialled the station and asked if the two detectives were genuine. "Why?" asked the copper on the other end. I told him about the call.

"I see - and you are going to be out before they get there."

"No I'm not, you cheeky whatnot,"

I was concerned, what would they want with me.

When they arrived they said

"We want you to look at a photograph and tell us if you know this man. Before you look we want to tell you he is dead. We also want you to know he has been in the sea for some time."

I stood there trying not to be alarmed as they asked

"Are you ready to look at the photo?"

They handed me a large picture of a man's face, his eyes were closed and the face was very clear. I stared at it for some time before asking,

"Who is it?

Isn't it your brother John?"

"Never," I said, "who told you it was?"

152

It was so unlike John it was laughable. The body had been washed up on the beach and the police had published the photo in the local paper. Betty had identified it as her brother, say no more. John had certainly disappeared; rumour had it he had to get out of town - why wasn't I surprised? Eventually he turned up in Bristol, he never came back to Southend, not even for Mum's funeral.

We didn't write or phone for the next twenty or was it thirty years, not until 2002. With Colin (my second husband) we were staying over in Bristol so on the spur of the moment I gave him a call and just said,

"Hi how about me buying you dinner?"

He was just thrilled to bits and we hugged for ever. After all those years of silence the first thing he said was

"I wish I had never sold you that car."

"God, that was a lifetime ago," and sadly it was. Colin had laid the law down as men do, happy as he was to have dinner, he reminded me we had already had a long day and were due an early start, this wasn't going to be a long evening. By two a.m. I was yawning my head off, dying for my bed, while the two men were talking their heads off. Finally I was the one who insisted we went home but that wasn't the end of the night.

"No need for a taxi, I'll drive you" said John.

Then he proceeded to give us a tour of Bristol until three o'clock. By then it was too late to sleep so we sat quietly discussing the evening. Colin thought John was terrific, charming - a real character. For me it was unreal, sitting there with John I could have been sitting with Dad, they were so alike.

Colin wouldn't have a word said against John.

"I know, I totally agree with you. He's all you say, lovable, silver-tongued, just like Dad." Memories came flooding back, I know all about silver-tongued lovable charmers. Sadly for me that's the way to lose all your money.

153

Chapter 14

As quickly as Mum and Harold had bought the shop they had sold it and had retired to Thorpe Bay and I was job-hunting again. It was a desperate daily search, looking through the papers and visiting the job centre. In despair I took a job as a delivery driver in a feather factory. Yes, feathers, millions of them. They had to be delivered to ladies at home making Indian head-dresses.

I had never given much thought to those things, although I had bought a few for Stephen. They have the main feather in the front, then as the feathers go round the head they get smaller, with left and right sides in matching colours. The outworkers would phone for about a thousand head-dresses a week. I had to count the feathers out, collecting them from holding bays as high as the ceiling. I'd begin with the main one in the front. One thousand main feathers, one thousand next size down left, blue, etc, etc, another thousand down right to match. It drove me bleeding crackers, but I had to stick at it for the time being, with the two kids at home depending on me. I worked as many hours as possible but there was never enough money.

When my delivery duties were over for the day, I was expected to help out on the benches, pressing even more bleeding feathers. I was bored to distraction and praying that Stephen and Ruth were keeping their side of the bargain, working as hard as I was to make sure they didn't end up like me. They were holding their own at grammar school so I couldn't have been prouder. It was worth the effort I was making to see them doing so well.

They always had a cooked meal in the evening. I missed my café dinners and in the evenings I was quite hungry but I told them I had already eaten. When they'd finished I would rush into the kitchen and lick the plates. If it was a pork chop I would suck all the juices out of the bones.

The feather stint was ended by some surprising news - Mum and Harold had come out of retirement and they had bought a third shop. I had never been so pleased to be working with Mum. She said I was to have nine pounds a week but Harold had a quiet word with me and said it would be twenty pounds. And not to say a word to Mum and I never did.

Many a time my day would start at 3.30 a.m. - if there were particularly heavy magazines to be delivered, I would do that first, then help Mum and Harold mark the papers for the rounds. Then it was home to get the kids to school. They ate their breakfast in bed, much quicker and it saved any tidying up afterwards. Once they were dropped off at school, it was back for a full day in the shop

Mum and Harold lived over the shop so the children made their way there after school. Their dinner was always ready; prepared between busy periods. I would dish it out, saying

"Get on with it" then fly back downstairs to carry on serving. On one occasion when I dashed back upstairs I noticed their plates hadn't been touched,

"It was awful," they choroused.

They were left in no doubt of what I thought, I wasn't being messed about.

"Make sure those plates are clean next time I come up."

Later, when I was washing up, I was suspicious about something on one of the plates, I put it to my nose and smelled soap. It must have slipped off the draining board into the saucepan in my rush and I had forced them to eat their dinner. Poor kids, it must have tasted dreadful. Life was at full stretch for all of us, I'd no time for anything, nor for the children and certainly not for myself.

As they do, the years were passing and it was 1974, Stephen was fifteen and six feet tall, Ruth was coming up to being a teenager. Alan was totally out of their lives, there had never been a birthday or Christmas card. He must have come to Southend as his father and stepmother lived not far away.

It was Mothering Sunday I returned from my morning in the shop and was surprised to see there were no parking spaces.

"I'll just stop here for a moment while I check the kids are alright,"

I knew it wouldn't be long before there would be a knock on the door and some irate neighbour would be complaining. Sure enough the bell rang. I opened the door with the words,

"Yes, I know, my car's...." coming out of my mouth as I looked at the stranger standing on the step. My brain was telling me to shut my mouth as stared at the grey-haired man with the fat face I couldn't remember how many years it had been and I hardly recognised Alan. I showed him into the lounge, where his first word, even before he greeted the children were,

"So you do keep that photo there."

For some reason the photo was still in the centre of the room.

Sitting on the floor looking up at him was his clone. Ruth had his hair, eyes, skin, nose, mouth and teeth. I will never forgive Alan for daring to suggest the day she was born when we both almost lost our lives, that she wasn't his.

I didn't occur to me straight away that he would be out of the navy now. He'd done his twenty-two years and would have received a golden handshake It was 1974 and he was still only paying two pounds fifty a week for each child. He didn't ask about Stephen's blazer, bought in his first year at Grammar School, the sleeves now stopped at the elbow. Ruth's shorts had been bought to grow into, when she left to go to University she still hadn't grown into them. No he couldn't even go to a packet of chewing gum. After the brief visit it was some years before we heard from him again. When he left I finally removed the photo, the children were in no doubt about their father, they were old enough now to make up their own minds. I didn't want that miserable looking bastard staring at me anymore. Then I went upstairs and cut up every photo I had of him, especially our wedding photos. The ringing of the doorbell had ended an era.

Chapter 15

It started off as just another normal week. Mum and Harold seemed their normal self on Monday. I had long regarded Harold as a friend I could trust, someone who was on my side, we had always been able to talk to each other.

On Tuesday I thought Mum was fussing a bit, getting me to tidy this, or sort that and by Wednesday the fussing increased so much I began to smell a rat. A small boy came in for a comic on Thursday morning: Mum took a pile of out dated ones and trust them into his arms, saying

"Here take these."

Mum never gave anything away; and putting this together with her behaviour during the early part of the week I knew something was very odd. Come Friday afternoon and she began emptying a cupboard, big time.

"Do you know, Mum," I said, "if I didn't know better I'd think this shop has been sold."

But of course it wouldn't have been sold, I was working with her every day. I'd have seen people coming and going, heard something, perhaps a phone call. Besides she would have told me. I wish! Not only had the shop been sold, the new people would be moving in the very next day bringing their own staff so I wouldn't be needed. Reminding her I had two adult children to support, I asked

"So what's going to happen to me next week?"

Not even a pause in her chores

"You will soon get another job."

I felt hurt that Harold had let me down. They had bought a bungalow not a mile from where we lived and would be moving out as soon as the shop shut on the Saturday. So when did they do all that? The mind boggles, there'd been not a whisper to me.

I returned to my old pattern of thinking. – why should Mum owe me anything, she had given me shelter of a kind when I was young and after all it wasn't as if she was my Mother. The funny thing was she honestly expected me not to mind a bit and asked me to help with the moving.

Harold had thought I wasn't entitled to know, that it was none of my business. Although he did consider I deserved a handsome reward for the years I had supported them. He bought me a brand new car - UJN 191S - lovely, but I couldn't feed the kids with it.

As I helped her carry her bits and pieces into her new home she said,

"This is my last move, you will be carrying me out of here in a box."

It wasn't quite like that. Towards the end, the question became which of the two of us would be carried out first?

So it was back to Paul again, just like the old days. Little had changed. He did had a new manageress,

Mary, who although she was quite matronly she was great fun.

Stephen had joined the T.A.S. in the Parachute Regiment, he was enjoying his weekends away. He had taken Math's A level a year early and was studying hard for Physics and Chemistry. Ruth was at the Convent up the road from me. At dinner times I would hear a quiet

"Hello, Mum," and she would be there with her friends. I would give them the best table available and whatever they wanted to eat which wasn't much, on the house. For me the struggle was getting harder and with two children at grammar school both of them bigger than myself, I had no choice but to work longer hours.

One Sunday evening a party of six men down from the North on a six week engineering contract came in for a meal, Nick was gorgeous, a Paul Newman look alike, with the same blue eyes, crinkly dark hair and smile, He chatted me up and this time I was ready and willing. On our first evening together we walked the length of the pier, it was a cold misty night and I snuggled up, feeling like a schoolgirl on her first date.

As the weeks passed I knew on my part it was love. As we returning home one evening Nick said, "Lets go."

If Stephen and Ruth had been that few years older I would definitely have thrown caution to the wind and gone with him without a second thought.

Life had been a continuous slog so   a little recklessness wouldn't have gone amiss. But the kids and I had come a long way and I had vowed to see it through. I would rather have cut my throat than rock the boat now at this stage of their lives.

158

The six weeks flew and before Nick left Southend he bought me a ring and put it on my engagement finger, I was so thrilled. Parting was so tearful, with all the usual promises to love each other forever. It wasn't long before he was back for the weekend,

I met him off the train in London on the Friday evening and we went straight home to bed with a bottle of whisky and a bottle of vodka and got stoned out of our minds. We stayed in bed the whole weekend, too drunk to get up, although, I did surface now and then to see if the kids were still alive. After the weekend was over and Nick had left the kids went mad. They were so ashamed of me, I felt awful. Stephen was outraged and told me in no uncertain terms,

"While I'm here and head of this house, I won't tolerate such behaviour."

I didn't know whether to smack him one on the chops for being so cheeky, but I was ashamed of my behaviour and knew the relationship wasn't going to work out. Over the next six months I gained the strength to make the break with Nick but I will always be grateful for the lessons he taught me. They were to play an important part in my life later on.

Stephen had his A level results and was off to Manchester University. Not bad for a kid from a violent broken home and a council estate. Remembering my own school days I tried hard to see he wasn't too short of the things he needed. He didn't want me to run him to Manchester, only the station in London and then he didn't even want me to come on the platform. I could see how pleased to was to be on his way, leaving behind the poverty and that awful estate.

As I drove home I was so upset I cried buckets, at times the tears flowed so freely it was a wonder I didn't crash. My little curly-haired baby had made it, he was on his way, that was what I had worked so hard for, my heart was bursting with pride.

If I continued working at the cafe, Ruth would be alone for too long. In his retirement Harold was doing the books for a friend who owned a baker's shop. There was a vacancy there for an assistant five days a week, Mondays off, I could do something else that day. After Lord knows how many years I was finally away from the seafront.

It was a decent job and I felt a lot cleaner doing it. No longer did the whiff of fish and chips come over me as I moved about.

I was still plodding along with the Conservative Party.

"Why the Conservatives?" people would ask.

Perhaps they didn't expect it of a one parent family poorer than church mice and living on a council estate. I was never very political, it was back to that old chestnut "respectability." I had no support when I was being beaten and abused, nor when I was evicted from my home. All I can say is,

"I felt safe."

Nothing else, I simply felt safe.

The baker's shop was a step in the right direction. The past was behind me, none of it would ever be mentioned until I was old and grey. Then one day it would all be put down on paper for my children to read when they are old and grey.

Right now I needed some extra money and was looking hard for ways to get it when I ran into a very old long-standing friend. Colin. His two sons had been at St Helens with my two, and the three of them had just moved into a large block of flats on top of the cliffs at Westcliff. Colin told me the agents were looking for someone to scrub the miles of landings and stairways once a week for five pounds. That would do me, I was free on Monday's, still no time to be proud.

On my first Monday Colin was waiting for me.

"I'll leave you a set of keys to my home, treat it as your own. You may need the bathroom or to get yourself a drink,"

That had to be the lousiest job on the earth. A strip of red lino ran down the middle of the stairs and on each step was a strip of black rubber. If too much water was used the red of the lino ran everywhere.. I hated the job more than I had ever hated any job. It was like being back in Dickens' time with my bucket of dirty water and rag. Funny that! Me on my hands and knees scrubbing just like my grandmother and even my own mother. Now I knew how they must have felt; at least I wasn't pregnant,

That was exactly what this was all about. No way would my children have to do what I had to do. They would have the best education going, be able to have proper career's.

During my first day at the flats I decided I didn't have a degree in scrubbing so I hurried along - spent the time making an apple pie for Colin's tea. He had been good to me that morning -I wanted to repay his kindness.

It was now the 80s, Stephen had completed his degree and spent the summer in the United States teaching Judo at summer camp. I loved his graduation day. Ruth and I sped up the motorway to take him out for a well-deserved meal. He had accepted a job in Kent and had found someone to share digs with, I was pleased he had done so well.

Ruth had gained A levels in Math's, Physics and Chemistry and in her final year had won "The girl of the year award." It was a wonder my heart didn't burst I was so proud. I wondered if anyone told Madam Mildred that the daughter of that waster of a Merriman's girl had won the award. Ruth chose to go to Nene, in Northampton.

Now I really was alone but I still had to keep a roof over the children's heads. It had been over sixteen years since the divorce and I allowed myself to feel as if I was nearing the end of the road. However tired and stressed I was, it was always a joy to be free. No words can never explain how wonderful it is not to be afraid.

Ruth was back and forth and she seemed very settled. I was busy in the shop and still scrubbing stairs. When Ruth was home she would come to work with me on Saturdays to earn some cash. The Christmas just before her twenty-first birthday, she put her arms around me, hugged me tight and sobbed and sobbed. "Whatever is it?"

I asked time and time again. She assured me it was nothing, she just felt like a good cry and afterwards she seemed her usual self. But her sobbing had sounded as if she was distraught and I couldn't help worrying.. She was going back to Nene just before her birthday at the weekend, Saturday night all her friends were eating out at a restaurant, which was already booked. On the Sunday it was open house. I was upset that I hadn't been included in the arrangements but grateful to have had her home all over Christmas and the New Year. Mum had baked a big fruitcake and I had it iced professionally and I packed two boxes of goodies for the Sunday celebrations.

On the Saturday night Colin, had a Builders' do to attend and he asked me if I would keep him company. I went along and feeling quite sad and lonely I asked the band if they would play something for Ruth. They announced, "The next number is for Ruth who is celebrating her twenty-first birthday away from home."

They played, "Take the ribbons from her hair." Now it was my turn to sob, I wanted so much to be with her, to give her a birthday hug.

The following Wednesday evening, there was a letter from Ruth waiting on the mat. I walked into the kitchen and leaning against the sink hurriedly opened it. Mum, my birthday was wonderful, something I shall remember all my life.

I was thinking, that's how it should be and was feeling so pleased, when there was a knock on the door. I was amazed to see Ruth standing there. We all think we know our daughters, I knew Ruth pretty well, I knew she wasn't involved in drugs or pregnant. I looked at her and asked,

"Why have you run away?"

It was a good thing I was numb with shock and for once kept my big mouth shut, I might have said something I regretted. I put the kettle on and we settled in the kitchen, Ruth was quite calm and not at all upset.

"Mum," she said, "I woke up this morning and I knew I couldn't face another day studying. I went to see my tutors, told them I was leaving, when went out and got a job selling lampshades in an electrical shop then caught a train home to tell you, I couldn't put it in a letter. I'm going straight back to Northampton on the next train."

Dumbfounded I took her back to the station, praying to God to give me the strength to act correctly, struggling for something to say that would sustain her. In the end all that came out was,

"Promise me you will keep yourself clean."

How naff can you get? I waved her off with a big smile after a hug but my heart was broken. Not because she had left Nene but she had chosen not to come home. When I got home I sat on the stairs and cried my eyes out, I wondered how many times I had sat on those very stairs and had cried over my children.

It must have been what I didn't say, on the Saturday morning there was another letter from Ruth. She was ready to come home as soon as I had the time to come up and help her with her luggage. She didn't explain anything, why the change of heart, just a short cheery letter. I was pleased the post had been early, I was able to plead a sickie at work. Ruth wasn't on the phone, so I couldn't tell her I was on my way.

When I arrived she was out but that was no problem, I would wait, for however long it was. Finally she came strolling along the street looking as if she hadn't a care in the world, which is how it should be at twenty-one. Her things were packed in minutes and we were on our way home.

162

My next move was away from the bakery. One of my customers ran the jewellery department in Keddies in Southend High Street. They had a vacancy and she offered me the job. I had started my working life in jewellery, making and designing it, I had always loved being with pretty things so I grabbed the chance to work there.

Wednesday afternoon would now be the only free time I had for my stairs. So Wednesday it would have to be. One old bat opened her door wanting to know what all the banging was about. Seeing me she said,

"You're supposed to be here on Mondays."

I explained that this was now the only free time I had, thinking she would understand. She really was a sour-faced old witch, talking to me as though I was a piece of dirt. I was sorry to let down people who pay me but she really got up my nose. Handing her the bucket with the wet rags I said,

"Here you do it," and walked off.

Everyone gets a strop and that day it was my turn; my children had finished their education, I had finished my scrubbing.

My lovely son was getting married. The happy couple invited me down for lunch as they wanted a quiet word about the wedding plans. Foremost on their minds was not to have me upset on the day. They were assured anything they did was OK with me. After all, the bride knew nothing of the past and when it came to the crunch that was where the past should be, in the past. They had to accommodate Alan and Margaret and if sitting them on the top table was the way things were going to be, I would accept it. Not Mum – when she heard she went ballistic. There was no way they were sitting on the top table, she would have everyone boycott the wedding. Mum could always be relied on to start a fight.

The happy day arrived, Ruth was bridesmaid, so we travelled down the night before and stayed in a hotel. Mum drove down in the morning with Harold, my lovely cousin Maureen was there with her four children, so also my equally lovely cousin Sheila. The Harold Wood mob were there, no one was left out. It was a beautiful wedding, top hat and tails, the bride was gorgeous, the weather glorious, nothing could spoil anything for anyone. It was a wonderful family day. The top table looked scrumptious. In her place of honour was the new Mrs B, then there was me, still Mrs B. The place setting for the third Mrs B just said Margaret. It didn't enter her head that she

163

was sat at the top table and should be pleased, she just went mad. The bride, bless her little heart, said,

"I felt we had enough Mrs Bs at the top table, I didn't want another ."

Margaret saved her revenge for Ruth wedding, when she turned down the invitation.

Ruth got herself a part-time job in a newsagents and then a full-time job in a sandwich bar. She insisted she gave me housekeeping which I refused. She had very little for a girl her age and I wanted her to get herself straight. To make her feel that was acceptable I said

"If you've any money over at the end of the week, save it until I needed it." She had already arranged to go to summer camp in America to teach swimming and she still wanted to do that. I tried not to worry about her choice of jobs or lack of ambition, I figured the trauma of leaving Nene was still around and she was still a bit lost. I told myself that one day she would work it out and for the moment I wouldn't nag or fuss.

The young people who go to Summer Camp have a great time. I waved Ruth off at Gatwick with a lump in my throat. She wrote home about seven of them piling into an old banger and driving down to Washington, D.C. They bought lobster and cooked it, something I couldn't afford to do at home. After Summer Camp ended Ruth still had time to spend in America, she didn't want to come home a minute before she had to. She phoned home, "Mum, do you have your cousin Brendan's address in Canada?

I told her I hadn't been in contact with him for years and the address I did have was probably out of date.

"That will do," she said with great determination, "I'll start there."

Now I began to worry. Canada was a big place but Brendan was still at the same address, which was lucky for Ruth but less so for Brendan, who had broken his leg. At least he was able spend time with her. Finally her visa was running out and she wrote home.

Dear Mum, I'll be landing at Gatwick, etc. etc. What am I going to do in that boring old place Southend? That summed up her frustration, she came home, took a job in a record shop and settled down to a boring old life.

The Conservative Party was taking up a lot of my time

especially at elections, delivering leaflets, canvassing, always fund-raising. At a cheese and wine evening in '82 I met a lovable old rogue, Ken Cater. Over a glass of wine (several glasses for him) he invited me to join his committee, Milton Ward.

"I'm going to be Mayor in five years and I'd like you to be my Mayoress"

Oh, yes, I thought, but took it quite seriously.

We never became friends, I think if we had the relationship, if that is the right word for it, would never have survived. Quite mature in years, Ken was at the front of the queue when they handed out the Oomph and he always had a lady in tow. Whatever he did in his personal life was no skin off my nose, we rarely spoke apart from politics and no way was I part of his circle. The Mayoress promise was never mentioned again, although I thought about it quite a lot. How would I manage if he had been serious and it ever happened. For now I can dream, "Mayoress of Southend." It was a long way from that barefoot little girl of eight who had lost her way on the death of her grandmother.

Meanwhile something else took my attention. Lucky, lucky me, if you can call something that keeps your daughter close luck. Ruth went to a disco in Basildon with a friend and met the love of her life. Rob was her first real boyfriend, I think for both of them it was love at first sight. Five months later they were engaged; he told her he would marry her when West Ham won the F.A. Cup. We were in for a long engagement, then.

Two or three weeks later Ruth told me she and Rob wanted to live together. I didn't say anything immediately but waited a few days before I asked her to come and sit down for a chat.

"Now young lady," I said to her, "are you serious about living with Rob?"

"Very serious, Mum, but we have no idea where. We've no money"

Our little house was now a palace, I asked her how she felt about it. She said it was very nice.

"But you live here,"

Everything she needed was there, linen, crockery, cutlery

"Here are the keys, my bags are packed, I'm off, Colin's got himself a lodger," I told her.

A few days earlier Colin and I had had a very serious

conversation, both saying we would never marry again. We were very good friends and I'd been on my own for over twenty years, a lifetime, I had no idea at that time Ruth's bombshell was coming and suddenly I would find myself redundant as a parent. Moving in with Colin was no problem.

Stephen, Ruth and I had kept that bargain we made when I was first divorced, all three of us had given it our best shot... Whether or not I had made a good job of it, well - the jury's still out on that one.

Meeting up with the children was now the most important part of my life, especially my weekly glass of wine and a bite with Ruth.

"Mum," she declared one day, "I don't fancy selling pop records when I'm fifty, I think I'll get myself a career."

She and Rob had bought the little house, so there was the question of finance. Now she thought she couldn't afford to go back to studying. I assured her she could afford it and I said to her,

"You have no choice, otherwise you will end up like me."

Ruth fancied a career in banking and applied to Barclays. At the interview she was asked what had happened, Ruth explained that things were wrong from the start, the wrong A levels, the wrong course at University.

"I knew, if I had stayed until I was one hundred I would never have got my degree." Then she was asked

"What do you think about Barclays sending you back to study?"

They wanted Maths, which she had, Bookkeeping, Accountancy, Law and Economics. She stuck it out and now has the career she wanted and I'm very proud of her.

It was coming up to election time, '87, and in six weeks Ken Cater would be the Mayor, he had been the Deputy for one year. I'd seen pictures of him in the paper opening this, going there, but I'd still not heard a word about the Mayoress. I was on my way to the supermarket one dark evening and suddenly I decided to knock on his door and find out.. He stood looking at me for a few moments trying to work out what I was doing standing there, then he said, "Don't tell me you have come to tell me you have changed your mind, because I'm counting on you."

"Of course not"

I went on my way, puzzled, it was the only time we ever spoke about such an important matter. When I got back from the shopping I was on cloud nine, absolutely thrilled. Colin was less impressed,

"I don't need it"

Whatever that might mean. I tried to explain what being born a bastard in the 30s did to you, what being in a violent marriage did to you. I told Colin this was something I definitely "did need." In the end he said I should do it if that was what I really wanted. He thought, however, that it would be nice for me to be married.

"We can't have our Mayoress living in sin," he declared.

Many people, including Colin, say I only married because I wanted to be the Mayoress, that old chestnut "respectability." Not true, not true at all, I love him more and more as we have grown old together.

It was a very quiet wedding on a Tuesday morning, no flowers, no photographs no cake. Just the four children and their partners and mum. I wondered if my lovely grandmother and granddad were watching. Afterwards we went to a local pub and had a meal, it was a perfect day.

Colin immediately took me shopping. He bought me six of everything - suits, dresses, evening dresses, hats, gloves, bags, and a couple of coats. Ken had gone to the Council saying he needed more money to carry out his duties. They doubled the Mayor's allowance that year which made the headlines on the front page of the local paper. The article went on to say the Mayor would have to buy the Mayoress clothes. People would say to me

"You do look lovely. Ken has been very generous."

The truth was His Worship wouldn't buy a cup of tea, to put it politely, he was a mean old bugger.

Finally the great day arrived. Mayor making, 1987, it was very nerve wracking. Fairly recently Colin and I were invited to another Mayor-making and I was amazed to hear him say it was the first time he had been to such an event. I'd completely forgotten that neither he, nor my mother or my children, had been to mine. I'd had no idea that guests could be invite. It confirmed my opinion that Ken, was selfish and thoughtless.

After my Mayor making there was a grand ball. Colin reserved a table for ten, a re-run of our wedding. Afterwards we went back with a crowd of friends to our flat and celebrated until three in the morning. The Mayor had gone his own way with his cronies and that was how it was from day one to the very end. One of Colin's friend's had just taken part in the American Cup Yacht Race and had been presented with a commemorative bottle of whisky, which he had passed on to Colin. I ran out of whisky and opened it, I don't think Colin will ever forgive me.

It was a wonderful year for me. I would never knock the Mayoralty, it is a great institution. I was and still am very grateful for the invitation. I learned so much about people and it gave me an inner confidence I sorely needed. I came out of it a much more rounded person ready to take on the world.

As for the Mayor himself, he gave me nothing and I needed to achieve something for myself. I asked Ken if I could have my own charity in my spare time and launched my appeal for the Premature Baby Unit at Rochford Hospital. It was hard work and great fun and at the end of the year I had raised eight thousand pounds.

My brilliant year ended as it began - on a sour note. It was entirely my fault but I was unaware of the procedure. It is customary at the end of the year for the Mayor to present the borough with a gift with his or her name on it. I would really have liked a little something to present to the town with my name on it.. I hadn't done much in my life to shout about and I was very proud of myself at this particular time.

The presentation came as a surprise to me. Ken's gift was supposed to be a silver centre piece. I thought it was appalling but my name objection was that my name wasn't on it. People may say he was the Mayor so he was quite right but if we had known Colin would have organised something for me. It was silly to take it so much to heart. I told Ken later, in private, that I was disappointed. Dribbling and sniffing, a normal state for Ken, he was very upset.

"I'm disgusted with that rubbish they made. They wanted seventy pounds off me for it, I wouldn't pay."

Why didn't that surprise me? I hadn't seen him pay for anything the whole year. "But someone must have paid." I asked

"So who did pay"

"The money was taken out of my charity fund."

I was well pleased then that I had no association with the gift, I thought his behaviour appalling.

After my very high profile year in the Mayoralty I was offered the opportunity to stand in Milton for a seat on Essex County Council.

It wasn't a Conservative held seat but I relished the challenge. I just loved the whole packet of an election, the canvassing, the speeches, the whole show. Many a time I would hear Nick giving me advice in my head.

There was one sad note which really upset me. Two weeks before the election Harold died, He had been a true friend to me and the kids, he and Mum had been married nearly twenty-five years, For two days I couldn't go out, I didn't trust myself not to burst into tears.

Harold had a Jewish funeral at Finchley, a wonderful service and I felt privileged to have been part of Harold's life. It was still strange to me, a Catholic growing up in Ireland to have had two Jewish stepfathers, both of whom I loved, especially Jack. I felt this strange bond with both of them, if I could explain it better I would. I knew Harold would want me to get on with what I was doing so I did.

At the count I couldn't look, I had put my heart and soul into the campaign and would have hated to lose. My legs went to jelly and I had to go and sit down away from it all, giving myself a good talking to, saying I had to see things through whatever the result. Finally Colin came over and said,

"You can come and look now."

But I was frozen with panic; he took my arm, lifted me off the chair and said, "Trust me."

We approached the table, me trying to look cool and casual as I glanced at the piles of votes being stacked up. I couldn't believe my eyes, I was well ahead, I was winning. I did win and I was thrilled.

That started a roller coaster ride which gave me the ten best years of my life although at times it plunged me into despair.

Mum was seventy-three now and widowed for the second time, a woman of substance with her own home and a healthy bank account. She told me she was going to associate only with people who made her laugh. Was she having the usual go at me, because I still made her cry? We still spat at each other as we had always done, she found it easy to forgot the many kindnesses I had shown her. My life's goal had been to finding my mother and find out who I was. I know now that this is a common and permanent anxiety for those who have been adopted or brought up by someone who is not their birth Mother. Time was getting on both for Mum and me I was beginning to think that time would run out altogether and I would never find the true "ME."

Colin was really good with Mum, they got on like a house on fire. He was quite happy on a Sunday to take her out for a drive in the country and a bit of dinner. She hadn't been back to Moortown all the years she was married to Harold, so the first thing Colin and I did after his death was to take her home. We took our own car so we could drive all over Ireland, visiting Mum's brother Joe in Galway and as many of her nieces and nephews as we could.

"It's been grand to see how well they're all doing" she said

She had a few gin and tonics in the old pub and popped into Tierney's. Old Mr. Tierney was still serving in the shop and reminded Mum about the times he chased her around the playground. She put flowers on Mick and Lizzie's grave. It was a great time for all of us but no matter how close we seemed to be I always remembered to avoid stepping over that invisible line where I asked "Who am I, are you my real mother?"

Life for me was the best it had ever been, I loved the flat and Colin had bought me a brand new car. We were both very busy people, I absolutely adored being at County Hall in Chelmsford and never got over the feeling of pride every time I walked through the door. My fellow councilors there were helpful and supportive and I never had to watch your back. It all seemed a long way from that barefoot little girl of eight walking along the bog road confused and unhappy and even further from that distraught person who had been abused, beaten and practically driven mad then evicted from her home.

Out of the blue, when everything seemed to be going right, Stephen's wife left him for another man. My son was devastated, no more than I was. It was like having a death in the family. Mind you when I first met the girl she told me she had been engaged three times while at University and I thought that was a bit over the top. This new bloke could offer her nothing but sex, as we all know that has the strongest pull.

Life on the political scene locally was getting tough for me. My Conservative colleagues made sure they gave me a hard time. The problem was that Southend wanted Unitary Status and I thought we were better off under the umbrella of the County Council. I'd been elected and I thought I was entitled to an opinion.

There had been three Conservative councillors in my ward with over sixty-five years between them, who thought they were God and you crossed them at your peril. On the grapevine I heard they were going to deselect me and this at a time when the Conservatives were at an all time low. My ward now had three Labour councilors; the voters sick to the teeth with the lot of them had thrown out anything calling itself Conservative. I was only to glad to get rid of the whole shower but I still held the seat at County for the Conservatives and you would think I would be put on a pedestal and be treasured, not knifed in the back.

The Chairman of my ward, Geoffrey Baum, was a fellow guest at a party in the Mayor's Civic home. A nothing of a little man with cement in his brain and concrete in his heart, totally pissed with power. Vanity oozed out of his veins, he was potty in the hands of anyone who flattered him. A little rat like him wasn't going to beat a toughie like me. I sidled up close to him and almost cooing, putting on my best and biggest smile, I said

"Good evening, Geoffrey."

I was met with his usual sickly imitation of a smile. Grinning even more broadly I asked

"What's this I hear about me being deselected?"

"Nothing to do with me, Dearie, it's your committee."

I could feel the knife pierce my back but I was still smiling.

"Now then, Geoffrey, you know what you say, goes."

I wasn't going to let him wriggle of the hook, I considered myself much the stronger person and I could fight just as dirty. The knife was about to twist deeper but I wasn't going to let this little rat get away with his games. With great confidence and authority I said

"I'm very surprised with your MBE in the pipeline that you would allow this to happen. John Major wants the Conservatives united and deselecting a sitting County councillor might upset him."

This ridiculous little nothing of a man puffed himself up like a peacock,

"Am I getting an MBE?

I thought he would explode. All I had to do was keep a straight face. As if I knew anything about an MBE – and anyway he would be the last person on this earth to deserve an MBE. I feel no guilt, I have to fight fire with fire.

Of course I was reselected. The fact that I worked hard and cared passionately about the Conservatives should have protected me from those three at Milton but it almost didn't. At a time when the Conservatives were almost wiped of the face of the earth not only did

I win but I was only three votes adrift from the previous election. I expected major trouble ahead, the petty Mr. Baum didn't get his MBE.

I sounded so surprised when he phoned to tell me, said I couldn't understand why not. He was gunning for me now and he would make sure if he could that my political life was at an end.

There was some fabulous news on the home front to take my mind off my worries. After more than five years together Ruth and Rob were getting married. West Ham hadn't won the F.A. Cup but I guess they both got tired of waiting. Rob had always said he couldn't face the big traditional white wedding. He thought something like Colin and myself, quiet and with no fuss would be perfect.

They married at the local registry office with just Rob's parents and grandparents and his best man. Ruth had Mum and me and her friend Marlesse and husband Hank with their baby, they had flown in from Holland. Lovely cousin Maureen was there with Stephen and Alan. Alan and Margaret had both been invited to the wedding – we wouldn't lower ourselves to her level and not send an invitation. Having waited all those years to get even after Stephen's wedding, she refused. How stupid - if she really wanted to upset us all she had to do was turn up - now that really would have put our noses out of joint. After the service we had a meal in the best restaurant in Southend and in the evening there was a disco for 150 at a posh hotel in the country.

Marlesse and Hank were staying with Colin and myself so after the reception lunch we went home to change the baby. Ruth phoned to say Alan had found out about the evening "do" and insisted on coming. I assured her that was OK by me.

"But Mum, nobody's coming back to Southend so how will he get back."

"OK. OK," I said, "I promise you I'll give your dad a lift at the end of the evening"

Colin hadn't been seen all day, he was busy looking after Ruth's guests. Although he loved Ruth like a daughter he never changed his stance about not wishing to be in the same part of the world as Alan.

The baby was restless when it was time to leave for the evening affair so Hank decided to stay at home with Colin and the two men could have a few quiet beers. It was a grand evening, Mum had arranged an open bar, then Mum had always been very generous, she wouldn't have had things any other way.

Alan hadn't changed, he propped up the bar all evening, I heard him encouraging people to have trebles

"After all" he said to our guests, "they're paying."

Normally father's help out with the expenses at their daughter's wedding, I wouldn't have wanted him to spoil the habit of a lifetime.

Time for the journey home, Marlesse sat in the front with me, and we chatted together most of the time. It must have been about one o'clock in the morning when we pulled up outside Alan's hotel.

"How about a nightcap?" he asked.

It had been over a quarter of a century, a lifetime, since our divorce, time to let bygones be bygones. I was pleased to accept; it would be pleasant to have a quiet chat, after all we had just seen our only daughter married. It was well time for him to say how proud today had made him. The hotel had only a small lobby with a few tables, the night porter-cum-watchman asked Alan what he wanted. It was really weird to be shown to a table by Alan and asking what I'd like to drink. I can't remember what Marlesse ordered, but I thought I'd have a brandy. I was quite relaxed, this was a fitting end to a great day with the bride looking as beautiful as all brides should.

Thinking Alan was in the same frame of mind I raised my glass to give a toast. I found myself looking into the same evil face that sat opposite me on the train the day I married him. White with temper he almost hissed at me,

"Don't you ever forget I know you, I know what a lying, conning, cheating, conniving, fucking bitch you are. You may be able to con the people of Southend but you will never con me."

I was absolutely dumbstruck, Marlesse put her drink down, burst into tears picked up her bag and left. Alan continued in his venomous, spiteful way,

"I'll never understand how you've got where you have, achieved all you've achieved, but I can imagine."

I was gone before he could say any more. Marlese and I arrived indoors in floods of tears, Colin and Hank wanted to go after him but decided he was the kind of rubbish not worth dirtying their hands over.

173

Chapter 16

Mum had always suffered from arthritis. When Harold was alive she would wash, cook and clean the bungalow and as she was the driver, take Harold out in the car but after his death she no longer had to get up in the mornings and could take things easy. As the first year of widowhood came to an end she had stiffened up considerably. I found it odd she didn't have any friends to go with her shopping or on holiday or an away-day. This fantastic life she had planned for herself wasn't materialising. She'd never had any interests in life other than work, cards and gambling. She often said how she missed her many brothers and sisters. They were all long gone, she had outlived them all. Her only friend was the old lady next door who shared her love for gin. There was always a glass being passed over the fence, usually one way - from Mum.

The second and third years passed and the stiffness with the arthritis became more and more noticeable.

I was still doing my best to establish a mother-daughter relationship. We would be making good progress then something quite trivial would happen and Mum would destroy all the good that had been done. It couldn't be that she was jealous, mothers aren't jealous of their own kids but she attempted to be totally in control of our lives.

Colin and I went abroad for a two-week break, we were working very hard, Mum was well and we deserved it. We were relieved to arrive home without incident, but Ruth was soon on the phone to tell us Nan had been quite ill while we were away and had demanded our return. Much to Nan's annoyance she made the decision to let us have our holiday. Next morning I went straight round to my mother.

It didn't take long to work out what had happened. Mum was so determined to ruin our holiday, she had drunk two bottles of gin and taken some tablets. She had laid in bed for eight days without eating because she had nearly killed herself. Her weight had plummeted and she looked half dead. It showed the lengths Mum would go to spoil things for me. This time she had almost gone too far and in my heart I knew she would never recover from the damage she had done herself.

It was time for me to begin saying my prayers. The ideal situation would have been for Mum to go into a nursing home, she had her own home, money and could afford it. She would get the care she already needed but she was determined to stay in her own home. She came from that old brigade who thought children should care for their parent's and had conveniently forgotten abandoning me all those years ago and never admitting openly that I was her child. Care in the community was now law and there was nothing that could be done against the client's wish.

We still hadn't had even a brief chat about things but I had long realized she was my mother. I could see myself in her every move, her smile, hear myself when she laughed. We were two identical peas in a pod, the only difference being my colouring. Strange as it may seem although I never liked my mother, I loved her dearly. You have to love your mother, you might not like her, but you love her. The decision I made in the end was almost one hundred per cent from my deep desire to find that Mother I never had before it was too late. Even if it was on Mum's deathbed, if we could just hug each other close and say "Sorry" even that would be wonderful. I would never give up trying for that breakthrough. It was the most important thing in my life. I wanted to put the past behind me and move on before it was too late for me.

It hadn't yet come to the stage where I went round to check her every day. Sometimes, it would be three days. One Sunday Colin and I popped in on our way out for a meal. I was all dressed up fit to kill, wearing the latest shade of lavender eye shadow. Never one to miss a chance to exercise that sharp tongue of hers she asked

"What do you think you look like? I've seen people who have been dead for days looking better."

It was always a battle trying to be a good daughter, doing all the things expected of you. One day I thought I had everything under control. I felt I could approach her trying to explain.

"I've always felt I'm the odd one out with my cousins. Is there anything you can say to make me feel any different."

It was perhaps not the best way to put things but how else do you put it. What came next sent me reeling. Mum appeared to have a fit.

"How dare you speak to me like that! You horrible, rotten little cow. Don't you ever come near me again or touch me. I never want to see you again. Get out! Get out!"

175

I was shocked and just stood there looking at her in amazement.

"Get out!" she screamed.

It took me three quarters of an hour to walk home, sobbing openly. What was it all about. Over the years I've wondered about this big secret a lot. Was it a terrible rape when I was conceived? What was so awful to make her react like that? When Colin came home that evening he found me distraught. Three days passed without a word from Mum. She would rather rot in hell than let her guard down. Finally, Colin couldn't take my distress any longer. He knew I was frightened to death of her so he phoned her.

"Look here, Mum, she is your daughter and she needs you - you need each other," he said. Mum wasn't in the least bit bothered. She showed no emotion.

"The trouble with Leila is she's mad."

Colin replied,

"Mum, you know she's mad, I know she's mad, but we have to put this quarrel behind us, I'll bring her round to see you."

So Colin bundled me into the car and presented me to my mother. By now I am almost an old age pensioner myself, my hair was thinning and grey, the lines etched on my face weren't all laughter lines. Yet I was being treated like a naughty child. All I had done was ask a question and I was being made to feel I wasn't right in the head.

Mum sat there all cool, calm and collected and made me wonder what it was all about as she continued her act.

"This is the cross I've had to bear all my life," she told Colin.

To me things didn't look that way. I had seen Mum for two days when I was two and again for a few moments when I was eight. We lived together for about six years from the time I was eleven. After that it seemed to me I was always the one to support her. Certainly she forgot a lot, once again she got away with her act. Colin thought she was a sweet old lady, which in reality she was. If only she could come to terms with this awful burden she carried all her life. Easier said than done, who knows what goes on in a person's mind.

The first nightmare began all too suddenly. It was winter, freezing cold and Mum had turned her fire off to go to bed. Clad only in her nightie, she fell by the side of her bed and laid there for eighteen hours before her chum next door wondered about her. The police had to break down the door to get in. At the hospital they were amazed she had survived. If I knew anything about it, she would have been pickled when she fell, that would have saved her.

The next incident came when her neighbours, concerned when they hadn't seen a light on all evening decided to check and found her in a flower bed, drunk. They put her to bed as she was. It seemed she had been eating dirt, it was all in her mouth when I checked her the next day! That evening Colin said he had something very serious to talk to me about.

"What are you going to do about your mother?" he asked.

"Not a lot," was my answer.

"Now it's time to be serious," Colin told me.

"Your mother came to see me today and with tears streaming down her face asked me what was going to happen to her.

Mum wouldn't talk to me but Colin was a real softie and she fancied her chances. At the end of the day I wasn't going to turn my back on my mother, I never had and I wouldn't now. Mum was determined she was staying in her own home. After months of discussions, Colin and I agreed we would keep an eye on her if we could build an extension to her bungalow in her back garden. She very reluctantly agreed. We put our home on the market. Whatever mixed feelings I had, my gut instinct told me I was mad, totally crazy, a leopard never changes its spots. But I was full of hope. I was a great believer in fate, this was all planned in the stars. Now I would find the mother I never had and had desperately needed all my life.

Colin being in the trade drew up our dream home. We were going to build most of it ourselves. It would be no bigger than a doll's house with one bedroom, lounge/diner, bathroom and a kitchen - so small you couldn't swing a cat. It would be very modern, central heating and double glazing. Mum had neither and Colin suggested while ours was being done we could keep going and do hers, but she wasn't having any of that, her big old storage heaters plus her free-standing fires were good enough for her. She was going to stay in the dark ages. Our only problem was we weren't allowed to put a front door on the side. It was one plot, one building, so one front door. We would always have to come in and go out through Mum's place.

Finally we sold our flat and while our new home was being completed rented a flat for three months, which went over Christmas. By then we had been married for five years. We were both flat out at work and the additional building work make each day very long. We hoped, in the evenings, we would relax for five minutes by the fire. It would be good having that little time to ourselves. How long were we looking at keeping an eye on Mum? She was only seventy-seven. It could be fifteen years or more before we would be in a place of our own again.

Everything was going well, the foundations were prepared. Mum's garage had to come down, a big tree plus her blackberry bushes to be dug up. She made no secret of her distress, although she never gave one thought to ours. We had survived the trauma of giving up our home. Our furniture was far too big for the little place we were building and had been passed through the family. We had already spent a considerable amount of money and whatever happened now it was too late to turn back.

One morning when I arrived I was surprised to see how ill Mum looked.

"What on earth has happened to you?" I said.

"Haven't you heard?" Mum asked?

"Heard what?"

This time when she fell she let out such a scream the neighbours heard. The police broke in through the kitchen window and the door we had just mended, through to the hallway was broken again. She had been taken to hospital and after an examination brought home. That night when it was time for us to go home Colin seemed surprised I had my coat on.

"What about your mother?" he asked.

He thought she didn't look fit to be left and after we talked it over, we agreed Colin should go back to the flat alone as it was more important that he got some sleep. I dozed in the armchair. The next day Mum didn't seem any better, I found it difficult to get her up and she kept crying out in pain.

A week went by like this. She wanted to go to the toilet and I had almost got her out of bed, bum on the edge, feet on the floor, with a bucket between her legs, then she became unable to move. I called an ambulance and she was taken into hospital.

A young doctor, Sam came to see her.

Arms folded across her chest, she looked at Mum and in a very arrogant tone said,

"So you've got a pain have you?"

I stuck my shoulders back and glaring at this young woman said,

"No, she hasn't got a pain, she's got more than a pain."

Another X-ray – although I couldn't swear she had had an X-ray after the fall a week earlier, but she definitely had one that day. The verdict - nothing wrong. I had had her for a week, I certainly wasn't taking her home again. I stood so firm the hospital agreed to give her three days' bed rest, which stretched to a week and then fourteen days.

Mum was a terrible patient, abusive, hating everyone but she did look desperately ill. On one occasion, she protested that she was in such pain she couldn't walk to the toilet. When the nurse asked her,

"Are you going to play me up again?"

Mum stepped bravely forward and fainted. Another X-ray was taken and still they found nothing wrong. She asked for the phone, then phoned the police and asked them to investigate, saying she was being slowly murdered.

The fourteen days were up on the Monday, on the Saturday, she looked so ill I was convinced she was dying. I phoned the grandchildren to warn them and they visited her on the Sunday.

I made it quite clear to all concerned that Mum lived alone and that Colin and I worked full-time, so there was no one to support her. Monday came and Mum arrived home in a wheelchair with two occupational therapists. I sat quietly in a chair and watched.

"Jump onto the bed, let's see if you can do it,"

They echoed each other like a pair of parrots.

"Go into the kitchen and make a cup of tea,"

"I'll cook bacon and eggs if you like!" joked Mum.

Anyone with a brain, which these two occupational therapists obviously lacked, could see this pathetic, frail, old lady was very ill, she was hanging in there by the skin of her teeth. As they pushed her in the chair back out to the ambulance I told her not to worry, I knew how determined she was to get home.

"I'll see you this evening," I told her,

Convinced that they would certainly keep her in hospital. I was amazed to be told that evening her living conditions were excellent and she would be home in the morning. It was about 7pm. the next day when the ambulance arrived and Colin, full of good cheer went in to see her.

"Well, Mum, you've made it. Nice to see you," and he planted a kiss on her cheek.

"Yes! I'm here despite the efforts of that fucking cow, that bleeding bitch who didn't want me in my own home but she won't get it."

"Who are you talking about?" asked Colin.

"That fucking mare there," pointing at me as I arrived with a nice cup of tea for her. I stood in her kitchen for ages, unable to deal with this. My view had nothing to do with not wanting her home. I wasn't a medical person but anyone with a grain of sense, doctors, nurses, occupational therapists could see she wasn't fit to be out of hospital.

"What have I done?"

I yelled aloud, banging the table with my fists. Deep down in my heart I always knew this wouldn't work.

Colin interrupted my rage

"Come on now, show your strength of character, go on in and cheek her."

I walked through with a heavy heart to find my mother collapsed on the settee. She had got up to answer the phone.

"Up you get,"

and I pull an arm around her to pull her up. This nightmare was to last four years and almost take my life.

While all this was happening, as if I didn't have enough problems, there was rumblings in my local Conservative party. Southend was about to gain Unitary Status and I was going to be redundant. That's fair enough, it's how the cards fell, but the three past councilors at Milton in their jealousy and spite couldn't just let it be. Oh no, being the muppet's they were they passed a vote of no confidence in me. It was a put up job; there were only six people at the meeting and the other three all told me it was fixed. They were so ashamed, they couldn't post the letter they were ordered to write to me, but came round with it personally with an apology I was distraught by their nastiness which seemed to have no end but every cloud has a silver lining as the cliché says and in my darkest hour I was offered one of the safest seats for the new Authority. But there is always a snag, a fourth little rat was in my new ward. He had lost the last election, the voters, like those in Milton, had made their feelings clear they didn't want him. All these past councilors, a load of has-beens who hated each others guts, found that united they kept each other in and everyone else out.

My selection didn't go down very well with them and very soon I read letters in the papers asking the voters not to vote for me. Naturally they were all anonymous. With so much bad feeling out there I reluctantly offered my resignation. I felt awful for the lovely people who had adopted me, but they wouldn't hear a word about me quitting, saying they thought I had more fight in me than to give up.

It got worse; one of the little rats stood against me. Conservative against Conservative – that's a new angle for the Conservatives. It goes without saying that I won. I never had to bother about the labour or liberal opposition, my main opposition was always my own party.

Having being elected safely on to the new Authority I found it nothing like being a County Councillor. I had to watch my back all the time. With the traumas at home I didn't need it, so I served my time with as much good grace as I could muster and then retired. At least I can say I retired under my own steam, that nobody got rid of me. I still support the Conservative's and I am so grateful for those wonderful ten years at County Hall.

By now, luckily, my workload was easing off for the Christmas recess. In my eyes, Mum was as ill as ever so I saw nothing of my cosy little flat, as I spent my days watching Audrey Hepburn films. On some days we would watch four of them. Mum was in such pain that finally I managed to get a physiotherapist to visit. Mum was in bed and the physio threw back the bedclothes. One look at Mum's body and she said:

"You have a broken hip."

"I knew it," shouted Mum "I knew it."

Mum was triumphant; at last she would be proved right. I said

"Don't start all that nonsense again, Mother's had two or three X-rays and we've been told her hip definitely isn't broken."

Only this time it was I who was wrong, as I later discovered.

The lead up to Christmas was hellish, we hadn't even moved in and we were already totally stressed. The building work may have been progressing but Mum certainly wasn't. Christmas had always been my favourite time of year so I tried to keep my spirits up. I managed to get Mum in the car and take her to visit the grandchildren before the big day but Christmas dinner was subdue and immediately after Christmas dinner, Mum took to her bed and seemed to give up.

She had been assessed and told there was nothing wrong and no support of any kind had been offered. I was worried about the future and now Christmas was over I took drastic action. I phoned Social Services at Southend, explained my mother's plight and was completely dazzled by the description of support available.

"Sounds absolutely wonderful," I said. "I'll have a little bit of that, please."

"Who's the client?"

That was the problem, Mum didn't qualify. In a fury I asked "Why the hell not?"

I asked if they were absolutely sure they had got it right and I said I would like a second opinion.

It was a bitterly cold day a few days later. I was outside sweeping up the building rubble and putting it into a skip. I had a woolly hat pulled down over my ears, an old coat, jeans that had seen better days and a pair of old wellie boots. I was a good advert for a tramp. A car pulled up and out stepped a young man from Social Services.

"Come round the back," I invitation and we stood amongst all the rubble in the half-built extension. I explained I was quite happy to do all my mother's housework for nothing, money didn't come into it. I would do her washing, ironing, cooking and shopping. All I wanted was someone to check she was up, washed and had eaten in the morning and put her to bed in the evening.

"Can't you wash your mother yourself?" was his first question.

First, I doubt my Mother considered it the kind of relationship where I washed her. Second, everyone involved, every prat (i.e. jumped-up official connected with Social Services who thought they were something) connected with my mother had it explained to them.

"I WORK. You haven't been listening," I said. "I might be at work."

"What hours do you do?" was his next question.

"Enough," was my reply.

It wasn't a nine to five job. Most days I liked to be on the road by 7.30 a.m. To do that I had to be up by five. Colin had to be fed and his packed lunch prepared. Mum needed her breakfast, plus a tray with all her needs for the day - a flask with a hot drink, sandwiches, etc. Then I like to have most of the preparation for the evening meal completed and potatoes and vegetables prepared. After that I would bath and got myself ready for work. Sometimes it was evening work, sometimes I'd be away two, three days - Birmingham, Leeds etc. I didn't know what hours I'd be working. His next question was, "Why doesn't your mother walk?"

Who knows the answer to that one either.

"She just doesn't,"

Next question:

"Is your mother lazy?"

Now that was out of order, the interview was going nowhere. I looked down on the ground and there in the dirt was one of my cards. I picked it up, rubbed it on my sleeve and handed it to the young man and said,

"There, that's me, that's my job."

That to me was what you call pulling rank and it was something I hadn't wanted to do.

"Right," I said, "Shall we go and meet mother now?"

Mum was up, sitting in her armchair. She didn't need any help she told the young man, she was quite capable of looking after herself. If she did she certainly wouldn't go to Social Services. Her friends were queuing up for the privilege of caring for her. The young man told her,

"I'm not so concerned about you. My only concern is helping your daughter."

I was very grateful for the support I was promised. I only needed the minimum but it would enable me to continue some sort of life for myself. After the young man's departure, I would now get a second opinion on my mother's health. I would take her privately. A nearby nursing home lent me a chair. The task of getting my mother out of the house and into the car was horrendous. Now I'm no shrinking violet but I just stood in the street and cried. It was the same the other end, trying to get this frail old lady who had been through hell (thanks to Southend Hospital, Rochford Hospital and all the doctors, nurses and occupational therapists) out of the car and into the chair. It couldn't have done her any good, it certainly hadn't done much for me. Finally we got there.

The surgeon had my mother's notes in front of him and there was the broken hip. A subtle break, that's what the surgeon said, hard to detect, nevertheless it was a broken hip. The very next day Mum had her operation, six weeks overdue.

This time Mum was an even worse patient. I asked what drugs she was on because they didn't seem to agree with her. But I was assured she was on none. According to Mum, there was a dungeon under the hospital. If a patient was moved, possibly to go home or be sent for other treatment, to Mum they had been taken down to the dungeon and murdered. She told everyone they were killing the patients off, one by one. I told her she was hallucinating and none of it was true, her response is unprintable. It seemed the doctors and nurses held wild parties at nights and raped all the patients and I checked again what medication she was on. One night Mum asked if she could use the phone.

"Of course you can," she was told, "You're not in prison."

When the phone was brought to her she dialled 999 and said she was being held against her wishes.

Her stay in hospital gave us time to do things while she was out of the way; make a bit of noise and get things straight. We moved in and spent our first night in our new home twenty-four hours before she was due out of hospital. It would be four long weary years before we were going to have a night on our own again.

Chapter 17

We had received some fabulous news, Stephen was getting married again. It was his fiancee Lyn's first wedding, so she wanted the whole white affair, top hat and tails. Stephen asked Colin "Would you do the honour's for us? You've been more of a father to me than my own Dad."

"I'm not sure."

Colin is a very private man and had to be persuaded to step into the role. Ruth was Matron of Honour and Mum and I were just thrilled to see Stephen settled. It was a picture-book sunny day, Alan and Margaret hadn't been invited - and the newly-weds looked wonderful and very happy.

More than a year later I became a grandmother for the first time. A pensioner by now, I had began to think I wouldn't live to see the day I'd hold a grandchild. Of course the Christening was going to be a magical occasion, with Auntie Ruth as Godmother. Then right out of the blue, after over three years without a whisper, Alan phoned Stephen.

"Why didn't anyone tell me you had re-married?"

When he learned he was a grandfather he was not a happy bunny.

"I'm coming to the christening, that's for certain."

Stephen had no choice. My turn to be unhappy, but even though I felt like kicking Alan's teeth in I would rather die than upset my children and would behave. I had kept my mouth shut all these years and not one unkind or snide remark would pass my lips. Once he knew he was back on the scene Colin firmly refused to come; he would not be in the same room as a man who mentally and physically abused a woman, he would have given Alan a pasting where it hurt.

Even though Mum was at her most frail now and was nearing the end of her life, she wouldn't hear of missing the day, so Ruth and I set of with her to drive to Kent, in my brand new bright red Hurricane Hyundai. As I pulled up outside the church I thought the brilliant red sent out just the right signal on a day when I needed a

185

boost. With Mum and Alan together and remembering the way he spoke to me last time we met I felt I was sinking fast.

When Mum and I arrived at the Christening party it was in full swing. I had a job getting her out of the car, even a blind man could see the end wasn't far away. She was driving me bleeding crackers but that was between Mum and me, nobody had the right to upset my mother and would do so at their peril. Suddenly the pig - can I think of a worse word than pig, because I'd hate to upset a pig - anyway I'm talking about Alan, he was standing in front of us. Anyone with a mind, and with Alan it was always doubtful, anyone with an ounce of compassion, decency, humanity in their bones could see this frail little lady's time was limited. You would think that warning bells would be ringing. He'd been snubbed by not being invited to Stephen's wedding and might have worked out it was time for him to behave himself, as I was determined to do.

If he hadn't the strength of character, (but then how can one expect someone who hasn't got any character to have any strength) to be polite and say "hello," all he had to do was walk away, that wouldn't have hurt. But no, not Alan. Rubbing his hands and sniffing, with that evil leer on his face he said to Mum, who was almost on her death bed,

"So you're still alive then." And with an even worse leer continued, "Of course you would be, you're too wicked to die, you must be the wickedest woman on the earth, even the devil wouldn't have you."

My heart went out to my little mum, Alan's mind was still in the dark ages, we were nearing the end of the twentieth century and had long learned that it was years since children born the wrong side of the blanket – their Mother's too - were reviled, many women locked away in asylums for the mentally ill; many more too ashamed to do other than keep silent about the child all their lives. Even I understood that; I might not appreciate it, my life was scarred by the silence. There were times when not knowing who I was tempted me to ring my mother's neck with my bare hands.

However having a dogmatic, pathetic little squirt like Alan talk to someone who had more guts in her fingernail than he had in his whole body disgusted me. Perhaps this is where I should say, "May God forgive him or may he rot in hell"

There will be quite a few of his type in hell: he seems to be fond of the devil, perhaps Alan can be in charge of the whips, that would suit him.

On Wednesdays, Mother went to the day centre and once a month, now back in the folds of the Catholic Church, she went to Mass.

Luckily for me from day one I set down some ground rules explaining to Mum that we would eat in our own place during the week and at weekends we would all eat to-gether. Colin was in business and very busy. When he came home in the evening, there was the post to deal with, phone calls, and all the chores of just living. He was lucky if he got his meal in peace. I was probably worse, my post every day was enormous, and I too spent half my evening on the phone.

Mum would have preferred it if we both flopped out on her settee and argued about the TV all evening but life wasn't like that for us. Everyone knew the set-up, we went to great lengths to explain it. The first time I served her dinner to eat alone I noticed a tear in her eye, but that was the only way it could be.

Our next task was to sort our legal position out with Mum with regards to our home. If people couldn't be contained in their own home that home would be sold to pay the fee's in a nursing home. I totally agreed with that and voted for it and I now found myself in the position where my mother owned my home.

We had spent our own money building an extension in her back garden she owned. I went to Social Services who said I hadn't a leg to stand on. If my mother had a stroke my home would go. I approached Mum and explained the situation and she agreed that our Solicitor should call.

The Solicitor said what a sweetie Mum was. Hang about, I thought to myself, something's wrong here. Sure enough a couple of mornings later I heard Mum yelling.

"Look what that crook has done."

Going in to see what the noise was about I said,

"What crook, who are you talking about?"

"That Solicitor, he's only suggested I give you half my bungalow"

"Well," I said, "We are going to give you half of ours."

I knew that if we laid a single finger on one brick of our home, she would have us for damaging her property.

"You can take that building down, I didn't want it there in the first place. I'll tell you something now," she continued, "you won't get one brick of my home."

Worse still it gave Mum the ammunition she craved for to gain great sympathy with her mates at church and at the day centre. We were living in her home rent free and we even had a Solicitor in to try and get her home from her. Talk about being caught by the short and curlies. Colin and I were both getting older ourselves and our total frustration cannot be described.

The day centre was concerned because Mum was always crying. She was totally dependent on support. The Social called in the morning to wash her, check her at lunch and put her to bed in the evening. I worked long hours and when I got home there was endless washing and ironing, cooking and housework had to be done, as well as sorting out Mother's problems. All the time the Social Services were encouraging her, it didn't matter how many times I said,

"Mum, I know differently, I make the rules," she would give that false laugh, knowing she had us tied up in knots. Her big mouth never let her down and she felt she could always afford to go for broke.

One day she was really taking the piss out of Colin. I turned on her angrily and told her not to keep doing that. As always, Mum thought she held the trump card and could go for broke. Her reply stunned me, she really had gone too far but still there was nothing we could do.

"I've been to Social Services for advice and they have told me I can get an injunction against you to stop you abusing me in my own home."

Abuse her! - it was she who was abusing us. I got straight on the phone and called Colin home from work.

"Now then, Mum you really have gone too far."

"I've got two words to say to you," was her reply, "Good Bye."

It was a turning point: we weren't going to give up our home and we had to take drastic action. Knowing what we were facing, we decided to buy ourselves a second home. Mum was never to be told. Many a time I would have loved to have had a chat, to have confided in her and shared my worries, but I could no longer trust her.

A third year passed and Colin's health was deteriorating. He had two more years to go to sixty, but having his own business there was no set retirement date. He came home washed out, racked with pain. My mental and physical health was beginning to worry family and friends. I was losing weight and beginning to look ill and it began to look as if Mum would outlive us both.

When we built the extension we agreed to keep Mum's home up to scratch. Her windows were so rotten you could put your fingers through the wood and the front wall would have fallen down. We reluctantly agreed to double glaze her bungalow at our expense and while we were doing that remove what was left standing of her front wall and crazy pave the lot, so we could get our cars off the road. It seemed sensible while we were at it, to go the whole hog and modernise her kitchen and provide hot water for the Social Services. Mum went bananas.

"You leave my home alone, no way are you taking over."

"Look here," Colin said, "If the health people came in they would condemn your kitchen and I'm fed up seeing Leila have to cook in there."

"When does she cook?" asked Mum.

"You have dinner every day, don't you?" said Colin.

"Oh, call that cooking do you?" replied Mum.

One afternoon I was feeling so low I got out the whiskey bottle. Time to drown my sorrows. All the time I was drinking I was getting more and more wound up about my father. I must have had at least three doubles and in the end I stood up, brushed myself down and decided that after over fifty-five years I was going to walk into my mother and ask her about my father.

This was it, I had to steady myself and I faced Mum.

"Who's my father?" I asked.

"Whatever are you asking a question like that for?" Mum completely taken aback.

"I did have a father, didn't I? Most people do. Who was he - or was I a virgin birth?"

Mum was still looking bewildered.

"You don't know?"

"No, I don't know. How should I know?"

Mum asked

"Why do you think I keep the photo of my little great-granddaughter on the TV? Because when I look at her eyes I'm looking at Jack's eyes!"

"You're not telling me Jack was my father!"

I could hardly keep my voice down.

"Of course he was,"

I stormed out of the room back to my own lounge. I didn't believe that for one single moment, That my parents, my real mother and father, were married to each other all along and nobody thought to tell me! I had " FATHER UNKNOWN" stamped across both my birth certificate AND my wedding license.

That has to be even richer than being called a bastard! All the suffering, my children deprived of a father all their life, the hard time we'd had surviving after the divorce. Was all that unnecessary?. How was I to come to terms with this? I walked unsteadily back to my mother.

"I wish you had told me years ago," I said.

"Why did you want to know?"

I looked at my mother and thought what a stupid cow she was to ask such a question. I still hadn't taken in what I had just been told and I answered

"Because, Mum, I would have liked to put my arms around his neck, give him a big hug and say, "Daddy Dearest, I love you."

One consolation was that Jack knew I loved him. Why? God alone knows. Besides being the world's biggest gambler he was the world's weakest man. Well all gamblers must be weak to be unable to say "No" to putting the very food from their children's mouths on a four-legged creature. We were always so close but he couldn't tell me he was my father. I didn't believe Mum for a moment. Anyone as weak as Jack couldn't possibly be my father. I felt there was absolutely nothing of him in me. Once again I asked

"Why ever wasn't I told?"

Mum said that when Granddad brought me over from Ireland when I was eleven, she and Jack, after lengthly discussions, made a decision not to ever tell me Jack had wanted to adopt me but they both agreed a Jewish name would be a disadvantage to an Irish Catholic. So being labeled a bastard hadn't been a disadvantage then! Mum looked at me.

"I can't take the blame for your inadequacies as a wife,"

"What!" I shouted at her, "Inadequate on my wedding day, you really are the pits, Mother!"

It was awful that this old lady should be shouted at but I found it impossible to explain the depths of my frustration. Mum looked upset. She rarely got upset but even at that stage an apology would have gone a long way. She was quiet for a while, as if lost for words, then she muttered,

"I thought no one would notice."

"You thought no one would notice. Of course they would notice. What did you think no one would notice - FATHER UNKNOWN - on a wedding certificate."

Dropping her chin on her chest and still muttering said,

"I took a chance."

"YOU took a chance,"

Looking at her, for once I felt really sorry for my mother. She had taken a chance and of course it would be noticed, but what other man in the whole world would have behaved like Alan. I understood exactly how her mind had worked but could never fathom why she never had the backbone to talk to me.

Mum's health continued to deteriorate. Too weak to be dressed, she lived in her nightie, and was becoming incontinent. Morning, noon and night when the Social Services came in they would slip off Mum's woolly, nightie, socks and sheets and place them in the bath for me to wash. Finally, I went bananas.

"But," said the Social smugly and speaking to me as if I were a couple of jelly babies short of a quarter, "we have a laundry service, there's no need for you to do the washing."

"Right I'll use it," I replied.

"We will pick up your washing on Tuesday and, wonderful as we are, we will return it on Thursday."

"So what happens when my mother shits (vulgar or not, that is what it is, SHIT) all over the bed on Tuesday after your collection. Am I supposed to keep the soiled clothes in the house until the next Tuesday?"

I told them I thought their "wonderful" laundry service was crap.

The good news was that on doctor's orders Colin and I were to have a holiday, It was March and we decided on a two-week break in Cyprus the following January. Mum agreed to go into respite for the two weeks and treat it as a holiday for herself. We had long since stopped going out, all parties and other social events were cancelled and we spent as much time as possible at home. Shopping was always done in a hurry although a lot of thought had to go into it. I had to buy the right food to leave for Mum when I was out. Rushing around

Sainsburys as always, one day I bumped into Margaret, a friend from the old days. There's nothing nicer than bumping into an old friend in a rush or not, it was time to catch up on some gossip.

"Amazing," was Margaret's greeting, "Pat and I were just talking about you last night saying we hadn't seen you for ages. Whatever has happened to you?"

I explained about my mother. We stood for ages reminiscing about the good old days. Did we enjoy ourselves! We painted the town red many a time. We'd had some wild times and drank gallons of whiskey.

"Isn't it a small world?" I said innocently, "Pat's daughter is the manager of the team caring for my mother."

"Yes," said Margaret, "and I've never seen her sober!"

We laughed. It was a good joke. If I had thought anything serious of Margaret's remark I would have gone straight away to Social Services and had the lady in question suspended while an official enquiry was conducted into the allegation. But it was a joke, even if it wasn't, even if the woman was paralytic while she was working, so what. I wished good luck – and a drink – to anyone looking after people like my mother.

When I got home the two lunchtime ladies were changing my mother. What I actually want to call them now is unprintable. Laughing - and there wasn't much laughter in the house those days - I said,

"I've just been talking about your boss. Like the rest of us, apparently she is never sober." It's amazing with all the stress in the world and all the effort looking after our elderly, people have nothing better to do than run around telling tales

When I was little we would sing,

"Tell tale tit, your tongue shall split and all the little puppy dogs shall have a little bit."

I'd like to have fed those two ladies' tongues to a Rottweiler.

A couple of days later when the post arrived my world took a tumble. There was a letter from Sir Teddy Taylor, M.P. a letter from the head of Social Services (Southend), a letter from this lady's (I'll call her a lady for the purposes of this story) solicitor. She, this lady, was going to have my guts for garters.

Dropping everything I jumped into my car and headed for Chelmsford. The woman might have thought she had good advice but it wouldn't match the advice I had from County Hall.

The Solicitor saw me straight away and told me I wasn't in any trouble. I may have given myself a bit of hassle but whatever this lady did she would get nowhere. The Solicitor assured me however hard she tried I would hear no more as no Solicitor would touch it. As I got up to leave he leaned forward and said,

"Whatever you do, don't apologise. It will look as if you have done something wrong and you haven't."

Happy with my situation, I headed home. The lady was determined to fight, for what I don't know, until the bitter end.

Somehow we got through the summer, but Mum was now in a pitiful state and she needed full-time nursing, not care in the community. I went to the Head of Social Services again to see if I could override their decision to keep her at home. Mum was being totally neglected and abused by the system. She was actually in the last few months of her life. The situation with this lady drinker left me even more stressed. I felt I was on trial. I'd get letters –

Dear Mrs S, would you please not turn your mother's heating off before you go out. We found your mother frozen at lunchtime...etc. etc.

The health visitor's were as concerned as I was, they felt that Mum was being allowed to rot away in her bed. One day they spent an hour on the phone to her doctor asking the reasons why she wasn't getting better care away from the home. They got nowhere.

Mum had used the threat of suicide all her life now she was too weak to even do that.

"But YOU know what to do," she said to me one day.

I thought back to the days when I'd have dearly loved to knife my ex-husband. It was the same now. I was determined there would be life after Mum and there was no way was I going to do her in. It caused me real concern. Carers get no training in coping through the night with the numerous sleeping pills, painkillers, medicine etc. I felt extremely lonely, with this vindictive woman from Social Services waiting for me to slip up. Ruth was concerned and she warned me,

"Don't keep giving Nan all those tablets. If anything happens they will have you for manslaughter."

Mum had always been a very difficult patient. Still of sound mind and wanting to go to the toilet independently she would try to get out of bed. I understood this, there was no way she was going to soil the bed. I tried to explain to her that she had no choice but she was having none of it. One morning, frightened that she would hurt herself, I just flung the front door open and yelled for help. The next door neighbour came rushing in and helped me put Mum back to bed. Mum's mouth was in full flow.

"Stop fucking trespassing on my fucking property and get out of my fucking sight"

One more person I could no longer call on for help. Two hours later Mum was at it again and I rushed to stop her trying to get up. With a face full of hate and vindictiveness she shouted at me:

"You come near me and I'll kick your fucking teeth in."

I ran from the room to my own place and dialled 999. The operator asked

"Where is your Mother?"

"I'm too frightened to look."

"Stay where you are, we'll be with you straight away."

Thank goodness it was now the end of November and our holiday in Cyprus was near. It was a Saturday morning and I woke quickly aware of my mother yelling.

"Leila, Leila."

"OK, Mum, what now?" I asked gently.

Looking at her closely I saw death in her face. Waking Colin I told him I thought she was dying.

"What makes you think that?" asked Colin.

"I can see it,"

Worried out of my life, I called the doctor. Although it was still not 7 a.m. he had already been out to another emergency and came round straight away. He examined Mum but didn't agree with me. Standing in her lounge he said,

"We're not looking at a crisis here, your mother hasn't even got a temperature." He prescribed more medicine, this time with a touch of morphine telling me to give her a stronger dose.

After the doctor's early morning visit, Social Services called.

"Your Mother is cold and dehydrated, we think you should call a doctor."

"He's already been"

Mum was so ill the doctor was called four times that Saturday. Every time I asked for her to be taken into hospital. The doctor insisted she wasn't a hospital case.

194

"She's dying" I kept saying.

"No she isn't" said the doctor.

"No" said the Social Services, "She's just having a bad day"

I knew the score, cheaper to let this old lady die in her own home, that way it won't interfere too much with the budget. With all the criticism I was getting from Social Services I felt they considered she was being neglected by me, but in truth she was being neglected by them, by the system. It was criminal that it should be allowed to happen.

Chapter 18

Colin and I cancelled the holiday we'd waited for so eagerly, stopped switching on the TV and radio and just read quietly. All Christmas parties and outings were cancelled, we told the kids and grandchildren to have a bloody good time without us and our thoughts would be with them.

At night I stayed up to be near Mum. I would put on my pyjamas and dressing gown, close our bedroom door so Colin would get some sleep then sometimes doze on our settee, sometimes on Mum's. It didn't matter how much medicine I gave her throughout the night nothing settled her. You only have one Mum and they only live once and ideally I would have been curled up in bed with her, hugging her close. But all the hurt had gone too deep, anger, frustration and humility had left its mark. I knew soon it would be too late and I would no longer have one of life's most priceless gifts - a mother - but the wall between us just wouldn't crumble.

The days and nights passed. It was getting embarrassing

"Yes," I would reply to enquiries about my mother's health, "She is still with us."

The neighbours were concerned at my appearance. I had got very thin myself and they were convinced Mum would still outlive me.

All was calm one night when she quietly asked

"Can't you just put me in your car and take me home."

"You are home," I told her.

"Can't you do anything I ask you, you stupid fucking bitch!" She was screaming now.

I tried to tell her gently that she was home.

"What! at number eight?"

"Mum, you have never been anywhere but home."

Her reply to that was unprintable or just plain boring, there were so many F words all rolled into one. She was so rotten to me that next morning I re-booked the holiday. On January 14th, come hail or come shine I was going to be on that plane. Social Services still had a respite bed for her and agreed she could be moved.

Mealtimes were difficult. I knew she wasn't getting enough

food and would lift her head off the pillow and try to get her to eat a spoonful. When I tried to spoon some tea down her there was an awful hollow sound, she was so empty. If I said to Social Services,

"This is ridiculous." They would always reply,

"She is just having a bad day again."

Not all Social Service's were at war with me. The young girls who had to clean up my Mum's bed had my full support. They were wonderful, as were the people from the Health Department.

Mum still had the strength to have a go

"How much longer are you going to let me suffer? You know how to end it, you f——ing cow" she would hiss.

We had a quiet Christmas and New Year. The doctor gave me his home number which I could ring direct day or night but in the past he's simply told me to double her dose. It was almost a week into the New Year and I hadn't been to bed for a month. I was completely worn out, Mum was rarely quiet for more than a few minutes. It would be

"Leila, Leila"

"What's it now, Mum"

"Give this bloke ten shillings and ask him to leave"

"Right Mum, now try to sleep"

Minutes later

"Leila, Leila"

"What now"

"Who are all those people in the lounge – who's paying for the fire?"

"Don't worry Mum, try to sleep"

It went on all night until by 4am. I thought I would explode. I had to get help, it was no use phoning the doctor at home, I'd phone and take whoever was on call. It was after 7am when the doctor arrived. As I opened the door Mum shouted as loud as she could

"Leila, Leila"

"What's all this about?" he asked her "Don't you think your daughter needs a break"

"Have a break? She does nothing else, she's a lazy f——ing mare"

The doctor turned to me and very sympathetically said

"This is care in the community gone completely mad, I'll have her taken away now"

197

Somehow, exhausted as I was, I felt a great sadness at those words.

"Have her taken away" as if she was a sack of potatoes. She was my Mum.

Colin took the necessary paper's to Mum's own doctor who was very put out.

"What's all this about? Why wasn't I called?

As far as I was concerned he could take a running jump. I had no support from him and now I was having his decisions overriden.

It was five o'clock when the ambulance arrived and ten o'clock before Mum was settled in a ward. I assured her she was in hospital to get better and come home, then said,

"Good night."

"So, you're Leila," the nurse said the next morning. "Mum has called for you all night."

What's new, I thought, it wasn't necessary for me to ask anyone how she was, I knew. Word soon got around that I was there and strange a doctor came in, introduced himself and asked could he have a word in the corridor. He looked at me with suspicion.

"Your mother is very ill," he told me.

"I know in my opinion she has been close to death for the last month and I've tried everything I could to get her into hospital but care in the community wouldn't have it."

His expression changed immediately to one of kindness and he asked,

"How have you managed?"

"Look into my face and you will have your answer,"

"It's over now," he said.

Mother wouldn't be allowed to live in the community in that state again. She had enormous strength and with a bit of tender loving care Mum rallied. I firmly believe if she'd had expert help a few months earlier she would be alive today. As it was, fight as hard as she could, she was very weak and the mountain was too high to climb. But she hung in there. I was sitting by her bed when a nurse came in. Mum beckoned to her and signalled that she wanted her to bend over so she could whisper in her ear. I wondered what she was up to now.

"Please give my daughter a hug for me," she asked the nurse.

I immediately went over to her

"Don't be silly, I'll give you a hug."

Bending down close I tried to slip my hand under her frail body but she cried out.

"Don't do that, you're hurting me."

So it was now too late to hug her. The days passed, getting nearer to the 14th.

What should I do?

"Go," said the doctor, "you need some tender loving care. I don't want your funeral on my hands."

"Go," said the children, "you are exhausted."

Torn in two. I changed my mind every few minutes. The night before I left Mum was lucid and I brightly reminded her that I was away in the morning. If it had been just Colin and myself things might have been different, we were going with family; I felt a responsibility to them, I couldn't let them down.

"People are in place to visit you every day. The time will fly and I'll be home before you know," I told her, bending down to kiss her and holding her paper thin hands I said,

"Now then, you just hold on till I'm back."

"I'll try," said Mum, "I'll try."

We'd been away nearly a week, regularly making phone call home. When I rang on the Sunday, Ruth said

"I've just been to see Nan. She wants a box of Black Magic to pass around and some drinking straws so it's easier for her to drink.

I was relieved, it sounded O.K.

"Oh, yes, and she's out of soap."

"Please God I'll make it home in time. I'll ring you Tuesday"

On the Tuesday we all went to visit a monastery. It was gloriously peaceful and beautiful. We strolled quietly around the cloisters where the monks walk in the evening. I visited the chapel with it's gold statue of the Blessed Virgin Mary, Mum's favourite, She would have loved to have seen it. I lit a candle and prayed with all my heart for her.

We decided to stop at a taverna outside the monastery for refreshments before the long journey back to our villa and the men dropped us two girls on the pavement while they went to park. I explained to the waiter who rushed out that we were waiting for our men. He understood very little English

"I'm a man."

"No! No!"

I tried to explain.

You've pulled, I said to myself, there's life in the old girl yet. As the only wine drinker I ordered a carafe of wine and some dry bread. The others wanted soup which was served with dry bread and I had to point to that, then to myself to make the waiter understand my request.

We were concerned with the time, leave it much longer and Colin would have that dreadful drive home in the dark but for now I was more at peace sitting there with my wine gazing out over a vast vineyard, than I had been for a long time. Alone with my thoughts, it was as if the others didn't exist. I glanced at the clock, it would be exactly 5 p.m. at home. I would always remember this moment. I felt a strange peace.

When we arrived back at the villa it was time to cook dinner, then too late to phone.

"I'll get it done early tomorrow" I told Colin.

Next evening he walked down the hill with me. But as we neared the phone box I suddenly couldn't go any further. Standing in the middle of the road I froze.

"It's too late," I said.

Colin made the call home and I knew from his conversations that I was right, eventually I was able to talk to Ruth.

" Nan had died at 5 p.m. yesterday" she told me.

"The hospital phoned me at work but I was stuck in a traffic jam" She hesitated, I could hear her crying.

"Oh, Mum, I missed her by ten minutes"

I knew I would never get over the shock of my little old Mum dying alone and I would never forgive myself for not being there but my first thoughts were for Ruth's distress. I should have been there to take the responsibility of it all and comfort my children. Something else I would never forgive myself for; I held back when I left Mum, couldn't say the word's "I love you, Mum," now I'll never have the chance.

I had to endure another week on holiday and when I returned home there would be another week before the funeral. That's good I thought, time to get organized and give Mum a good send off. I wasn't going to have a Requiem Mass, just a cremation with a Catholic priest. I couldn't face all that Catholic mumbo jumbo after the pain of the life Mum and I had shared. This was my Mum and I was dealing with it my way.

On returning home my first task was to go and see her in the chapel of rest. She looked so small lying in the coffin. The flesh had left her face and her skin was like porcelain, white and drawn tight. A frown crossed her brow. Mum's thick black eyebrows almost met at the top of her nose and it was definitely a frown. I was so taken aback that I had to speak to the undertaker about it. I had always thought people died peacefully. It was almost as if she was reluctant to go, things had been left unsaid and records had to be put straight. Making myself comfortable by the coffin I held her hands.

"Mum what the hell has it all been about? Couldn't you ever have found a word of comfort?" I said to her out loud. Remember the time when I was dressed to kill and you asked

'What do you think you look like? I've seen people who have been dead for days look better!' Well, Mum," I said, "You've been dead for days and I can tell you, you don't look that bloody marvellous!"

I sat for ages talking to her. Perhaps she was listening, you never know, she never listened when she was alive.

"I bet you always planned it this way," I told her. "I don't think you ever intended having that great moment when we hugged and let all the pain flow out of our hearts, when we came together and said all our, 'Sorry's' There were many times but you always let your big mouth get in the way. Now you have gone and left me with an aching heart, a great pain that I know will never go away; there will always be a great sadness in my life, an emptiness that nothing will fill.

I realize your misery was such you couldn't break the mould and my anger was deep. Between the two of us we dished it out and just couldn't bridge the gap. I can't think of anything to make it up to you for letting you die alone, except to take you home. I'll take you home Mum, after the funeral. I promise you.

There wasn't much more to say. I held her frozen hand in mine, such little hands, I didn't want to let go. Suddenly I had a weird feeling, if I held them any longer they would thaw out and Mum would come back to life. It was unreal sitting alone in the chapel of rest, knowing it was the end of a life. It had been a very difficult life for Mum, as it was for me, but I hoped the great faith which she had rekindled in the last stages of her life would sustain her. I stroked her hair. It was soft and warm.

"Goodbye, my old dear, I'll see you in heaven." Searching for a copy of her favourite hymn proved unsuccessful so I had to settle for second choice. I put up new curtains at the windows, scrubbed and polished her bungalow, emptied out her spare room and placed her big oak table in there with a few chairs. The food would be served there, she'd always put on a show so she wasn't going to be let down. All her photos were put out for everyone to see, the doors to my place were open so people could wander through. Everyone would be welcome. One last item to organize - flowers. I wasn't going to get Mum a wreath but a single rose to be left on the coffin so she cold take it with her to heaven.

It was amazing the years I had spent with Mum, now she was dead I was looking for answers. I know I could have asked her myself but never did. All I know was when she came over from Ireland as a fourteen-year-old she lived with Lily. I thought I would phone lovely cousin Sheila and ask her if she could tell me anything. It was the first she had heard about Mum staying with her mother.

"When was that?" Sheila asked me.

It turned out to be the year cousin Sheila was born. Her father was away in the army. Her mum was pregnant and had a haberdashery shop to run.

"But Mum wouldn't have been able to pay your mum any wages. The recession was still biting between wars and the big stores were taking over - in the end Mum went broke."

"Where was this shop?" I asked.

"Barkingside,"

Barkingside. To me what was like a bomb exploding. Auntie Lily's shop had been only a few doors away from where Jack had his fruiterer's and greengrocers shop. Mum would have gone in there to buy vegetables, so they would have known each other. Perhaps the story that Jack was my father was true and not the rantings of a dying woman.

It took four trips to the tip with junk to make an impression on the rubbish Mum had collected. I was still busy clearing out her things when at the bottom of a drawer I found an old brown envelope addressed to Leila Merriman.

It had been well over forty years since I was Leila Merriman. They say people with secrets always leave a clue, was this my mum's clue? I sat down at her old oak table and, feeling very pensive, opened the envelope. It was full of certificates - birth and marriage, some so old I was almost afraid to open them up. There was her marriage certificate to Jack. His birth certificate, his parents, etc. etc.

Was this the other half of me I had been searching for all my life? I had never been one hundred per cent sure of Mum although by the end I was sure she was my mother. I always hoped when I found the rest of me I would be looking at names like Smith or Brown from say Dagenham or Plaistow. Here I was looking at names like Lazarus and Abrahams from the suburbs of Russia. I still haven't worked out who "Hannah" is. She signed her marriage certificate with an 'X' so obviously she couldn't read or write. What was her story? What is the story behind all these immigrants in the eighteenth century? For the time being I shall put this envelope away. I have a mother to bury.

Up to now I had no definite proof of my parentage. Luckily Dad was buried so if it meant digging him up and doing a DNA test so be it. Then there are his two children, I prefer to think they are not my flesh and blood, much as they would think the same of me. I thought of Betty and her hatred for the young girl who married her widowed father. Sixty-five years later, was I discovering that not only had Mum married her and John's father, she also married my father.

For now I can't get my head around all this. In years to come I'd like to get the records straight for my grandchildren's sake.

Now I understand the silence. In those days brother and sisters often didn't know if a sister had a baby out of wedlock. It was such a shame on them all she would be sent away with some cock and bull story, like she had got a job working for a duchess, etc. etc. Mum was here in England with her brothers and sisters so everyone knew I had been born, but the father's name had been kept a dark secret. There was not one word from Mum and now I knew why. If the family had known I was half Jewish they would have taken me for a ride in my pram to the River Deel and let the handbrake off.

The Priest phoned to ask if someone would give the eulogy. On the morning of the funeral, all the cousins arrived including Uncle Tom's son, Michael. I had only seen him once in the forty years since his father had committed suicide and was very grateful for his presence although sad that the family had been estranged for almost a lifetime.

There was a large whiskey for anyone who felt the need, that would have been Mum's way. When I asked who was going to do the eulogy there were loads of excuses but no offers. As we arrived at the cemetery, I couldn't believe the number's of people there. Who the hell were they? They were probably all Mum's church cronies come to see this wicked daughter, who wouldn't give Mum - that wonderful, good devout Catholic - a Requiem Mass. Life had been too difficult for me to go through all that load of rubbish. I was doing this my way. God would understand.

Again, there were no offers for the eulogy from the crowd so I told the Priest I'd do it. I sat shattered at the prospect and tried not to get too emotional. All too soon the Priest nodded and it was time for me to step forward. I stood up in front feeling very self- conscious almost in a daze. I looked at Colin sitting in the front row with my lovely son and beautiful daughter their eyes focused on me. Time to begin, take a deep breath, I told myself and take it slowly.

"My mum, Sheila, is the last survivor of twenty-three children. She outlived her brothers and sisters by many years. If we believe what we are told they will all be together up there and they will be looking down on us. The cards will be out, they will have a few hand rolled fags and a bottle or two or three, if anyone trumps my mother's ace, they will know she's arrived because there will be a fight. If the good Lord gives my mum pocket money for good deeds done, she will find something to bet on. Mum was never interested in material things - vases, plates on the wall, things like that. As long as she had the money for a bet she was happy. She worked hard and played twice as hard. Mum married twice, both times to men of the Jewish faith. I was brought up on Jewish history, customs, food and culture. That is why I find this so hard to cope with but if it has brought her peace at the end of her days I'm happy. I'm an only child..."

I wanted to say she left two grandchildren she adored and two great grandchildren who were the light of her life. Most important, I wanted to say she was dearly loved but emotion caught up with me and I sat down quickly. The Priest stood up, probably shocked by what I had said - his face changed colour, Colin told me - and began with: "We shall quietly pray for a couple of minutes for our dear departed sister Sheila. May God forgive her human faults and frailties."

I smiled through my tears.

It had been a good service and as I walked out into the day-light I had a funny feeling about my Uncle Tom. I walked over to look at Mum's flower's and realized Michael was standing close.

"Shall we put some of Mum's flowers on your Dad's grave?" I asked

Suddenly I had this feeling he was there, why I should think that, I have no idea, just that at that moment, I felt it. To my amazement Michael said

"I've no idea where my father is buried."

He went with Colin and Ruth to the office to find out if in fact he had been laid to rest in Southend. He was there, they couldn't give the exact spot as Uncle Tom was in a communal grave with twelve others. That was awful, beyond belief, that no one would pay for a spot of ground to bury him. This was the holy Roman Catholic faith who chucked on a heap a lost soul who committed suicide? Where's their compassion, their humanity, their forgiveness? Where was the love of God for all his children?

What about his widow and three sons? He had been a bloody good husband and father to them and me when we were small. Even a dog would have been given a decent burial. What of that bitch Mina, who put so much energy into beating my mother up and verbally abusing the rest of us? It was a pity a little more energy couldn't be put into seeing Tom had a resting place of his own. Tom wasn't a tramp but part of a large loving family, there were dozens of us. I still hang my head in shame to think of it.

One of my regrets in life is that I didn't phone Michael, Sean and Tommy on the day he died. After Mina's intervention on their behalf I was totally shell-shocked and the anger is still with me. Uncle Tom was closer to me than anyone else, it was he who held me in his arms on my first night in Ireland, who walked me down the aisle on that dreadful day I married. After his death, with my small baby I had to work for almost a year to pay off his debts. If I had known about the community grave I would have seen to it that he had a proper grave even if it meant working all my life to pay for it.

Colin and I walked round to the cemetery yesterday, May 2003. I had a map with a cross that marks the spot roughly where Uncle Tom is buried.. We put a few flowers on the grass and I thought of the other poor souls there with him who probably had no one. I'd like to dig Tom up and rebury him but how do you sort out who is who out of twelve of them? It's appalling.

In the circumstances I was glad I hadn't put myself through a Requiem Mass for my mother. All that hypocrisy, those wonderful, devout, holy Catholics who turn their backs on a lost soul who ends his life yet expect the whole works when their turn comes. They want all the blessings on offer, the Priest shaking incense over them, chants of hallelujah for the good pious life they have led. I'd like to think they get a couple of turns on the devil's barbecue as he gets to give them a few pokes with his red hot poker. I'd be there to watch. I booked my place by the fire when I was eight.

Losing a mother is traumatic, perhaps more so for me because we had never really settled our differences and now it was too late. Colin and I set out on the sad, sentimental journey home to Ireland. We made our way to Moortown, passing over the crossroads, down the road to the little cottage where Mum was born. She wouldn't have recognised the old road now, it was quite posh and well used by cars, not at all like when Mum and I were young!

We drove slowly past the cottage and carried on down to the river, where I got out of the car and leant over the bridge. The bridge there now is wooden and dull, the lovely old stone bridge with the three steps carved out by loving Granddad had long gone, the river had been drained and was now a little trickle. Although it was early summer it was cold and the rain was falling gently.

Time for a wee dram. There would be a difficult time ahead and I felt in need. Sipping the whiskey, my thoughts went back to when I was child and the river flowed. The fun all of us had fishing, swimming and just running wild and free. It would have been the same for Mum. She would have played and fished here with her many brothers and sisters, they would have been 'Grand' days, definitely the best years of her life, free from the pain that was to envelop her in later life. She always longed to be here in Moortown. I thought of her as that beautiful young girl who never had a chance: now she was just ashes in the boot of the car.

It was time to make our way back past the little cottage again. It had changed, the old hay barn on the opposite side of the road had gone and the cottage itself was quite smart. This was the road Mum walked to school every day of her young life, like her brothers and sisters she started and ended her school days at Ballinvalley School.

Next stop was in Delvin to buy a large bunch of brightly coloured flowers and then in to see the Priest. I had a ten pound note handy to give him. He was such a lovely man I felt my offering was inadequate. Discreetly, I reached into my bag for a second but he refused my offering and I left it on the table. After all I've said about the Catholic Church, he was so kind and comforting. I wondered if perhaps he have a direct line to God.

Our final stop was in the church itself. I lit a candle for Mum, recalling the incident with my grandmother when I was just a child. I was standing on the same spot where I stood as that eight-year-old. That day was probably the last day I knew peace. I lit a candle for Lizzie and Mick as well then took a seat next to Colin. We were in no hurry. There was plenty of time for me to be alone with my memories.

This is where Mum had been baptized, where she had made her First Holy Communion and where she was confirmed. Mum, until her dying day, liked to tell the story of her First Holy Communion. She was one of the brightest pupils and had a one hundred per cent pass, so she had to wear a different coloured ribbon from the rest of the girls. So did I, Looking back there was very little in Mum's life to be proud of. This is where she had probably spent her happiest years and that's why I've brought her back here, hopefully to rest in peace.

Colin and I looked at each other; we had been sitting there for ages and now it was time to make the short journey to the cemetery. Taking the casket and flowers we made our way to where my beloved grandma and granddad lay. I knew the way as I had visited in the past. The funeral had been so crowded, I'd been surrounded by family. Now I was alone except for Colin.

This was such an unknown area, no one explains how you are supposed to feel coping with scattering your dearest ashes. Panic came first - this was very final, I scattered the ashes and placed the flowers on top and felt immediately calm. Now my mum had her flowers, not on a cold winter's day in a cemetery in Southend but here in the privacy of her birthplace, back home where she longed all her life to be.

I watched the rain fall gently on the blooms, roll down the leaves and rest gently on the ashes. I stood close to Colin, his arm tightly round me for support. Feeling emotionally drained I chatted away to Mum.

I realize now how upset you must have been when you conceived me, so upset that it turned your mind against me. You never once put your arms around me and hugged me. You never claimed me as your own. You've kept me at arm's length all your life and now you are gone. If only you knew how desperately I needed you.

I don't know what happens now, I've not been there yet, but

you are. If God lets you take a peep down on me I'll be trying to be kind to people and lead a good life.

Well, Mum, I think that's it. I'm not just dumping you here. I couldn't think of anything else to demonstrate my love for you. One day I'll bring Stephen, Ruth, Hannah, Adam and Georgina here. I'll try to show them the beauty of this place and tell them of the happiness and peace of mind you and I experienced here. I doubt if I'll ever manage that but I'll try.

Till we meet again, dearest Mum, 'God Bless.'

Chapter 19

Ten years have passed since my Mothers death. No one could have mourned a mother as I mourned mine. I missed her like crazy and would have given my very soul to have her back for one moment to give her a hug. It took five years before I settled down and shortly after I published my book. It is my story, I needed to write it to give me closure on all the pain. If members of my family were upset reading it – I'm sorry – they only had to read it, I've had to live it. I drew great comfort from the letters I received. I went home to Moortown four times in twelve months. On one occasion I had tea and cakes with the Lord Mayor of Dublin at the Mansion House. She gave me a wonderful book on the history of Dublin. I cheeky gave her a copy of my book. I had lunch in Dublin with a girl who started school with me in 1939 and hadn't seen since 1945. I was having a great time.

Waterstones in Dublin had my book on sale, to promote it, I took a leaf from my Grandmother book, I went back to my roots. She was born in Dublin in Victorian times. I dressed in full Victorian attire, hat, earrings, beads, shawl, long skirt and boots and carrying the biggest Victorian basket, I walked down O'Connell Street handing out literature. I was hoping to be arrested, that would get me into the papers. As the manager at Waterston's said

"A girl's got to do what a girl's got to do"

Then out of the blue, forty six years after his death I received a letter from a grand-daughter of my lovely Uncle Tom. Having introduced herself, she said she wanted to come to Southend and visit his final resting place. Also learn what he was like as a person and what he looked like as she had never seen a photo of him.

I wondered what terrible crime he had committed that his family had destroyed every photo of him.

Colin wasn't part of my family when Tom died, I went over old ground with him. He considered he was well up on Police procedures and said,

"You would know everything. It was a terrible crime in those days and if as you say a letter was left for you, the Police would have

209

interviewed you and you say they didn't and I can't believe that"

I was alarmed at what he was saying and protested

"I know absolutely nothing" His reply was even more alarming.

"If you were in court now, you wouldn't be believed. I'm your husband and I don't believe you"

I know he was trying to be helpful but he had un-nerved me. If my own husband didn't believe me, these strangers coming to Southend wouldn't either. I decided to spend a day playing detective and see what I could find out.

I made my way to the Police Station, it was quite a struggle getting in along a passage that seemed to have various glass doors. I greeted the officer on duty with a laugh

"Good morning, I must have had a wasted life, I couldn't even find my way into a Police Station"

Things had certainly changed. Gone was the familiar old front counter, instead there was a small table and chairs.

"What can I do for you, Madam" the officer inquired once we were both seated.

"I want to go back to 1960, I want to know where I can find out the details of a suicide"

"We don't keep any records at the station, you can try the library or the local paper. You could of course try the Coroner's Office.

"Can I do that" I asked in surprise.

"Just a moment" he said, looking thoughtful.

"I can give you the Coroners name and phone number. It's half an hour away by car, perhaps you would do better phoning"

"Can I tell you something before you go" the officer volunteered.

The suicide law hasn't changed since 1960. The police are very much aware who they talk to at a time like that. He was watching me closely possibly sensing how important this conversation was to me.

"They would only have spoken to his nearest, his wife, probably not even his children" he continued

"They certainly wouldn't have spoken to you"

I went straight home to bring Colin up to date.

"I'm very surprised at that" was his comment. I felt exonerated.

When I had collected my thoughts I phoned the Coroner's Office. They too were so helpful, they didn't keep records after twenty

five years. They would phone around, somewhere out of town might have stored old records. Give them a few weeks and they would let me know one way or another.

Receiving that lady's letter had opened up old wounds I had put to the back of my mind. I was once again deeply upset, I'd lie awake at night, tears spilling down my face wondering where I had failed. Tom was so close to us here in Southend and we had allowed this to happen. I had forgotten the heartbreak of it all and I was surprised it was still there just as strong. I was glad that at last someone in his family wanted to know about him. I got my box of family photos out, happy ones of Tom with his many brothers and sisters, photos of him in his army uniform and him by my side on my wedding day. I wouldn't part with a single one but I got copies, two or three in some cases.

It couldn't have been two weeks when I got the call from the Coroners Office, they had his files. Next morning the large brown envelope was on the mat. I nervously picked it up and walked straight through the house to my chair.. I sat down very apprehensively. In my hands I had all the answers, why he did it was the paramount one.

The very first page gave me my first surprise. I wondered why it was my Mum the police interviewed and it was she who said there would be no objection to a post mortem examination and why she declined the invitation by the police to be represented. I can only think it was because she was still the proprietor of the café.

The next pages described how fit he was. Never had an illness in his life but he was very dead.

The next pages made terrible reading describing how he had ended his life. It was the week before Christmas, he went out for a few drinks, a freezing cold night still dressed in his overcoat he had made a cushion for his head in the oven with egg cartons. Then he had put a black plastic mac over the oven, weighed down each side with steel saucepans, he had tucked the mac in around the oven and around his neck. He was determined to finish things.

Then came a really whopper of a surprise for me, the letters. I had always believed he had left only one and that was to me. Reading the first letter it was obvious I had never seen it. If I had I would have known all along what this was all about. Somehow with all the distress that morning Mum managed to pull the wool over my eyes. It amazes me that in that desperate hour she was still thinking of

"Survival" for herself. According to her my letter read,

"This is a five minute wonder, you will soon find something else to talk about. Give the boys their share" But it said a bit more,

"I'm sorry about this but there is no point in carrying on to give her £5 a week. I do not want you to imagine anyone or anything but "MAGGIE" is at the back of this. The biggest surprise, having carried the can for forty six years; being the cow who never gave his boys their money, the letter wasn't to me. It was to my Mum.

Tom was quite young when he and Maggie married. She was a 'GOOD' woman, a real Norah Batty type. Never a trace of make up, didn't smoke, drink, gamble, a real staunch Irish Catholic. He was only fifty when he killed himself, his three boys (men) were in their twenties, with almost thirty years of marriage behind him he wanted out. In the Catholic faith in those days they didn't do 'out.' You had three choices, murder your other half and hang, get them to kill themselves or you kill yourself. The Catholic faith only did 'till death us do part', however that was achieved.

The letter explained something else to me that I could never understand. The complete silence at home after Toms death. I wondered why nobody phoned to ask about his funeral. Of course they all knew because Mum knew, she would be on the phone to them from the office. They wouldn't have supported Maggie in the circumstances, they would have gone to Church and grieved in private and probably had a Mass said for him.

The second letter was to his son's. I think I'll leave that private but it was clear they were well aware of the situation. I can see them supporting their Mother, she was always there with her apron on, cooking breakfast, dinner on the table when they got home, everything spick and span, the door step scrubbed, knocker polished, she never had to worry about going out to work to earn a penny. Who kept the roof over their heads, put food in their bellies, clothes on their backs and shoes on their feet, saw they had a present on their birthdays and at Christmas, they never went without. Surely that entitled him to at least one of his son's having the guts and love to stand and say a prayer when he was thrown on that heap of poor souls.

The letter to his son's had a major revelation. His mind had been made up for some time but his eldest had been to see him and tell him he was getting married, he didn't want to spoil his day. Reading their letter, I would imagine my Mum's cry for help gave him

a way to finalize his plan. He would give her all his money, that way there would be nothing for Maggie and Mum could gave it back to his son's when the Café was sold. I have no idea what arrangement he made with Mum over working, as he was just marking time, I can imagine he worked for peanuts and all the takings went to prop up the betting shop, The trouble for me was he only had half the money Mum needed to settle her gambling debt. I don't mind about the money, he could have the lousy stuff. But I was really hurt to think that morning his question,

"How about you and me going into business together" was just a great big con, as his only plan for the future was to kill himself.

I can imagine when the news came out that 'I' had given the boys not a bean, the reaction of the Merriman clan. I know what Mina would have to say, Lily would have her fag stuck to her lip and stuttering worse than ever would declare, "Somebody should have drowned the F---ing bastard" Una would play the old tune, I had always been a liar and a thief. Mum would be going for the sympathy vote, knowing, without a trace of conscience she had unloaded all the guilt on my shoulders. Making me the bad guy I had been since the day I was born. Mum would declare "This is the cross I've had to bear all my life." It was beyond me, we were now in the 1960's and nobody would think of saying to Mum

"Leila didn't get here on her own" They were all as bad as the husband I had, I wondered what was in their warped minds.

I can remember how distraught I was over Uncle Tom's death and the times I would ask Mum "Was it my fault, leaving him alone to carry on?"

She had read the letters, she could easily have told me, it was nothing to do with me. Then she would have to admit it was her who never paid me any wages and her debts I opened the café to settle.

Today, December 13th. 2007, the forty seventh anniversary of Uncle Tom's death, armed with a bunch of flowers I walked the half mile to the cemetery and placed half on the grass. There had been a fire in the offices years ago, so I don't have the exact spot but near enough. A little distance away I put the rest of the flowers on my Dad's grave, odd that they are almost side by side, the two men who played such a big part in my life. When Dad was buried three years after Uncle Tom I had no idea he was there. But after the service for my Mum I knew Uncle Tom was close by. How strange is that? I'm

sure they have been watching out for me over the years. I know Uncle Tom wouldn't have wanted me to have been so hurt over the café and sent to Coventry where I remain to this day.

It's all a long time ago now and it's sad we are still estranged but I haven't lost out on life. I'm no further in my quest to find out if Jack was my Father but I would say it's 99% he was. I have found out my Grandparents came from Russia When I was growing up, in the 40's, 50's, 60's etc. I was always searching to find 'Me' I wonder how my Catholic Irish half would gel with my Russian Jewish half, I think they would have gelled beautifully and it explains the very complex character that's Leila. I wish I had known, I would like to have embraced who I am, I know I shall always feel cheated.

But it has been a bloody good life, a few tears on the way but a lot of laughs. In fact I don't know how I got to be so lucky. That young man I married over twenty years ago because I wanted to be the Mayoress, he is my soul mate.

My wonderful son and his lovely wife have given me three of life's most precious little people, three grandchildren. Each day I count my blessings each of them I count twice.

My beautiful daughter, that baby I needed like I needed a hole in my head, she is my best friend, life wouldn't be so sweet without her.. The teenager she brought home years ago, we have just been out celebrating his fortieth birthday. West Ham still haven't won the F.A. Cup but he has played a blinder..

I thank that young lady for her letter, making me go out and find the truth and unravel another twisted thread. In writing this book I never set out to hurt anyone. I needed to search and find a meaning to my life. This last chapter has brought me the peace I have been seeking since I was that little girl of eight, lost my Beloved Grandmother and lost my way. Now it really is time to let the past go and let my lovely Uncle Tom and my Dearest Mum rest in peace.